The Church and Residential Desegregation

THE CHURCH AND RESIDENTIAL DESEGREGATION

A Case Study of an Open Housing Covenant Campaign

HENRY CLARK

Union Theological Seminary

COLLEGE & UNIVERSITY PRESS · *Publishers*

NEW HAVEN, CONN.

MANUFACTURED IN THE UNITED STATES OF AMERICA BY
UNITED PRINTING SERVICES, INC.
NEW HAVEN, CONN.

To My Father

ACKNOWLEDGMENTS

The burden which any author feels in attempting to acknowledge the help given him in the preparation of a manuscript is felt even more acutely by one whose book includes data gathered in field research. Without the patience and cooperativeness of all the persons who answered questionnaires and granted interviews, this work would not have been possible. Any reader whose understanding of residential discrimination and church social action is deepened by this volume shares the author's debt to the people of the city referred to herein as Newfield.

The author owes a particular debt to the teachers who advised him in conducting this study: Professors Kenneth W. Underwood, John D. Maguire and William Hughes of Wesleyan University; Professors James M. Gustafson, William Lee Miller, and, most especially, Erdman B. Palmore of Yale University. Gratitude is hereby extended also to Mr. Nathaniel Kaplan of College and University Press, who served as the editorial adviser for this book.

A word of appreciation is due, finally, to the officals of the National Committee Against Discrimination in Housing, located in New York City, and to officals of various agencies, both public and private, in Washington, D.C., who aided the author by granting interviews or by directing him to important written materials.

Excerpts from Kenneth W. Underwood's book, *Protestant and Catholic* are reprinted with the kind permission of Beacon Press; and excerpts from Gibson Winter's *The Suburban Captivity of the Churches,* with the kind permission of The Macmillan Company.

CONTENTS

The Church and Residential Desegregation

I hate, I despise your feasts,
    and I take no delight in your solemn assemblies.
Even though you offer me your burnt offerings
    and cereal offerings, I will not accept them,
    and the peace offerings of your fatted beasts
    I will not look upon.
Take away from me the noise of your songs;
    to the melody of your harps I will not listen.
But let justice roll down like waters,
    and righteousness like an everflowing stream.

Amos 5:21-24

INTRODUCTION

CHAPTER *1* IN THE SPRING OF 1963 THE NATION focused its attention on the state of Alabama, where a dramatic confrontation between protesting Negroes and a recalcitrant white power structure was taking place. Exclamations of disgust and disapproval resounded in all parts of the country as reports from Birmingham told of police dogs and fire hoses being used against peaceful demonstrators. The irony of this situation was captured perfectly in a Herblock cartoon showing a group of well-dressed executives standing at a commuter's rail depot labeled "North Suburbia." One of the men looked up from his paper and said to a companion, "Those Alabama stories are sickening. Why can't they be like us and find some nice, refined way to keep the Negroes out?"

The nonviolent protest movement (sometimes aptly called the "passive insistence" movement) and the Civil Rights legislation of 1964 promise to put a speedy end to legal segregation in public facilities. Accomplishment of this task will represent an important step forward; yet it will only make nation-wide an unsatisfactory status quo in race relations which has existed in the North* for some time. It will mean that full national attention can be given to what has for several years been acknowledged as "by all the odds the most pressing civil rights problem outside the South: housing discrimination."[1] It will mean that community resources throughout the entire country can be mobilized to overcome the type of racial discrimination which is "most institutionalized and resistant to change,"[2] the type of

---

* For the sake of convenience "the North" is used here to mean any part of the country outside the eleven Southern states. Needless to say, migration of Negroes to the West Coast has occurred at a very high rate, and the number of Negroes in this part of the country is comparable to the number in New England.

discrimination which has been designated "the root of all Negro frustrations."[3]

Why so much emphasis upon the housing problem of non-whites? How did the problem assume its present proportions? One important answer to these questions can be summed up in these words: the Negro is no longer "staying in his place." Statistics indicate that Negroes have changed location geographically as they have moved upward in recent decades on the ladder of socio-economic status; furthermore, there is every indication that they will continue to do so.

At the turn of the century, almost nine-tenths of the Negro population lived in the South, most living on farms. By 1940, only three-fourths of the nation's Negroes were in the South, and more than half of the national total were now located in urban centers. At the time of the last census, just over half (56%) of the nonwhite population was still in the South, and more than two-thirds were concentrated in cities exceeding 10,000 inhabitants.[4] When one takes into account that it is, by and large, the younger element of any group which migrates and that the birth rate for nonwhites is sliqhtly higher than that of the national average, one realizes how great is the increase in the demand for housing by Negro families outside the South, and in urban areas in both the South and the North.

In the early years of the northward migration, the low-income Negro felt most painfully the pinch of the housing shortage. Men who came to Chicago to work in the meat-packing plants, or to Detroit to work in the automobile production lines, or to Boston, New York and Philadelphia for a variety of reasons, had to crowd their families into the oldest and the most unsafe tenements of the city; and they usually had to pay outrageous rents for their miserable living accommodations. With few exceptions—Los Angeles is one, for the move to the surburbs on the part of whites in that city has created, temporarily, at least, a "spacious ghetto" for nonwhites[5]—conditions in urban centers have not changed for working-class Negroes.

Negroes with moderate and high incomes are also beginning to feel with new intensity the shortage of reasonably priced housing. There is just not enough room in the few "gilded ghettos" which have been established. Figures recently released by the Housing and Home Finance Agency, based on a study of twenty-one representative areas throughout the United States, reveal "a large and growing unmet housing demand among middle-income nonwhite urban families." Between 1949 and 1959, "the total number of nonwhite persons earning more than $4,000 a year increased nearly fifteen times," and "an even greater increase —nearly seventeen times—occurred for those with incomes of more than $6,000." The study concludes that "if nonwhites had shared in home ownership equally with whites in the same income group, both the rate of home ownership by nonwhites and the value of homes that many minority families could have owned would have been much higher."[6] Another study conducted in 1957 disclosed the astonishing fact that since World War II, only two per cent of newly constructed housing was available to Negro buyers.[7]

Thus the first major reason why housing has become the top priority item on the civil rights agenda is to be found in the population changes and the advance in socio-economic position of Negro Americans. A proportionately larger Negro population is moving into metropolitan areas, especially those of the North, and a proportionately larger group of middle-class Negroes is eager to obtain better housing in the neighborhood of their choice.

But the logical consequences of demographic changes often do not take place so long as public awareness of these changes remains low. A second important cause of the new concern over minority group housing is the realization on the part of large segments of the American public that residential discrimination is a serious social problem which demands an immediate solution. The emergence of widespread acknowledgment of this problem as a matter of the most serious concern is a story in itself.

Sizable numbers of sensitive spirits have always cried out in the wilderness of national complacency for Negro rights, but the shock of Nazism was needed to awaken America to the horrors of racism. Denials of equality and outright racism in our own country could no longer be overlooked when we found ourselves engaged in a death struggle with an antidemocratic power which perpetrated unbelievable evil in the name of racial supremacy. The publication of Gunnar Myrdal's *The American Dilemma* in the early 1940's is a milestone in the development of the consciousness of conflict between "the American Creed" and the condition of Negroes in America, which he describes.

As World War II ended, social philosophers drafting blueprints for a just world order stressed racial justice as an essential ingredient in any enduring peace. A number of seminal works by Jewish, Protestant, and Roman Catholic authors served notice that the major religious institutions of America were awakening from their lethargy regarding injustice in race relations.[8] Thus the beginnings of Christian social action pertaining to Negro rights can be traced to the stirrings of conscience within the Church, which took place during the late 'forties.

The war also increased the resentment and the impatience of Negroes, and this change of mood expressed itself in spectacular ways. The threat of a gigantic "March on Washington" by Negroes in 1944 brought about the issuance of a presidential Executive Order barring discrimination in many government-operated or government-sponsored facilities and activities.[9] The success of this maneuver encouraged Negroes to hope that protest actions could lead to progress. Returning Negro veterans had experienced (many of them for the first time in their lives) the benefits of a social environment unclouded by Jim Crow laws, which further augmented their determination not to settle for second-class citizenship in the land they fought to defend.

Added to the uneasiness of conscience felt by more and more white Americans and the hopeful resolve of Negroes was a third force intensifying both of these factors: the independence movements of former European colonies in Asia and Africa. As world opinion became progressively more outspoken in its condemnation of racial discrimination in the United States, cold war considerations made a thorough attack upon this violation of our democratic heritage a vital imperative for national policy. The humiliation of foreign nationals in American restaurants, educational institutions and on beaches became an intolerable embarrassment to our government. The difficulty encountered by dark-skinned diplomats in securing housing in the nation's capital was discomfiting. In view of the fact that only eight of 211 large apartment houses in Washington as late as 1961 were open to colored occupants, it is small wonder that "many Africans consider Washington a hardship post."[10]

Discrimination in housing has become a central concern, finally, because of the accumulation by social scientists of evidence demonstrating the far-reaching ramifications of inadequate and restricted housing.[11] The relationship between crowded dwellings and family disorders or juvenile delinquency is just as evident today as was the relationship between unsafe or unsanitary housing and bad health or frequent accidents to an earlier generation of social analysts. As for segregated housing, the Herblock cartoon, mentioned above, implies correctly that this condition results in segregated schools and public accommodations. Confinement of one group in a ghetto leads to, most of all, a heightened sense of racial difference and a lack of communication between persons of dissimilar racial backgrounds.[12] For reasons which will be analyzed in some detail below, segregated neighborhoods are more likely to suffer greater deterioration than would normally be the case in all-white or mixed neighborhoods. Thus the ghetto typically causes a waste of what Eli Ginsberg has termed "the Negro potential" which the nation can ill afford: it causes a lack of economic opportunity for Negro entrepreneurs and workers, which leads to the setting up of inferior standards of performance and aspiration in the minority group subculture.[13]

The housing problem of minority group families is a very complex phenomenon. The discriminatory aspect of the problem must be considered in the light of, but not confused with, at least three other aspects of the situation of Negroes in the United States today: social disorientation, acculturation, and economic inequality.

The question of social disorientation should be clearly differentiated from the question of residential discrimination, because the former is frequently used falsely as a pretext for the latter. There is a small group of individuals in our society who are victims of various psychological and social ills. That many of these individuals are Negroes is hardly surprising in the light of the emotional lynching to which nonwhites are subjected in our country. (One has only to read the ferocious essays of James Baldwin to appreciate the resentment of Negroes, or the preachments of the Black Muslims to see how savagely scarred the psyche can become.)[14] Persons of this sort are a sore problem to themselves, their families, and the communities in which they live. But the problem presented by such cases of maladjustment should not be used as an argument justifying discrimination; on the contrary, they constitute one of the strongest proofs for the urgency of finding a solution. The fact that some Negroes fall into the category of those persons who do not pay their rent on time, or get drunk and fight, or fail to support their families cannot be allowed to stand as a legitimate explanation for the exclusion of the vast majority of respectable Negro citizens from desirable apartments or neighborhoods of their choice.

Nor should the acculturation gap between rural and urban people be used as a justification for discrimination. Certainly a great disparity exists between the housekeeping standards of many country folks and city landlords: housewives who formerly lived in a wooden shack devoid of modern conveniences have little in their experience which has taught them how to use and care for plumbing facilities, electrical equipment and the like, or which has provided an incentive to take pride in the home. Landlords can hardly be blamed for not wanting tenants who are careless with their property. The trouble is that the lack of familiarity with conventional standards of home care that characterizes some migrants from rural areas, including Negroes from the South, is attributed to all Negroes and considered a racial characteristic.

The confusion is compounded when, in addition to stereotyping all Negroes as negligent housekeepers, landlords and realtors make the further erroneous assumption that Negroes cannot learn new cultural standards or are congenitally opposed to them. Since some families (Negro or white) may choose not to change their habits of home care, they may be perfectly content to live in what middle-class people would call inferior housing. But because some families take this option, it is foolish to conclude that all families presently living in inferior housing

are satisfied and do not aspire to better living conditions, or
that a housewife living in a dilapidated house in a run-down
neighborhood has no inclination to keep a neat home and has
no capacity for pride in her dwelling. She may simply have
been driven to a "don't care" attitude because of the irresponsibility of the landlord and/or city officials who have neglected
street maintenance, police protection, schools, and zoning regulations in nonwhite residential sections. Her apparent careless-
ness might vanish if she were given an opportunity to live in a
home and in a neighborhood where there was some incentive
to neatness and pride. Moreover, just as it would be foolish to
impute to all Negroes of lower-class background a desire to
adopt a middle-class style of life and to obtain a place of residence commensurate with this, it would be a mistake to impute
genuine and complete satisfaction to all Negroes who do not
express active dissatisfaction with their neighborhood or the
rent and upkeep of their dwelling. Silence on these matters
might best be interpreted as avoidance, that is, refusal to think
about an unpleasant fact of life.[15] Silence might even be a
sign of a feeling of relative status in comparison to a reference
group which considers as normal a high degree of deprivation.[16]
For example, an apartment which would be considered inferior
by middle-class standards might seem a great improvement over
the tenant farmer's shack where one used to live, and where
one's friends—now considered less fortunate than oneself—still
live.

The economic aspect of the minority group housing problem
is especially important. For many Negro families, the most pressing consideration in finding a place to live is financial: they
have little chance to worry about discrimination because they
cannot clear the economic hurdle that stands between them
and the kind of home they want. Needless to say, since the
problem of discrimination in housing makes contact at this point
with that of discrimination in employment, a direct attack upon
the latter is at the same time an indirect assault upon the economic dimension of the former. When the Smith family moves
out of its $80 per month apartment into a home of its own, then
the Joneses (who could not afford to buy a home) can move

out of their cold water flat to live in the Smith's old residence. And when a large number of Mr. Smiths get better jobs and are able to buy their own homes, the Mr. Joneses of the central city may not have to pay such high rents, the pressure of excessive demand for a limited Negro housing supply being alleviated.

Residential discrimination may be defined as the denial of a dwelling to a Negro family simply because it is Negro. When a thoroughly responsible household head is excluded from a desired apartment or neighborhood solely because he is a member of an ethnic group which is looked upon with disfavor, he is the victim of unjustified discrimination. His rights as an American citizen and as a human being have been denied. It is this aspect of the Negro housing problem which is especially odious in a democracy founded on Judeo-Christian principles, and it is this aspect of the problem of racial injustice that is challenged directly by the type of citizen action to be described in the following pages.

The mechanisms used to deny equal opportunity in housing may be classified as private or public, depending on whether they are the result of action by private or governmental agents. One of the private mechanisms grows out of (or hides behind) what we normally call the laws of the market. If there are more Negro buyers seeking certain types of housing than the supply can accommodate, landlords or home vendors charge them higher prices. If Negro buyers have little money for a down payment, and will therefore submit to an arrangement which gives them nothing but a contract of sale instead of title to the property, the seller can drive just as hard a bargain as he wishes. (In 1950, more than one of every seven first mortgages on properties occupied by nonwhite owners was not actually a mortgage but merely a contract of sale, whereby the buyer, who does not actually take possession of the house legally until he has finished paying for it, has far less freedom to modify or improve the house than he would otherwise have.)[17] If Negroes have greater difficulty in securing loans, it is accepted practice to charge whatever interest the desperate traffic will bear.[18] All of these versions of the "Negro tax"—the amount of extra money which a Negro must pay in order to obtain housing or financing

—make it inevitable that many nonwhite home buyers will be forced to scrimp on maintenance or take in roomers to meet their payments.[19] Thus neighborhoods deteriorate as the indirect result of discrimination against Negroes, but Negroes are blamed by casual observers for causing the decline.

Another private mechanism of residential discrimination is lack of equal employment opportunity. The first effect of this factor is obvious: the less money a man makes, the less he will have to pay for housing and the less able he will be to find desirable, or even adequate, housing. The second effect, even more subtle, does have a bearing on the question of residential exclusion. If Negroes are seldom seen in white collar jobs or professional and semi-professional positions, that fact can be and often is subconsciously interpreted by whites as proof that Negroes either are not qualified for such positions or are happy with more menial occupations. Jumping to this conclusion further consolidates the stereotyped notions about Negroes which make whites resist having Negro neighbors because, as the saying goes, "They're just not our kind of folks."[20]

The most blatant private mechanisms enforcing residential exclusion are those practiced by the real estate industry, including the financial institutions which are associated with it. Restrictive covenants were ruled legally unenforceable by a Supreme Court decision of 1948; nevertheless, clauses forbidding resale of land and homes to various ethnic groups continue to be written into real estate contracts.[21] Negro real estate brokers are almost universally barred from membership in local associations of realtors: indeed, they cannot even use the term "realtor" in advertising their services, but must list themselves as "realtists."[22] Although realtors and bankers protest their innocence in public hearings, few realtors who value their professional associations will dare violate the unwritten laws of the fraternity by selling to a Negro in an area that has not been "cleared for colored."[23] Collusion between realtor and banker to prevent entry of Negroes into a white neighborhood by refusing mortgage credit is difficult to establish in court, but many instances of this have been discovered.[24] Contractors are subject to the same powerful informal sanctions: they sometimes find it difficult to secure loans for the construction of homes for Negro families, and they run the risk of being boycotted if they build a home for Negroes in a Caucasian preserve.[25] In justice to the men of the real estate business, however, they are in many cases simply reflecting the wishes of their clients when they resort to these practices. Even homeowners who are themselves without prejudice are intimidated by the assumption that their neighbors would hate them if they sold their home to a Negro. Workers in fair housing groups are all too familiar with the remark, "Well, I really would like to sell to a Negro, but I couldn't do that to my neighbors."[26]

Public mechanisms of discrimination can be seen at work on both the local and the federal levels. The crudest form of discrimination by public policy was outlawed in 1917 when the Supreme Court declared that racial zoning ordinances were unconstitutional.[27] The same results can be achieved, however, by more devious means. The notorious Deerfield case, in which land purchased for the construction of a planned interracial community was condemned for a public park, has highlighted one such device.[28] Another way to accomplish the same purpose is to draft zoning codes which, when followed strictly, call for lot or house sizes that rule out everyone except the very wealthy and then make exceptions for whites but not for Negroes.[29] Uncommonly rigid enforcement of building codes can be used to get rid of Negro home builders or open-occupancy contractors who have violated some technicality in construction.[30] If these *de jure* measures fail to do the trick, a number of *de facto* stratagems may be utilized. A neglect of essential public services —garbage collection, water, electricity, even sewage—in a short while will effectively discourage most occupants.[31] Or the hint can be dropped to a prospective Negro buyer that the local fire department is, after all, a volunteer outfit, and if someone's home just happens to catch on fire when the volunteers are not available, the owner will just be out of luck.[32]

The public agency which has discriminated on the grandest scale, though, is the federal government. As of August, 1961, "more than 80 per cent of all public housing projects were racially segregated in one fashion or another"—sometimes by projects, sometimes by buildings, occasionally by floors—and "PHA daily was approving plans and entering into new contracts for more segregated units."[33] There is another kind of discrimination in public housing, too, albeit well-intentioned discrimination, resulting from the so-called "benign quota." This is a device used to maintain integration by preventing the number of Negroes in a public housing project from exceeding a hypothetical "tipping point" beyond which it is feared that all the whites would move out, leaving the project totally Negro. Strict observance of this policy involves "sometimes withholding vacant apartments from Negroes while waiting for white applicants."[34]

As the concentration of Negroes grows in cities, the effects of this concentration have been aggravated by a public policy —urban redevelopment—ostensibly designed to improve the lot of the low-income city-dweller. The bitter certainty of Negro leaders that urban renewal means Negro removal can be amply supported by the record. In the first place, urban renewal has reduced the total available housing supply in central city areas. As of 1959, 190,500 original dwelling units had been destroyed, but only 115,000 had been built to replace them: this represents a net loss of 75,500 units. About fifty-six per cent of the families displaced were nonwhites.[35] Secondly, "the relocation of displaced families largely has been in the old slum neighborhoods in poor housing at substantially higher rents." A four-year study of the consequences of renewal in California indicated that "two-thirds of *all* relocated families tend to relocate within twelve city blocks of their former homes."[36] In the light of this finding, it is hardly surprising that many sections of a city which absorb relocatees from a renewal area one year become deteriorated to the point of being selected for clearance a few years later. This means that numerous families, especially Negro families, are shuttled from one clearance site to another within a matter of a few years.[37] Finally, the assistance given to displaced families has often been woefully inadequate. "The official authorities in housing, planning and urban renewal are focused on physical and economic rehabilitation of the city, rather than on its social needs; in general, they are little concerned and fail to involve the traditional social services of the community, and . . . they do not reach out to engage in minority housing social services."[38] Symptomatic of this condition is the fact that "top policy committees in urban renewal seldom include professional social workers or human relations personnel," and also the fact that "the handful of professional social workers employed by (public) agencies . . . are used in routine and non-professional ways."[39] In the words of a prominent Negro lawyer and publisher,

> urban slum clearance does become Negro clearance in all too many, if not the majority, of cases. Seventy per cent of those displaced under such programs have been Negroes. The Negro finds himself locked in a battle with the power elite of his city, and because the members of that power elite are white, the tug of war over slum clearance pits Negroes against whites with the Negro seeming to stand in the way of progress.[40]

But the most important form of federally supported discrimination is that which has come about from the lending policies of the Federal Housing Adminstration and the Veterans Administration. Before 1947, FHA lenders were clearly directed to go along with prevailing real estate policies perpetuating segregation; since that time, it has ruled out contracts with restrictive covenants and has officially affirmed "the right of all citizens to receive the benefits of its mortgage insurance system irrespective of race, color, creed or national origin."[41] Neither FHA nor VA has, however, enforced a nondiscriminatory policy in loans for housing construction and purchase, and the same is true of the Housing and Home Finance Agency in its College Housing program.[42] The United States Civil Rights Commission Report on Housing of 1961 asserted that in the seven states where it conducted hearings—only in these seven—68 million dollars had been loaned to educational institutions that are compulsorily segregated.[43]

Federal banking policies have supported discrimination indirectly, too, because most banks depend heavily on the Federal Reserve System for the supplying of funds which they lend. Granting the fact that many working-class Negro household heads are poor credit risks, one may rightfully criticize most bankers for not having lending policies which reflect the equal fiscal reliability of middle-class and upper-class Negroes and whites.[44]

A set of circumstances which causes so much human misery cannot be ignored, and efforts to alter these conditions have not been lacking. In the area of judicial action, the two Supreme Court decisions outlawing racial zoning and the enforcement of restrictive covenants have been the major breakthroughs. Since legislative action has been taken by sixteen states and seven municipalities, other political jurisdictions—perhaps even the nation itself—will probably follow suit in the near future.[45] In 1963, drives were underway in eight states to secure the enactment of fair housing laws for the first time, or to extend the coverage of existing laws.[46] (Drives were also underway, though—notably in California—to challenge fair housing laws through lawsuits or public referendums.) Executive action began just before the 1948 ruling of the Supreme Court, when new regulations governing federal credit programs broke away from the previous pattern explicitly prohibiting loans which would serve to introduce Negroes into previously all-white areas. Beginning in 1947, explicit statements directing compliance with accepted real estate policies gave way to vague euphemisms carrying basically the same import but endorsing some "flexibility." Since 1949, however, official policy has supposedly required nondiscrimination in all construction receiving federal support. By 1952 "some preference" was given to interracial developments, and by 1954 official policy included "active steps to encourage . . . open-occupancy projects."[47] A similar swing from a "neutral" policy (which had the effect of increasing segregation) to an official advocacy of nondiscrimination is evident in the pronouncements of Public Housing Authority and Urban Renewal officials.[48] But issuance of the President's Executive Order in Housing in late 1962 was an admission that this policy had not been effectively carried out, as well as a further step in the direction of federal support for equal opportunity in housing.

The dismal truth of the matter is that all of these official efforts on the part of various branches of national, state, and local governments to eliminate residential inequities cannot possibly be sufficient to accomplish the task required. There are too many loopholes in all of the measures cited. Since the Supreme Court's ruling against the legal enforcement of restrictive covenants does not prevent the inclusion of restrictive clauses in real estate contracts, the average party to such contracts is apt to think this clause is legally binding although in fact it is not. Because they require extraordinary perseverance and sometimes rare courage on the part of individual complainants, fair housing ordinances are pitifully inadequate. Few Negro homeseekers are willing to undergo (and emotionally capable of undergoing) the delays, the expense, and the humiliation which are virtually inevitable under present laws. It is understandable, therefore, that between 1955 and 1960, "not more than 1,000 complaints alleging discrimination in housing have been filed in the nine states and two cities with administrative agencies."[49] When this figure is viewed in light of the fact that four-fifths of the complaints were filed in New York State and New York City, and that the jurisdictions covered have a population of more than fifty million persons, the small number of complaints is even more surprising. It is understandable, too, that a leading civil rights lawyer who has spent countless hours and substantial amounts of his own money on one housing case without having won it should despair of taking any more cases of this kind under present statutes.[50] As for executive action on behalf of civil rights in housing, the future is perhaps brighter as a result of the recent presidential Executive Order. In theory, this order will make it easier for Negroes to gain entry into large apartment houses and low-cost housing developments, and it will also add to the pressures on public housing authorities to eliminate discrimination. It is too early to assess fairly the impact of the order; however, civil rights leaders have voiced dissatisfaction with both the scope of the order and the slowness of its implementation.[51]

The inadequacy of attacks upon residential discrimination by public agencies highlights the need for action by private citizens. Without private initiative in the struggle to change the prevailing social attitudes which promote or tolerate housing inequities, neither judicial decisions nor laws nor the promulgation of new regulations in executive agencies of the government will suffice to do away with these inequities.

This book is a report concerning one type of grass roots action which is being taken by fair housing groups in many parts of the country. It is the story of an "open housing covenant" (OHC) campaign in a small industrial city of the North—and the story is a significant one, because in it are revealed many of the possibilities as well as pitfalls of privately initiated efforts to combat discrimination in housing. To understand the implications of the story of the campaign in this particular community, we must first show how the open housing covenant approach fits in with the total pattern of citizen activity on behalf of open-occupancy housing. According to officials of the National Committee Against Discrimination in Housing,

> the most dramatic indication of progress in recent years has been the spontaneous formation of literally hundreds of voluntary fair housing groups in many sections of the country. This proliferating movement appears to be contagious, spreading from town to town and state to state. It cuts across all economic lines: the wealthy Scarsdales have their fair housing committees, as do the middle-class Levittowns, and the upper-class avenues and workingmen's sections of the inner-city.[52]

The work of these groups may be summarized under three major headings: neighborhood stabilization, "willing buyer—willing seller" listing agencies which seek to bring together Negro homeseekers and whites who are willing to sell on a nondiscriminatory basis, and community education.

Neighborhood stabilization refers to the attempt of residents in a given area to maintain an interracial balance when there seems to be a danger that it will become either all-white or all-Negro. In practice, this usually means that a systematic effort is made to persuade whites not to move away in dread of an unprecedented influx of Negroes. Because of unfounded or exaggerated fears concerning loss of property values (or loss of face with one's friends in other neighborhoods), panic selling by white homeowners often occurs when the first so-called "invasion" of a residential area by a few Negro families takes place. This tendency is frequently intensified by rapacious realtors who frighten people into selling by relating fantastic tales of financial loss and general community disintegration in the wake of a sinister black tidal wave. Stabilization is typically brought about through neighborhood meetings in which anxieties are aired and calmed by a presentation of the well-established facts refuting the scare stories, and through sustained efforts on the part of an organized citizenry to insure that schools, sanitation facilities, streets, police protection, and all other community services are kept up to par. [53]

The listing service is self-explanatory; its aim is "to establish direct communication between the homeseeker and the seller or landlord, thus filling the gap created by the absence of normal marketing channels."[54] The underlying purpose, of course, is to open up neighborhoods previously closed to Negroes. The endeavors of the listing service are often supplemented by attempting to recruit "pioneer" Negro families to be the first to move into white sections, and (in states which have fair housing laws) by sending a white "checker" shortly before or after a Negro applicant to ascertain whether or not housing which is legally open to Negroes is in fact available to them.

The OHC campaign, or the "good neighbor pledge" campaign, is an educational device which attempts to change the climate of opinion in a community by demonstrating that there is in that locality a broad base of public support for interracial housing. The program begins when residents are urged to sign a statement affirming their willingness to rent or sell to, or live beside, any family of good character, regardless of race, religion, or national background. Although it is often carried out under the auspices of the religious organizations of the city, the program is intended to draw support from all segments of the population, not just the churchgoers. The climax of the appeal is the publication of a full-page advertisement in the newspaper(s) having the widest local circulation, the ad showing the text of the pledge, endorsements by religious and civic leaders, and the names and addresses of several hundred signers.

One focus of this study, then, is on the OHC as a device for changing the climate of opinion regarding residence and race: How useful is this device, and how may it best be executed? The other focus is on the religious institutions in our society as private agencies which often take the initiative in combatting discrimination: How much vitality does the Church possess as a prophetic force, how do churchmen approach social action, and how effectively do they carry it out?

This second focus involves an examination of a problem concerning which there is much disagreement, one to which conflicting answers have been given. There was a time, not long ago, when many social analysts predicted that we had reached the "twilight of Christianity."[55] It was predicted that with the rise of scientific thinking, industrialism and urbanization, the influence of religion in the lives of modern men would decline almost to the vanishing point.[56] Some sociologists, although they have admitted the Church does have some role in social reform, have argued that religious institutions are Johnny-come-latelies in this department; they argue that churches simply hop on an already rolling bandwagon after it has been set in motion by other forces in society.[57] A recent articulation of this viewpoint was made in regard to "The Role of Religious Organizations in the Desegregation Controversy" by a leading Protestant authority on this subject. The Reverend Will Campbell, for many years associate director of the Department of Racial and Cultural Relations of the National Council of Churches, concludes on the basis of his intimate experience with the controversy that churches will not be in the vanguard of reform, but will only serve to "clean up the mess" resulting from the struggle for civil rights.[58] If these assessments of the role of religion are correct, then the often remarked contradiction between America's highly publicized "religious revival" and her growing secularization—if by that is meant, in part, abandonment by religious institutions of ethical ideals which place them in conflict with society—is not surprising because it is not a contradiction at all.[59]

Other observers contend that there has been in recent years a "quiet revolution" which has released powerful prophetic forces within the churches of America.[60] These observers argue that the social witness of the church is becoming steadily more vigorous and more intelligent. They insist, furthermore, that a

religious institution cannot be true to its own nature as a re-
pository of transcendent values unless it is in the vanguard of
the fight for the just rights of the poor and the downtrodden.
They can cite official pronouncements of ecclesiastical bodies
as evidence that the churches have not been asleep on the
race question; they can point to the participation of hundreds
of ministers and laymen in reform and protest efforts as further
evidence of this fact; they can declare that the Conference on
Religion and Race, held in Chicago in early 1963, constitutes
a milestone in the commitment of American religious groups
to the cause for racial justice. This conference is notable for
the fact that it had the participation of all major religious
bodies in this country, and succeeded in gaining the approval
of all these bodies for a program of specific action, particularly
in the area of residential discrimination. Resolutions were
passed urging religious groups to refuse grants of land in suburban communities which developers intended to keep lily-white,
to withhold investment funds and all other types of support from
enterprises which practice racial discrimination, and to seek to
support, financially as well as in other ways, contractors and
entrepreneurs who were seeking to provide open-occupancy
housing.[61] Commissions were set up in many "target cities" where
extraordinary efforts are being made to overcome racial injustice, above all in housing in Northern communities.[62]

The summer of 1963 also provided evidence of a new vitality
in the Church's commitment to the cause of Negro rights. In
June, the National Council of Churches formed a special Commission on Religion and Race which began to function effectively
almost overnight. Teams of churchmen were dispatched to several trouble spots in the South, where an attempt was made
to demonstrate solidarity with the unjustly oppressed minority
group by having church leaders join Negroes in protest actions
and in jail, and also to visit white ministers to persuade them
that it was their especial responsibility to challenge segregation, even in the face of opposition from their congregations.
One of the most sophisticated operations of the NCC Commission was its effort to organize churchgoers in the Midwest
for the purpose of exerting influence on their senators and con-

gressmen in behalf of civil rights legislation.[63] On the theory that Midwestern votes hold the key to passage of this legislation, Commission sponsored teams visited churches and church gatherings in these states, urging citizens to let their legislators know that they do have a moral, if not economic, stake in the enactment of meaningful civil rights laws. A dramatic symbol of religious involvement in the struggle for racial justice was the March on Washington, in which thousands of clergymen and laymen of all doctrinal persuasions participated.

Thus the second focus of this study is doubly significant, for it promises illumination on the specific question of the Church's role in the desegregation movement and also on the larger question of the Church's vigor as a force for social justice. In seeing how the clergymen described herein define and carry out their roles in this particular area of social action, other clergymen may become aware of hazards to be avoided and potentialities to be exploited in their own performance of similar roles. In seeing how the churchgoers described herein respond to this particular moral challenge, concerned citizens in other parts of the nation may see revealed the poverty or the richness of response that is possible for them. And both friends and foes of religion will be able to judge the extent to which the religious institutions analyzed in this study* lived up to their responsibilities in providing moral leadership in their community.

---

* That the present study deals only with Protestant and Roman Catholic social action is by no means intended to imply that other religious groups are unimportant as influences in American society. The scope of the study was limited partly to facilitate the making of certain judgments about the relationship between theology and ethics, and partly because other groups were not sufficiently numerous in Newfield to make an analysis of their participation in the OHC appeal representative.

THE SETTING

IN 1800, NEWFIELD WAS A TOWN OF five thousand inhabitants, most of whom were engaged in agricultural or trading pursuits.[1] Already by that date, however, the town's importance as a shipping center was beginning to decline, and the growth of light industry had begun. During the nineteenth century and the early part of this century, the economic vitality of Newfield came to depend more and more on light industry—notably textiles, small machinery, and rubber goods.[2] Most of the workers employed in these industries were skilled craftsmen rather than unskilled workers.[3]

The manpower for these industries was supplied in great measure by the arrival of large numbers of immigrants. The Irish came first, then large numbers of Eastern Europeans (especially Poles), and finally a very heavy influx of Italians. The Italian group is of especial importance not only because it is the largest single ethnic group among the immigrants, but also because a very high percentage of the Italians came from one locality in Sicily.[4] Thus the Italian subcommunity in Newfield is remarkable for its continuing spirit of intense ethnic loyalty.[5] Even today, it is not uncommon for a girl of Sicilian ancestry to return to the village from which her parents came for the purpose of finding a husband, with whom she then returns to Newfield.

The tendency of various ethnic groups (not only the Italians) to resist cultural assimilation by maintaining their own language, traditions, and habits is of course a familiar one. This tendency was reinforced by the reluctance on the part of the "old Yankee stock" and the previously settled immigrant groups to accept assimilation with the newcomers. The pattern of resistance and reluctance manifested itself in, and was reinforced by, ethnically determined patterns of residence and religious affiliation.

As late as 1935, Cooney described the following picture of residential groupings in Newfield:

> For the most part the Irish, German and English inhabitants live in the one family type of house on the west side of [George] Street. The Italians are to be found chiefly on the east side of [William] Street, but in the last twenty-five years it is possible to detect a movement in the general direction of High Street. Whereas formerly they were located in a dense district in the vicinity of [Leonard] Avenue, near the railroad station, the Italian section now extends along the river to the north end of town, westward to the [Goshen] road, and then south to [John] Street, making an "L." Their diffusion has been slow. . . .

> The Polish inhabitants are centered in the vicinity of the south end of [William] Street and scattered from there out to the [Northwood] area, which vicinity is particularly available to those of the population engaged in the [Larkin] Company factory there.[6]

Part of the area which was inhabited principally by Italians in 1935 was occupied almost exclusively by Negroes in 1960.

The various ethnic groups were separated from one another by religious ties even more than by residential circumstances. One Lutheran congregation was Scandinavian; another was German. There was a Roman Catholic church whose membership consisted almost exclusively of Irish; another, of Poles; a third (the largest), of Italians.[7] The importance of the church for community life was very great. For the adults, the ethnic church offered a place to meet with friends and relatives who shared a common heritage, spoke the old tongue, and preserved the old customs. For the children, the church offered, in many instances, the only place where their parents would allow them to enjoy social intercourse with members of the opposite sex. (This was more true for girls than for boys, of course, and it was especially true for Italian girls, whose social life would have been almost nonexistent without the Friday night dances at San Stefano's.)[8]

In 1935, the last wave of migrants—Negroes from the Southern states—had not yet begun in earnest. The 1930 census showed only

227 nonwhites in a population of 24,554 (less than one per cent).[9] This is explained by the apparently few employment opportunities at this time for Negroes in Newfield: none of the principal industries of the city in 1935 had any Negro employees.[10] Since many of the Negro inhabitants were servants who lived in the homes of the well-to-do families which employed them, the housing problem for Negroes scarcely existed in the form that it was to take twenty-five years later.

But Newfield changed in many ways between 1935 and 1960: the basis for economic prosperity shifted; ethnic identification diminished in importance as assimilation and social mobility were achieved by hundreds of Italian-and Polish-Americans; residential patterns changed—and the Negro population of the community increased more than sixfold.

By 1960, the total population of Newfield had reached 33,250. But because of the decrease in immigration quotas which had been enacted shortly after World War I and renewed from time to time since then, the number of foreign-born citizens was considerably less than in 1930. A comparison of population figures from 1930 with those of 1950 reveals a substantial decline in the number of foreign-born citizens. The number of foreign-born citizens of the three largest ethnic groups was as follows:[11]

	1930	1950
Irish	1613	242
Polish	2406	900
Italian	3034	1754

Newfield was still an overwhelmingly Roman Catholic city in 1950; indeed, the membership of the four largest Catholic parishes included almost sixty per cent of the total population of the community.[12]

Not only were the bonds with the old country dissolving but also ties with the new country were being made. Hewitt, writing in 1957, reported that many persons of Italian extraction had recently moved up and away from the socio-economic and spatial confines of the Italian sub-community. Resistance to the assimilation of Italians was still strong as late as 1939-40, when an orderly yet determined battle was fought by various segments of the dominant groups in Newfield to prevent a housing development (which was to be occupied mainly by Italians) from being built in their area of town.[13] But World War II applied the *coup de grace* to all such efforts, and after 1946 it became increasingly meaningless to speak of "the Italian section" of the city.

Many socially mobile Italian families secured their status as middle-class Americans by buying real estate. Hewitt declares, "The Italian immigrant family worked as a tight, cohesive economic unit. Every member worked, even young children. . . . A frugal way of life led to savings and eventually to the purchase of property."[14] Sangree says that "a home—real estate—was almost invariably the first large investment [an Italian immigrant] made in this country," adding that "families endured all sorts of skimping and hardships in order to be able to buy their own homes."[15] After World War II, an increasingly large number of the noncorporation landlords of Newfield were Italian.[16]

The war also gave a boost to Newfield's light industry, which had failed to expand significantly from about the turn of the century.[17] But the temporary industrial expansion caused by the war was short-lived. The dominant post-war trend was for Newfield to become more and more a center for retail trades and services, and a "bedroom town" for larger nearby industrial cities. In 1957, more than two thousand residents of Newfield proper held jobs outside the city.[18] A survey in 1953 showed that Newfield was "the central city of an area with over 75,000 population." The same report stated that 55,150 persons lived within fifteen minutes of Newfield, and another 495,149 lived within thirty minutes of the downtown shopping area of the city.[19] The possibilities for new industry were severely limited by high taxes and by a scarcity of land near water and sewage outlets.[20] Said Hewitt:

> Because of the improbability of attracting new industry to the city, it is imperative that Newfield merchants continue to expand and improve their facilities to meet the competition of shopping centers and small business establishments . . . outside the city.[21]

He advised the city fathers of Newfield that "the key to her future is to be found in the trade and service fields."[22] The favorable vote in a referendum on an urban redevelopment program, which was approved in 1959 largely through the efforts of downtown merchants, indicated that a majority of the people of Newfield had become convinced of the accuracy of this prediction.

Equally important, and even more striking, was the large increase of Negro residents which occurred during and after the war. In 1940, the city's nonwhite population was only 320, but ten years later this figure had risen to 544. By 1960, 1,326 nonwhites lived in Newfield.[23] Housing for many Negro families had been made available by the substantial numbers of Italian families who had "moved to the other side of High Street"; however, housing conditions were very poor for many Negroes, and the restrictions on housing opportunities were tight. Even before redevelopment it could be said that "the local issue which concerns the Negro most is that of housing. Many Negroes have been admitted to public housing projects and many more would like to be. . . ."[24] The existence of racial discrimination in housing was beyond doubt:

> Those Negroes who do not live in projects are clearly segregated in certain areas of the city. . . .
>
> Private housing, in most areas of the city, is closed to the Negro. Most of them do not have the necessary cash for a down payment, and those who do are effectively barred through the use of the so-called "Gentleman's Agreement." Homeowners are reluctant to sell to a Negro family if it means, and it usually does, condemnation by their white neighbors. With the housing market an active one, it is just as easy to sell to a white family and keep your "standing" in the community.
>
> . . . I have not been able to discover a single instance in which a Negro has purchased property through a real estate agent. Negro ownership of property is limited, however, and I was able to find only sixteen local homes owned by Negroes in the entire city of Newfield.[25]

Four years after these words were written, the problem of residential discrimination had assumed such proportions that it could no longer be ignored by the socially conscious citizens and religious leaders of the city. The time for action had come, and a series of independently initiated actions by various groups and individuals culminated in the Greater Newfield Open Housing Covenant program of 1961-62.

EVENTS LEADING TO THE OHC CAMPAIGN IN NEWFIELD

In June, 1959, the citizens of Newfield approved a plan for redevelopment of two blocks in the heart of the downtown business district of the city. The area included a number of low-rent housing units, many of which were occupied by Negroes. The task of relocating the thirty-eight Negro families who were to be displaced by redevelopment focused the attention of a number of public-spirited citizens on the question of housing for Negroes in the community.

There was considerable apprehension within the Negro community as to what redevelopment would mean for the Negro families affected. Redevelopment projects through the country have often failed to relocate uprooted families in the "decent, safe and sanitary" housing which it is theoretically supposed to guarantee them. To this general suspicion of redevelopment among Newfield Negroes was added their mistrust of Ephraim Parker, the man appointed director of the redevelopment agency of the city. In the minds of many Newfield inhabitants, Parker was responsible for a deplorable incident which had occurred several years before when he was state highway commissioner. A large number of Negro families had been evicted from their homes and put into tents in order to make possible the construction of a highway through the city. Shortly after Parker was named to the redevelopment post, a feature story in the local press recalled the notorious "tent village" episode.[26] A follow-up story promptly exonerated Parker from blame for this occurrence; nevertheless, the image of Parker as the man who evicted many Negroes from their homes and into tents remains current in the Negro lore concerning Newfield. So Parker's appointment added fuel to the fires of concern about the housing problem which began to burn within the Negro community with the announcement that urban redevelopment was planned for Newfield.

The housing aspect of redevelopment was in the hands of Sean O'Malley, the relocation officer of the agency. O'Malley's significance lies less in his official capacity—although his efforts were instrumental in finding housing for many of the Negro families displaced by redevelopment—than in his unofficial capacity as one of the leading Roman Catholic laymen of Newfield. His long record of service in Catholic community affairs gave O'Malley direct access to the bishop of the diocese which includes Newfield, and he turned out to be the key liaison person between the Roman Catholic priests and the Protestant clergymen who were interested in conducting an open housing covenant appeal in the city. O'Malley's interest in the covenant received significant reinforcement from Miss Lois Rogers, the human relations consultant of the regional Housing and Home Finance Agency office, who visited Newfield several times to counsel with O'Malley about his task as relocation officer. Miss Rogers, herself a Negro and a Roman Catholic, was an enthusiastic supporter of the covenant program, and provided encouragement for launching it as an inter-faith venture by telling of the success of similar programs in other cities.

For several months following the approval of the referendum on urban redevelopment, the situation lay dormant. In March, 1960, the director of the redevelopment agency issued a policy statement regarding relocation of families displaced by redevelopment. In this statement he made it clear that no use would be made by agency officials of the state civil rights law on housing in order to force Newfield landlords to accept displaced Negro families.[27] This statement may have reassured the white homeowners of the city, but it offered no answer to the problem of how the families in question were to be provided with housing. It seemed evident that interested parties other than the relocation officer of the urban redevelopment agency would have to concern themselves in the matter.

Significant interest in the problem on the part of local church groups began to manifest itself in the summer of 1960. The Social Action Committee of the Protestant Council of Churches was informed of what seemed to be a clear-cut case of discrimination against a prospective Negro home buyer. Considerable discussion was held within the committee concerning how the matter should be handled. Dr. John Wallace of the chemistry department of the University felt that the civil rights law of the state should be invoked, if necessary, in order to persuade the realtor who was involved to sell the home. The Reverend Louis Dickenson was against this experiment, urging conciliatory talks with the realtor instead. His view prevailed, and the following letter was written to the realtor by the chairman of the committee:

July 14, 1960

The Excelsior Real Estate Agency
613 Horton St.
Newfield, ...

Gentlemen:

As you may know, the Social Action Committee of the Greater Newfield Council of Churches is concerned with the support and strengthening of any phase of community life which deepens the ties of brotherhood and understanding. Conversely, it is our task to be alert to any aspects of that community life which might weaken or even destroy them.

We are aware that the problem of finding adequate housing for minority groups, particularly negroes [sic], in the Newfield area is a real one now and, with the Redevelopment program in the offing, it is likely to increase. Old prejudices and misunderstandings of the facts can increase the tensions involved if they are not handled wisely and eventually overcome.

We are aware also that the Real Estate Agencies of the community are "in the middle" in this situation and that selling real estate to negroes [sic] in an "all white" neighborhood takes a good deal of courage. Nevertheless, you, as well as we, have no real choice provided the family wishing to buy qualifies in every other way. We are sure that you know this all too well.

It is because of this that our Committee on Social Action would like very much to talk with you at my office in the Parish House of the St. Thomas Episcopal Church at a convenient time within the next week or 10 days. Our attention has been called to the facts involved in the sale of the "Oldham property" at 234 East Street which we think ought to be discussed and clarified. We suggest this not in a spirit of criticism but in the hope that a future policy in the best interest of all our neighbors might be derived from sharing of views. (A copy of the "Chronology of Events" on the Oldham property as we understand them is enclosed.)

Please be in touch with me or with any other member of this committee at your earliest convenience.

Sincerely yours,
THE REV. MURRAY JACKSON
Chairman, Social Action Committee
Greater Newfield Council of Churches

A conference with a representative of the Excelsior Agency was held, but the disposition of the Oldham property was not affected by it, and little headway was made in facing the fundamental issue of the realtor's responsibility for discrimination in housing.[28]

This incident seems to have been decisive in triggering subsequent actions designed to combat discrimination on the part of church groups in Newfield. It was at this time that Dr. Wallace became chairman of the Social Action Committee of the Butler Memorial Congregational Church. It was also during this period that the Reverend Peter Everett, pastor of Butler Memorial, became chairman of the Housing Committee of the local branch of the National Association for the Advancement of Colored People.* Both men had been persuaded by the outcome of the Oldham incident that conciliation would not bring any tangible results. They were determined to try more vigorous tactics.

At the suggestion of Everett, the Butler Memorial Social Action Committee began to cooperate with the Newfield NAACP in trying to help Negro families secure new housing. The NAACP made it known throughout the Negro community that such help was available.

The NAACP then screened all applicants to make certain that they were financially reliable and socially acceptable. The Butler Memorial Social Action Committee then assigned one

---

* Referred to hereafter as the NAACP.

of its members to be a "checker" for each Negro family which passed the screening process. The white checker would answer newspaper advertisements of dwellings which were apparently suitable for the family concerned, and which were covered by the state public accommodations law. He would announce to the landlord that he was looking at the apartment to determine its suitability for some friends who wanted to secure a dwelling. If it were ascertained that the apartment was suitable, the checker would then ask if a verbal agreement of rental could be made. If the landlord were agreeable, the checker would then say, "By the way, there is one additional fact about the family you might want to know: they are Negroes." If the landlord showed no change of mind about the availability of the apartment, the Negro family would then sign a lease and move in. If the landlord refused to rent to the family—after just having said that he would be willing to rent it—a *prima facie* case of discrimination was evident, and it was up to the Negro family concerned whether or not it wanted to contact the State Civil Rights Commission to instigate legal proceedings against the landlord. This went on continuously from the late fall of 1960 through the late spring of 1961.

Dr. Wallace and his committee were perplexed by the reactions of several of the Negro families with whom they worked during this time. In the first place, they were struck by the fact that such a small number of Negro families seemed to be interested in availing themselves of the proffered help. Secondly, they were discouraged by the unwillingness of Negro families to follow through on their initial efforts by taking a case of obvious discrimination to the State Civil Rights Commission. Their perplexity over these developments led them to wonder if their knowledge of the Negro community was lacking in certain essential features.

As will be noted below, the membership of the Butler Memorial Congregational Church included a large number of faculty members from the University. Through conversation between members of the church Social Action Committee and faculty members at the University, the idea for a study of the Negro citizens of Newfield evolved. From this conversation emerged the idea of forming a University committee to undertake such a study. In February, 1961, a group of interested persons, which included faculty members, local Negro leaders and the Reverend Everett, formed a University Study Committee which began to investigate ways of conducting a study of the housing conditions of Newfield Negroes. In June, 1961, a team of thirteen University students visited every known Negro family in the Newfield area and compiled the data which will be presented in the succeeding chapter. The study was facilitated by the cooperation of the Newfield branch of the NAACP and by the ministers of local Negro churches.

During the spring of 1961 interest in the housing problem was mounting. On February 16, the Social Action Committee of Butler Memorial Church issued a sobering report based on the first few months of its activity on behalf of Negro home and apartment seekers. The report charged that many Newfield landlords were guilty of discrimination against nonwhites. The implication of the report was clear: it was virtually impossible for Negroes to obtain housing in Newfield outside the predominantly Negro residential areas.[29]

This implication was made explicit in a letter to the editor of the Newfield *Review* which appeared on March 27. Dr. Jake Lawson, a faculty member of the University Study Committee and a past president of the Newfield branch of the NAACP, asserted:

> We in Newfield must realize that a successful relocation of Negro families is not simply one which physically moves the families. . . . While we are at it, why not help to improve living conditions and further integration? To concentrate Negroes in ghetto-like areas, no matter how nice the physical surroundings, is to build a dike against progress. Nothing breaks down prejudice like associations. . . .
>
> Another point of the utmost importance needs to be made. The problem of Negro housing in Newfield is not confined to thirty-five families now residing in the Dock Street area. . . . Very few Negro families are properly housed in Newfield and environs, not because they necessarily lack economic potential but because the general community has not opened itself to them.[30]

Lawson's letter received editorial support in the Newfield *Review* the following day. An editorial entitled "The Old Excuses Won't Suffice" warned that "a city reaps what is sows." Deploring the failure of city officials to enforce municipal building and fire codes, the editorial reiterated Lawson's contention that "the city has its fair share of housing that is dangerous to human life and is uninhabitable by any reasonable human standard." The *Review* editorialist declared that "every landlord has a duty to provide safe housing"; furthermore, he maintained, "When the landlord does not [fulfill this obligation], there is a clear duty on the part of the city to see that this is done." The editorial closed with an endorsement of a civil rights bill currently being considered by the state legislature:

> We believe that the law should include any landlord with three or more apartments and that a landlord charged with a violation of the law should be required to post a bond. What is happening now is that landlords who wish to evade the law rent the apartment to white tenants before the state government agency can act.[31]

This flurry of excitement was minor compared to the full-fledged squall which broke in May. Angus McCrory, a realtor, angrily resigned from the mayor's Displaced Housing Committee—a committee which must be appointed by the administration of every municipality which participates in the federal urban redevelopment program. McCrory charged that the attitude of certain members of the committee rendered impossible any constructive democratic discussion of the matters with which the committee was supposed to deal. The Newfield *Review* diagnosed the resignation as the result of a dispute over whether or not the committee should support "legislation now in the General Assembly that would liberalize the Public Accommodations Act, making it easier for the State Civil Rights Commission to take action against landlords who refuse to rent to Negroes."[32] McCrory was the only member of the eight-man committee—which included Dr. Jake Lawson and, as chairman, the Reverend Peter Everett—who was not in favor of a resolution supporting this legislation. He was of the opinion that the committee should not "waste its time with the legislative resolutions but [should] get right to work on the business of finding Negro housing and of fostering a harmonious relationship in housing."[33] The text of the lengthy minority report, entitled "The Solution for our Local Racial Problem: Not Force—But Mutual Understanding and Mutual Good Will," which McCrory attached to his letter of resignation included the following comments:

> To my astonishment, I found that the leading members of our committee considered it the primary function of the committee, not to help find homes for displaced Negro citizens but to sponsor stringent and punitive legislation forcing people to do what they would not do otherwise. . . .

> Not one of my fellow committee members own any real property, and would, therefore, not be affected by the new law they so vigorously advocate. For them to want to lay down the law to others seems rather out of place; and to increase the penalties beyond those already provided for in the proposed laws before the legislature, seems almost frivolous. . . .

> I believe that to pass and enforce legislation of the type recommended by the majority of the subcommittee can do no good. One cannot force the mixing of races as one cannot force esteem, affection or respect—by legislation, or any other way. If any of our fellow citizens were deprived of any basic constitutional right, as the right of free speech, of worship or assembly, the right to vote or the right to education, I would be in the forefront of those who would fight to have those rights established or restored. But no basic constitutional rights are involved in the relations between races here in Newfield. . . .

> I do not believe that it was our Maker's intention to mix up the various races, but rather that He intended to have them struggle towards the stars, each in its own fashion, and live and work, side by side, in peaceful competition.[34]

The controversy was enlivened by hints of a personal feud when, at a public meeting later in May, McCrory added to his general complaints a personal attack upon Dr. Lawson. According to McCrory, Lawson had stated in a committee meeting that there was only one "real solution" to the minority group housing issue: "to line up the real estate men against a wall and shoot them."[35]

Lawson's protestations that his remark had been entirely facetious did not deter McCrory from relating the incident in ominous tones at every opportunity.

While the lines of battle were being drawn publicly, interest in the housing problem was gathering momentum within the Protestant community of Newfield. The annual "May Day" gathering of the United Church Women was devoted to discrimination in housing. The Social Action Committee of the Greater Newfield Council of Churches passed a resolution urging the state legislature to pass the more stringent civil rights bill under consideration. Leadership of this committee passed into the hands of the Reverend Harold Baldwin whose intense interest in the housing problem was soon to become manifest. Most important of all, perhaps, the Social Action Committee of the Butler Memorial Congregational Church continued its efforts to place Negro families in housing advertised through the local press.

In late June, Dr. John Wallace, chairman of the Butler Memorial group, wrote a letter to the editor of the *Review* summarizing "The Story of a Search" for landlords willing to rent to Negroes. The gist of the story was that out of sixty-three calls on landlords who had dwelling units for rent which were suitable for the prospective tenants in question, only four had been willing to rent to a Negro family. Fifty-two had given a flat "No" when they learned that the prospective tenant was Negro. Contained in the latter was an implied indictment of the hypocrisy of landlords who claimed, "I'm not prejudiced, but—" and who then placed the blame for refusal on their other tenants, their neighbors, their relatives, or anyone but themselves. The letter closed with this appeal to personal integrity and community pride:

> Talk it over with your neighbors and friends. Talk it over with your priest, minister, or rabbi. But don't let the talk keep you from asking yourself the question which we will be asking you or your neighbor: "Will you accept a Negro family in this neighborhood?" Because when that quiet question is asked you will be on trial. And so will your neighborhood. And so will your town and your country. You must decide soon whether or not Newfield's present answer to this question is the answer you want the world to hear.[36]

An immediate response was forthcoming from Angus McCrory, who resented what he perceived as "veiled threats" in Wallace's letter. McCrory seized the occasion to reiterate his contention that the majority of the persons on the mayor's housing committee "were not interested primarily in housing for Negroes but in sponsoring punitive legislation against our white fellow citizens." He also reasserted his belief that "races and racial problems were created by God and no man-made interpretation of religious doctrine or man-made laws can change them." He went on to say that "the reaction of the white people to the question of racial integration in housing is the result of a sound instinct based on the God-given laws of life and self-preservation." After reminding his readers that Dr. Wallace did not own any rental property, McCrory declared that Wallace and anyone else who is "continuously promoting racial antagonism and, perhaps, interracial warfare" is also helping "to seal the doom of your country and mine."[37]

A series of letters to the editor followed this exchange between Wallace and McCrory, support being registered for each man's position. From this point on the "Negro housing problem," as it is commonly alluded to, had become a significant public issue in Newfield.

Shortly after this, at its meeting on July 26, 1961, the Social Action Committee of the Greater Newfield Council of Churches decided to make the housing problem its central concern for the next few months and determined to recommend to the executive body of the Council that this concern should be expressed in an interfaith housing covenant campaign during the fall. Plans were made to establish contact with local representatives of the Roman Catholic and Jewish clergy, and to make use of the September meeting of the Protestant Clergy Fellowship for the purpose of stimulating support for the covenant approach. All members of the committee agreed that the covenant program could not be successful in predominantly Catholic Newfield unless it had the full backing of the local Catholic clergy. The Reverend Peter Everett had already approached one of the local Roman Catholic priests with the idea of an interfaith open housing covenant; he reported that this priest was personally sympathetic to the idea but was certain that the approval of the diocesan bishop would have to be obtained before Catholic sponsorship of the covenant would be possible. According to Everett, the priest anticipated considerable resistance to the covenant on the part of Newfield Catholics, for in explaining the importance of having the bishop's backing he had wryly commented to his Protestant colleague, "Our people can tell us to go to hell just as quickly as yours can." The Committee decided to ask Sean O'Malley and Miss Lois Rogers to explain the idea of the interfaith open housing covenant to the Roman Catholic bishop and to seek his approval of the plan.[38] O'Malley and Miss Rogers agreed to do this, and at the next meeting of the Committee the latter reported that the bishop was planning to send a priest who was a specialist in the housing problems of minority groups to Newfield for the purpose of informing them of the need for an open housing covenant and instructing them as to effective methods of presenting it to their parishioners.[39]

Plans for the covenant appeal received added impetus in early September when public attention was once again focused on the housing issue through the release of a preliminary report on the housing conditions of Newfield Negroes by the University Study Committee. Press coverage of the report, which was a condensed, nonacademic version of the full analysis which will be given in the following chapter, placed emphasis on "Race Bias [as a] Main Factor in Shaping Negro Ghettos." The lead sentence of the six-column front-page story on the report alluded not only to discrimination in housing, but also to job discrimination:

> Many Negro families here are able to purchase adequate housing but they as well as others with insufficient resources are confined to several concentrated areas primarily because of racial discrimination and low income, which is caused, to a high degree, by discrimination.

Any reader who found himself unwilling to believe that the housing plight of most Newfield Negroes was as bad as the report indicated was invited to go and see for himself certain designated streets which were adjudged "typical of the housing environment for the majority of Newfield's Negro citizens."[40]

On September 20, the Council of Churches Social Action Committee presented an explanation of the planned open housing covenant program at the meeting of the Protestant Clergy Fellowship. The director of the housing study was present at this meeting to give a full report of the findings and to answer questions about them. After this report, Harold Baldwin urged all of the ministers of the fellowship to participate in the housing covenant program. In the discussion which followed, none of the ministers voiced serious misgivings about or objections to the idea of sponsoring the covenant campaign. It was agreed that all would, if practicable, preach on the theme of the injustice of prejudice and discrimination, when presenting the covenant to their people on October 22. In private, some negative sentiments were expressed: The Reverend Murray Jackson, a member of the Social Action Committee of the Council, reported that he had been the butt of some kidding remarks from another clergyman who chaffed him for being identified with those who were suggesting "this juvenile idea" to the Clergy Fellowship.[41]

The covenant program was scheduled for launching on October 16 at the semi-annual Council of Churches dinner. Since approval of Roman Catholic participation in the enterprise had not been received by the time of the October 5 meeting of the Council Social Action Committee, it was feared that the covenant cards would either have to be withheld from distribution at the dinner, or have to be distributed without the Catholic clergy's endorsement printed on them. As late as October 9, only one week prior to the dinner, no definite word of endorsement had been received from the bishop despite repeated assurances from Sean O'Malley that the endorsement would be forthcoming. The side of the covenant card containing the pledge of nondiscrimination was printed later that same week, and endorsements by representatives of the local Jewish and Protestant groups were prepared for printing on the other side of the card. On the evening of October 13, O'Malley called the Reverend Baldwin to inform him that Father Sloan had been appointed by the bishop to formulate an endorsement of the covenant on behalf of the Roman Catholic clergy. O'Malley delivered the statement to Baldwin the following evening (a Saturday evening), the printer received the three endorsements early Monday morning, and the cards were fully printed and ready for distribution that evening, October 16.[42] (The full text of the covenant card, both the pledge of nondiscrimination and the endorsements by clergymen of the three faiths, is given in Appendix B.)

The principal speaker at the Council of Churches dinner was Dr. Arnold Kerr, a high official in the Department of Racial and Cultural Relations of the National Council of Churches. Dr. Kerr set the stage for the covenant by describing discrimination as a moral challenge which forced the Christian Church to reform itself and society or else to forfeit all claims to a gospel with integrity. He also analyzed the components of the vicious circle which operates to perpetuate discrimination in housing, and recommended the open housing covenant as a means of breaking this circle by changing the climate of opinion in the community.[43] Kerr was followed by Dr. Wallace, who gave a brief résumé of the work of the Butler Memorial Social Action Committee and explained the covenant to the delegates. Approximately one hundred and sixty persons were present at the dinner. One hundred forty-nine of those in attendance signed the covenant that evening.[44]

Newfield's open housing covenant campaign was underway. According to the original expectations of the Council of Churches Social Action Committee, the participating churches were to have returned the signed covenant cards to the Committee by the middle of November, and the full-page advertisement based on the cards was to have been printed in the local press about the end of that same month. It was hoped that more than two thousand signed cards would be received. These expectations proved to be unrealistic. As the following chapters will show, the response of the Christian clergy and laity to the housing covenant was neither so immediate nor so numerically impressive as its planners had anticipated.

THE NEGRO POPULATION
OF NEWFIELD

CHAPTER *3*

IN THE SUMMER OF 1961, THERE were approximately 1,470 Negroes living in the Newfield area. According to the 1950 census there were only 713 Negroes in the city; thus, a population increase of 757 persons (106%) had occurred during the eleven-year period. The rate of increase accelerated steadily, moreover:

161 families (51%) have arrived since 1951;
94 families (30%) have arrived since 1956;
23 families (7%) arrived during the twelve months preceding the summer of 1961.

In addition, the "culture shock" which newcomers in a community often experience was augmented in this case by a high rate of residential mobility within Newfield itself: seventy-five per cent of the respondents listed their previous residence as "elsewhere in the Newfield area."

Most newcomers apparently take the first dwelling they can find upon arrival, and then move into another residence soon thereafter:

78 families (24%) have been in their present dwelling less than a year;
201 (64%), five years or less;
260 (83%), ten years or less.

An overwhelming majority of the Negro population was born in the South:

192 of the 471 wage earners reported on in the survey (41%) were born in the Deep South;

172 (37%), in the Upper South;
 10 (2%), in the border States.
_____
374 (79%) were born outside the Northern states.*

It is highly probable that the flow of Negro migrants from the South will continue during the next decade,[1] but even if in-migration from the South slackens somewhat in the near future, the family composition of Newfield's Negro population guarantees a continually expanding demand for housing. Of the 1,291 persons accounted for by this study,

112 are infants;
490 are children aged 4-18 (247 boys and 243 girls);
275 are young adults aged 19-35;
284 are middle-aged adults aged 36-60;
130 are elderly persons.

Thus nearly sixty-eight percent of the population is likely to reproduce itself, or more than reproduce itself, in the next two decades. The mean family size in the Negro population is four, but almost forty per cent of the families contacted have more than four members.

HOUSING CONDITIONS

Two hundred fifty-four families (81%) live in rental housing, the ownership of which is divided in the following manner:

109 have local white landlords;
 60 have local Negro landlords;
 34 live in the federal low-income housing project;
  8 live in the state moderate-income housing project;
 15 have non-local landlords;
 28 live in dwellings owned by other groups or agencies.
_____
254

* Because percentages for each category are rounded off to the nearest whole number, the total percentage does not necessarily equal the sum of individual percentages. Furthermore, because not every question was answered on all interview schedules, the total number of responses does not always equal the normal base figures of 314 families (254 rentals, 60 self-owned dwellings) or 471 wage-earning adults.

Virtually all tenants have running water, a flush toilet, electricity, and a refrigerator. All but nine families have a bath or shower, but nineteen families are forced to share it with one or more persons outside the family. Nine families do not have a private kitchen. All but twenty families have a gas or an electric cooking stove. Approximately forty per cent of those who rent do not have central heating; furthermore, twenty respondents reported that they have no heat or no heat other than that provided by a combination stove-heater in their kitchen. The average amount paid per month for all utilities, including heat, varies greatly, but it appears that the median price paid for rent plus utilities is approximately seventy dollars per month.

Sixty families (19%) own their homes. This figure is low in comparison with the national average for Negroes (36%), and it is less than half the average for Negroes in the state where Newfield is located (44%). Furthermore, even this percentage cannot be regarded as automatically "decent, safe and sanitary" housing simply because it is self-owned: about one fourth of the houses owned by Negroes in Newfield are of such low quality or are so undesirably located that they must be considered substandard housing. Some self-owned homes are included in the ninety-five dwellings which were classified as "overcrowded"—that is, dwellings which did not have a separate bedroom for every two persons or for children of the opposite sex.

It should be noted that home ownership is correlated with permanency of residence to a remarkable degree. Eighty-eight per cent of the self-owned residences belong to citizens who have been in Newfield longer than ten years. Sixty-one per cent of the self-owned homes have been acquired during the past ten years.

THE ECONOMIC SITUATION

Three hundred seventy (78%) of the approximately 471 men and women who belong to the nonwhite work force in Newfield have steady full-time jobs. Of the remainder, about half are seasonal or part-time workers, and about half are unemployed. The "last hired, first fired" employment policy traditionally applied to nonwhites still haunts many Newfield Negroes; quite a few respondents voiced pessimism or anxiety about job security. The fact that so many Negro wage-earners have very little seniority does not ease their anxiety:

268 (57%) have been on the present job 5 years or less;
 86 (18%) less than one year.

Even more striking is the existence of a very low job ceiling for Newfield Negroes revealed by the study:

249 (53%) are unskilled workers;
 56 (12%) are "service workers" (most of whom are employed in non-professional hospital jobs);
 47 (10%)—all females—are domestic servants;
 74 (16%) are skilled workers; but only
 17 (4%) are clerical workers;
 13 (3%) are professional men.

The percentage of professional and clerical workers is low even in comparison with the Negro average nationally, and the national average for Negroes is far below that for whites. On the other hand, the proportion of skilled workers is one and two-thirds times higher than the national average, and far fewer Negro women in Newfield are forced to work as domestic servants than in the nation as a whole.[2] Despite these findings, though, Negro wage-earners exhibit a high degree of satisfaction with the equality of job opportunities in Newfield: only forty-three (9%) thought they had been refused a job because of their race.

It follows from the occupational status of Newfield Negro wage earners that their income level is considerably below that of American whites, though it is above that of Negro Americans as a whole.[3]

131 (28%) of the nonwhite work force earn less than $50 per week;
290 (62%) earn less than $75 per week;
396 (84%) earn less than $100 per week; only
 51 (11%) earn $100 or more per week.

To state the matter in comparative terms,

> White workers nationally earn a mean wage of $79.72 per week;
>
> Negro workers in Newfield, a mean wage of approximately $70 per week;
>
> Negro workers nationally, a mean wage of $42.40 per week.

Total family income follows this pattern:

> 24 families (8%) live on less than $2,000 per year;
>
> 177 families (56%) live on less than $5,000 per year; only
>
> 11 families (4%) have more than $10,000 per year.

These figures show that Newfield lags slightly behind the statewide average for Negroes (47% under $5,000 per year; 8% over $10,000) and substantially behind the statewide average for whites (only 33% under $5,000 per year; 23% over $10,000).[4] Furthermore, the average family income for Newfield Negroes, which falls between $4,000-$5,000 per year, is substantially below that of Newfield as a whole, which is $7,069 per year.[5]

EDUCATIONAL ATTAINMENT

Information regarding educational attainment was sought in two different areas: formal academic training and vocational training. In respect to the former, it was ascertained that:

> 112 (24%) of the wage earners had not gone beyond 6th grade;
>
> 232 (49%) had gone beyond the 9th grade;
>
> 135 (29%) had graduated from high school (including 36, or 8%, who had received some formal schooling beyond the high school diploma).

The educational attainment of Newfield Negroes is slightly higher than that of Negroes in the country at large, but still lower than that of whites on a nationwide basis. In respect to vocational training, it was learned that 407 respondents (86%) had not endeavored to advance themselves occupationally through apprenticeship courses, correspondence courses, or other job advancement programs. The significance of the finding about job training is difficult to assess. If the job advancement is expected to come in the normal course of time on the job, extra effort and time in training might not be considered necessary. The very existence of job training opportunities might be unknown to many wage earners.

ATTITUDES

Although most of the questions on the interview schedule used in this phase of the study were concerned with quantitative data, a few open-ended questions provided some opportunity for respondents to express themselves on a variety of subjects. No system of coding for IBM cards can quite do justice to this kind of free response; however, the following findings can be reported with confidence.

Dissatisfaction with housing conditions is not unanimous, but it is considerable. Among those who live in rental housing,

> 153 (60%) are satisfied with the general upkeep of their dwelling by the landlord;
> 73 (29%) are dissatisfied;
> 26 (10%) are undecided or ambiguous in their reply.

Dissatisfaction was voiced concerning heating difficulties more often than anything else:

> 84% of the respondents had no complaint about the maintenance of plumbing facilities;
> 83% had no complaint about the maintenance of electrical appliances, stairs, porches, etc.; and only
> 2% volunteered* complaints about rodents;
> 4% volunteered* complaints about vermin; but
> 80 families (29% of those with central heating and 44% of those without it) complained of poor heating;

---

*Because it was feared that a direct question concerning rodents or vermin might offend the respondents and destroy rapport for the remainder of the interview, no such question was included on the interview schedule.

115 families (43% of those with central heating and 51% of those without it) complained of drafty rooms, insufficiently tight windows or doors, etc.

Perhaps the most serious complaint registered was that of the eighteen families who stated that their homes were subject to flooding. When asked about their general attitude toward the fairness of the rent they were paying,

99 respondents (39%) said it was fair;
104 respondents (41%) said they were paying too much;
46 respondents (18%) were undecided or ambiguous in their reply.

Dissatisfaction with the neighborhood was found less frequently than dissatisfaction with the house itself:

189 respondents (60%) liked their neighborhood, in general;
69 respondents (22%) disliked it;
56 (18%) had no strong feeling either way.

Among the criteria most often mentioned as a basis for a favorable attitude were:

108 (34%)—nice neighbors
84 (27%)—quiet
40 (13%)—convenience to town
34 (11%)—good place to raise children
25 (8%)—convenience to work

Among the criteria most often mentioned as a basis for an unfavorable attitude were:

65 (21%)—noisy
49 (16%)—bad place to raise children
30 (10%)—unpleasant neighbors
27 (9%)—dirty, run-down neighborhood

It is interesting to note that 172 (55%) of the respondents had nothing to say (or actually, in many cases, replied "Nothing" or

"I can't think of a thing") when asked about unfavorable aspects of the neighborhood. One hundred six (34%) gave a like reply to the question about favorable aspects of the neighborhood. The unconcern suggested by the large number of such responses is echoed in another interesting finding: only forty (25%) of the 159 respondents who live in housing classified by interviewers as marginal or substandard housing (most of which is in undesirable residential areas of the city) registered an unfavorable general attitude toward the neighborhood, and only forty-six of this same group considered the rent they were being charged too high.

Fifty-four per cent of the respondents indicated that they had considered moving from their present residence, and thirty-nine per cent had actually taken steps to find another place to live. These percentages would in all probability be significantly higher were it not for the fact that so many Negroes feel very pessimistic about their chances of finding better housing:

23 (7%) think that their large family would prevent
them from finding a better residence;
32 (10%) mention economic limitations;
146 (46%) mention racial discrimination.

Because discrimination is expected, only 112 (36%) of the respondents said that they consulted newspaper ads when looking for a house, and only fifty-seven (18%) bothered to consult a realtor. Unfortunately, the interviewers were unable to elicit detailed responses to their question about unofficial channels of information used in finding a place to live; however, the fact that fifty of the fifty-three persons who did give a definite answer to this question mentioned "friends" (rather than "employers" or "NAACP officials" or "church leaders") reveals how important informal word-of-mouth contacts (as opposed to quasi-official or organizational contacts) are in the search for housing. Only eleven (6%) of the 189 respondents who had been refused housing felt that the refusal had nothing to do with their being Negro—so the pessimism of those who have sought housing is based on unhappy experience.

A series of questions designed to probe the positive desires of the respondents concerning where they would like to live produced two interesting findings. In the first place, it appears that Newfield Negroes are hardly even considering a move away from this locale. Of the respondents who did not indicate a preference for some place in the Newfield area,

97 (31%) gave no definite answer;
16 (5%) mentioned another city in the North or West;
 2 (less than 1%) said they wanted to return to the South.

In the second place, it appears that there are in Newfield a substantial number of Negro families who want and can afford to pay for better housing. Interestingly enough, the effective demand for better rental housing appears to be much less than the effective demand for self-owned homes. When asked, "If you were to move into a community of your choice, how much rent would you be willing to pay, assuming that utilities are included in the rent?", respondents gave very conservative answers:

Only 18 (6%) were willing to pay more than $100 per month;
Only 58 (18%) were willing to pay more than $90 per month.

In view of the fact that the median total rent (rent plus utilities) now being paid is about seventy dollars, it does not seem likely that many better accommodations will be available for only twenty dollars per month additional.* But of the two hundred and eight respondents who said they would like to buy a house,

21 with a family income of at least $4-5,000 per year expressed a desire to buy a $10-12,000 home;
22 with a family income of at least $5-6,000 per year expressed a desire to buy a $12-14,000 home;

---

* It is quite possible that many respondents did not include payment of utilities in their estimate of what they would be willing to pay. If so, the findings would underestimate nonwhite demand for better rental housing.

9 with a family income of at least $6-7,000 per year
expressed a desire to buy a $14-16,000 home;
6 with incomes in excess of $7,000 per year expressed
a desire to buy a home costing $16,000 or more.

The housing market might not contain enough houses in the $10-12,000 price range to afford all of the twenty-one families who desire such homes an opportunity to purchase one, and other economic factors might prevent purchases by some of the fifty-eight families with apparent ability to buy a home. But it seems safe to say that a considerable number of Newfield Negroes would buy homes if they were given a chance to buy on equal terms with prospective white buyers.

A Profile of the Five Types of Housing

The Negro population of Newfield is very young and expanding very swiftly. An extremely large portion of this population has come from the South, especially from those Southern states along the Eastern Seaboard. Relative to the Negro population of the country at large, the economic position of Newfield Negroes is good, but their occupational and income levels are substantially below those of the white population of the nation and the state. Negroes of this city have less trouble than other members of their race throughout the country in finding employment, and the number of skilled workers is relatively large. But remarkably few local Negroes have professional or clerical positions. The level of educational attainment is somewhat higher that the national average for nonwhites; it is somewhat lower than the national average for whites.

Five types of housing are represented in the residences now occupied by Newfield Negroes: federal low-income housing project, state moderate-income housing project, inferior rental housing, adequate rental housing, and self-owned homes. Dwellings which were not in one of the projects and not self-owned were classified as "inferior" or "adequate" on the basis of complaints about poor upkeep, safety hazards, susceptibility to flooding, or other serious deficiencies in the dwelling itself (not in the neighborhood) registered by the respondent and/or the interviewer. A description of the occupants and the condition of their dwellings will now be given for each type of housing. (A summary of the same information is contained in Table 1. In the Table, the number assigned to each housing type corresponds to the order in which they are listed above: "Type I" housing is the federal project; "Type II" is the state project; etc.)

Self-Owned Residences

Almost nine-tenths of the families which own their homes have lived in Newfield more than ten years. This group is divided about equally between those families which have four or less members and those which have more than four. Three-quarters of the respondents affirmed satisfaction with the neighborhood in which they live, and four-fifths had made no effort to find another residence. About twenty-nine per cent have graduated from high school. In terms of occupational level and income, this group is better off than any other:

Less than 50% of the wage earners in these families have low-grade occupations (i.e., "unskilled," "domestic," or "service" occupations);

20% make more than $100 per week, and only 18% make less than $50 per week;

Only about one-third of these families have a total income of less than $5,000 per year.

Approximately two-thirds of these houses were rated by the interviewers as needing no paint nor repair work, but these figures include the responses given by persons who live in the low-quality self-owned homes in East Newfield and in the ghetto area between Dock and Porter Streets, and answers from these respondents make the overall percentages for self-owned homes lower than they would otherwise be in some cases. Two-thirds of the respondents in this category say that they have not encountered racial discrimination in searching for housing, but forty per cent say they would expect to encounter discrimination if they tried to move into a house "in the community of their choice."

Adequate Rental Housing

Unlike the residents of self-owned homes, seventy per cent of the families in this group have been in Newfield ten years or less, and only one-quarter of them have families with more than four members. Like the homeowners, they are satisfied with their neighborhood in seventy-five per cent of the cases, despite the fact that about the same percentage have tried to find another place to live. Slightly more than half of those who have a definite opinion about the fairness of the rent being charged are dissatisfied; slightly less than half of this group are satisfied. This group of residents contains more high school graduates than any other group (55%). Regarding occupation and income,

62% are in low-grade occupations;
11% make $100 per week or more;
29% make less than $50 per week;
60% make less than $5,000 per year total family income.

Almost half of the dwellings in this category were judged to be in need of no paint or repairs. Forty per cent have experienced discrimination in housing, but only thirty per cent say they would expect it in the future.

State Moderate-Income Housing

Three-quarters of this group have lived in the city more than ten years, and a like percentage have more than four members in the family. The most striking difference between families in this group and those who live in the low-income project is that moderate-income project residents are all satisfied with their neighborhood. Sixty-three per cent are satisfied with the fairness of the rent being charged. Even so, six of the eight

TABLE 1

A SUMMARY OF INFORMATION ON FIVE TYPES OF HOUSING

		Housing Type I	Housing Type II	Housing Type III	Housing Type IV	Housing Type V
Attitude to rent:	Satisfied	65%	63%	31%	41%	....
	Dissatisfied	11%	25%	46%	43%	....
Attitude to Neighborhood:	Satisfied	47%	100%	50%	75%	76%
	Dissatisfied	35%	0%	25%	12%	18%
Have searched for another residence:		67%	75%	48%	70%	80%
Expect Discrimination:		44%	100%	50%	30%	40%
Have Not Experienced Discrimination in Searching for Home:		75%	50%	40%	60%	67%
In Newfield more than ten years:		68%	75%	35%	30%	88%

More than four in family:	53%	75%	26%	25%	46%
High School Education (or beyond):	28%	25%	26%	55%	29%
Occupation: Low-grade (unskilled-domestic service)	74%	65%	67%	62%	47%
Clerical or Professional	9.5%	15.4%	2.6%	10%	10.3%
Income: Less than $50 per week	30%	21%	31%	29%	18%
More than $100 per week	7%	14%	6%	11%	20%
Less than $5,000 per year	79%	25%	60%	60%	35%
Condition of Dwelling: No complaint	85%	63%	0%	47%	65%
Needs paint	6%	37%	75%	48%	22%
Needs repairs	9%	0%	62%	17%	20%
Visible Safety Hazards	0%	0%	44%	9%	8%

families in the state development are looking for another place to live. About one-fourth of this group are high school graduates.

65% have low-grade occupations;
14% make $100 per week or more;
21% make less than $50 per week;
25% have a total family income of less than $5,000 per
    year.

Three of these eight dwellings needed painting; otherwise, there were no negative comments about their general condition. Half of the respondents stated that they had not been victims of discrimination, yet all eight would anticipate meeting difficulty in finding another home because of their race.

Federal Low-Income Housing

Like the preceding group, most (68%) of the families in this classification have lived in Newfield more than ten years. Half of them have more than four members in the family. Slightly more than one-third of the respondents here expressed dissatisfaction with their neighborhood; about twice that number were looking for another residence, despite the fact that the rent was considered fair by sixty-five per cent of those consulted. Twenty-eight per cent are high school graduates.

Almost three-quarters have low-grade occupations;
Only three of forty-two wage earners (7%) make $100
    or more per week;
About 30% make less than $50 per week;
Almost four-fifths make less than $5,000 per year
    total family income.

Eighty-five per cent of the apartments need no paint nor repairs, and no safety hazards were observed by the interviewers. Three-quarters of this group of respondents have not experienced discrimination; however, forty-four per cent expect to encounter it in seeking a home.

INFERIOR HOUSING

One hundred fifty-nine Negro families—more than half of the families contacted in this survey—live in rentals that are definitely substandard. Two-thirds of these are relative newcomers to the city, having arrived here during the past ten years. Contrary to popular lore, not many of these families are large ones: only about one-quarter of them have more than four members. Even more surprising is the fact that only one-fourth of the respondents in this group expressed dissatisfaction with their neighborhood; furthermore, only about half of them have actually sought to find a new place to live. Likewise, only a quarter of the wage earners in this category have a high school diploma.

Two-thirds are in low-grade occupations;
6% make $100 per week or more;
31% make less than $50 per week;
60% have a family income of less than $5,000 per year.

In the opinion of the interviewers, all but sixteen of the 159 substandard housing units were in need of paint, repairs, or the rectifying of some visible safety hazard:

75% needed painting;
62% needed repairs;
44% had safety hazards.

Exactly two-fifths of these families testify that they have not encountered discrimination in searching for a home, and over half of them expect it should they look for a place to live in the future.

The general import of these findings was made known to several members of the Social Action Committee of the Council of Churches through informal conversation long before the preliminary report of the University Study Committee was officially released. The information thus communicated provided final confirmation of their conviction that the churches of Newfield must address themselves to the problem of housing for the community's Negro citizens. The findings made it quite clear, in the first place, that the dimensions of this problem were much larger than the immediate task of relocating Negro families displaced by urban redevelopment, for more than half of the nonwhite families of Newfield were inadequately housed. The findings also indicated that racial discrimination was the only barrier deterring some families: there were a substantial number of Negroes in the community who wanted better housing and could afford to pay for it. The study suggested, finally, that unless steps were taken to alleviate the problem, it would become steadily worse. If recent population trends should continue, the need for housing on the part of Newfield's Negro citizens would continue to expand during the near future. The Greater Newfield Open Housing Covenant program was undertaken as a means of alleviating the problem before it assumed unmanageable proportions.

CLERGYMEN

CHAPTER *4* IN ANY CASE STUDY OF CHRISTIAN social action, the attitudes and actions of the clergymen involved are of particular interest. Despite all the commendable efforts made by religious leaders to convince laymen that no man can lead the good life vicariously for others—that a pastor cannot release his people from their obligations to live righteously by being Christian for them —the fact remains that the clergyman is a model of the Christian life for his parishioners. In terms of group dynamics, the clergyman is the leader who sustains group norms by embodying them better than any other member of the group. Any norms not exhibited by the clergymen will cease to have authority over laymen; or to describe the situation as it more often exists, an equivocal interpretation of what the norms require will be perceived and adopted by laymen who for other reasons of their own are not particularly eager to live up to the norms. A study of what clergymen think about a venture in social action, why they think this way, and how they act provides an especially important key for understanding the social function of religious groups in a given culture.

There were substantial reasons for supposing that clerical support for the open housing covenant in Newfield would be virtually unanimous and quite vigorous. Roman Catholic priests had the backing of their diocesan bishop, Negro Protestant ministers had an obvious stake in any community effort to overcome racial discrimination, and none of the white Protestant clergymen had openly voiced strong reservations about, much less genuine opposition to, the covenant campaign when it was proposed in the Clergy Fellowship's meeting on September 20.

Virtually all of the clergymen contacted during the course of this study had a fairly liberal attitude about race relations.

There were no objections to integration as a desirable goal in the most important areas of public life and few objections to it as a desirable possibility in private life. Only one of the men who disapproved of interracial marriage did so on grounds that "mixing the races" was contrary to the will of God, and none showed the kind of negative emotional reaction to the very question which might have been characteristic of some clergymen in any section of the country and of a great many ministers in the South. A large majority of the clergymen favored civil rights legislation and the NAACP as necessary instruments for the achievement of racial justice, and a slender majority endorsed boycotts as a legitimate tactic. Other civil rights organizations and tactics did not receive majority approval or disapproval, but there were substantial minorities favorable to sit-ins and freedom rides.

Much in the attitudes of Newfield clergymen concerning the relationship between Christian faith and social concern was encouraging. There was almost no compartmentalization evident in their verbal affirmations of the essential link between belief and action, and they approved of official church pronouncements on vital public issues. With few exceptions, all of the white ministers were sophisticated enough not to expect any semi-magical guidance from prayer or from the Bible. Particularly noteworthy was the awareness, rather eloquently expressed by a few clergy respondents, that prayer is an awesome engagement with the Holy God that is not to be entered into lightly, or the realization that prayer may be answered by one's being confronted with decisions which are more difficult and responsibilities which are more sobering than ever before. Some clergy respondents showed considerable perspicacity in their discussions of criteria for making ethical decisions and in their awareness of the complexities involved in any assessment of a moral agent's motivation.

As for the open housing covenant *per se,* it did have the approval of virtually all clergymen and it gained some measure of active support from more than half of them. The Protestant ministers most instrumental in making the covenant campaign a reality were among the most influential and

best liked pastors of the city; therefore, the "cue" presented
to the other ministers and to the city's Protestant community
as a whole should have been a valuable asset for the covenant.[1]
The official support of the OHC granted by the organizational
or hierarchical bodies to which local congregations belonged
was highly publicized through the endorsements printed on
the covenant card, the dinner meeting at which the covenant
was introduced to Newfield Protestants, newspaper accounts
of planned distribution of cards, etc.

Despite their insistence that the Church should speak out on
public issues, however, most of the clergymen were very poorly
informed on the subject of public affairs in general and race
relations in particular. On the whole, they relied on denominational publications, daily newspapers, or the popular news
magazines (such as *Time* or *Newsweek*) for their knowledge
of these subjects. A Negro pastor reported that the major Negro
weekly newspapers were unavailable in Newfield, and the only
non-newspaper source mentioned by any of the Negro clergymen was *Jet*.

The denominational publications most often mentioned were
the "family-type" periodicals rather than the more analytical
journals, and only three ministers reported regular reading
of nondenominational publications such as *The Christian Century, Christianity and Crisis, Worldview*, etc. Only one man
kept up with any of the semi-popular public affairs magazines
that offer reasonably good coverage of racial news, and only
two men demonstrated familiarity with social science literature in this field. Most of the ministers had no recollection of
ever hearing about the Congress of Racial Equality (CORE)
or the Southern Christian Leadership Conference (SCLC),
even though they had all heard of the Reverend Martin Luther King. All of the men reflected a knowledge of the NAACP,
but almost without exception they prefaced their remarks on it
by saying something to the effect that "I don't know very much
about it, you understand, but . . ."; and they nearly always
qualified their approval if they gave it.

There was a discrepancy, too, between the clergymen's assertion of the absolutely necessary link between Christian faith

and social action, on the one hand, and, on the other, the low priority they assigned to the minister's role of community leader. As Table 2 shows, all other ministerial roles were considered more important in terms of what the clergyman actually did with his time, what he enjoyed doing, what he felt his parishioners expected of him, and what he thought a minister ought ideally to do. The clergymen of Newfield apparently see themselves primarily as men of verbal and interpersonal skills. They feel that they ought to devote most of their time to preaching, calling and counseling, with teaching in the position of next greatest importance. Furthermore, these are the things they most enjoy doing. Conversely, they do not see themselves as called primarily to exercise administrative skills within the church or organizational skills in the community at large; nor do they enjoy these activities as much as the others mentioned above. As the table reveals and as numerous comments made in the interviews confirm, ministers are often disgruntled because they are expected to spend such a large portion of their time in administrative work and because they actually do find themselves so engaged. Both ministers and parishioners agree, moreover, that the minister should spend a relatively small amount of time in community activities. This ideal on the part of the ministers and these expectations on the part of the parishioners are reflected in the fact that the role of "organizer" is actually allotted very little time.

Indifference to the Church's role in community organization is also reflected in the almost total absence of lines of communication between Newfield clergymen of different faiths and races. Catholic priests and Protestant ministers barely knew each other, and there were no informal friendships among men of different religious persuasions to lubricate the machinery of interfaith cooperation when the need arose. When asked to name other clergymen of the city with whom one would like to work in the performance of some community task, Protestant ministers named only other Protestants, and Catholic priests named only other priests. Priests declared, in fact, that they could not name any non-Catholics because they had never worked with Protestant clergymen before and simply did not know them

TABLE 2

White Protestant Ministers' Ranking of Their Role Responsibilities[1]

	Actual	Enjoyed	Ideal	Expected
Preacher	2[a](65)	1 (69)	1 (69)	2 (66)
Pastor	2[a](65)	2 (67)	2 (66)	1 (77)
Priest	5[b](26)	4 (40)	4 (51)	4[c](30)
Teacher	4 (41)	3 (57)	3 (56)	4[c](30)
Administrator	1 (74)	5 (27)	5 (27)	3 (58)
Organizer	5[b](26)	6 (24)	6 (17)	6 (25)

[1]The numbers in parentheses indicate the total number of points scored for a particular role, scoring six points for each ranking of "1", five points for each ranking of "2", etc. In each of the four columns, the role with the highest number of points is assigned a rank of "1", etc. Ties are indicated by identical letters.

The meaning of the six roles was explained to respondents as follows: "Preacher," any activity directly related to the prep- aration or delivery of sermons; "Pastor," any activity the primary purpose of which is to bring solace, encouragement, or advice to a parishioner (such as visitation and counselling); "Priest," the performance of any liturgical act prescribed by the Church (such as funerals, weddings, and the celebration of the Eu- charist); "Teacher," any activity the primary purpose of which is to communicate formal knowledge to a group of parishioners; "Administrator," any activity the primary purpose of which is to promote the proper maintenance of church property or the efficient operation of staff, committees, and organized groups in the internal life of the parish (such as meetings, the printing of church bulletins, etc.); and "Organizer," par- ticipation in denominational or civic affairs not directly con- nected with one's own parish.

Because of the division of labor practiced by the several priests in each Roman Catholic parish, and the limited time available for their church responsibilities on the part of Negro ministers (all of whom had a full-time job in addition), only the responses of white Protestant clergymen are tabulated here. The answers given by priests and Negro pastors were similar on most points, especially in considering the role of community organizer rel- atively unimportant and devoting litttle time to this role.

well enough to comment on their ability or their personal qualities. Negro pastors were theoretically members of the Protestant Clergy Fellowship of Newfield, and they attended its meetings occasionally. But their participation in this group was marginal in the extreme, partly because of the 10:00 A.M. weekday meeting time (which excluded the Negro preachers, all of whom had eight-hours-per-day, five-days-per-week jobs) and partly because of an atmosphere in which some of the Negro clergymen felt unwelcome.

In light of these findings about the lack of informed social awareness and communication among Newfield clergymen, it is hardly surprising that the open housing covenant campaign did not call forth the wholehearted support of every minister and priest in the community. Interviews with twenty-nine clergymen revealed that some clearly opposed the OHC, some who professed approval did nothing (or virtually nothing) to support it, and some who made more than a half-hearted gesture in support of the covenant were ineffective in obtaining signatures. By analyzing the attitudes and actions of different clergymen who achieved differing degrees of success, we can gain a better understanding of the characteristic strengths and weaknesses of Christian social action in American churches.

A few introductory remarks regarding terminology will facilitate the exposition which follows by making possible a greatly simplified and shortened manner of description. In reporting answers given by clergy respondents to questions about their criteria for deciding between various social action alternatives, the following terms will be assigned the meaning specified here:

—"subjective interest": personal preference, as distinguished from commitment based on a calculation of what one ought to do.

—"immediacy": a tendency to regard as most worthy of support those actions which pertain to conditions and persons within one's own sphere of knowledge and influence—what is "close at hand," "right in your own backyard," etc.

—"vocation": a criterion giving highest value to those actions which are most closely in line with what one sees as a particular responsibility for someone in his particular position or someone with his training or talents.

In describing the techniques of presentation of the open housing covenant, these terms will be used:

—"the vestibule technique": the placing of covenant cards on a table in the vestibule of the church, the burden of responsibility for taking a card resting with individual parishioners who pass by the table.

—"sermonizing": concentrating the appeal for support of the open housing covenant in the sermon delivered as a part of the common pulpit emphasis on October 22, with little effort to procure signatures for the covenant being made after that occasion.

And references to "open housing covenant" will continue to be made by use of the abbreviation "OHC."

OPPONENTS

Three of the white Protestant ministers candidly disapproved of the open housing covenant, or were so lukewarm in their approval that they did nothing to offer their parishioners an opportunity to sign it. The reasons given for rejecting the covenant, and the whole complex of attitudes underlying these reasons, were quite different for each of the three men.

Frank Stevens, pastor of a small fundamentalist congregation, found no grounds for approving the covenant in either his theology or his understanding of society. He granted that "from the Christian point of view I thought it was a good thing"; however, in the next breath he declared that "in this world the good oftentimes has a hard time taking root." It was his opinion, then, that "they're rushing things." He felt that "these deep-seated antipathies that we're talking about are down much too deep to eradicate overnight, especially through legal measures." "Pressure from the outside" he regarded as self-defeating, and he objected especially to "pressure on you to sign some kind of a pledge," because "it has the aspects of a legal document, and I think we all have a reluctance to sign on the dotted line." In subsequent remarks, Stevens indicated a belief that

racial prejudice is not really unreasonable, considering that
"the Negro, the dyed-in-the-wool Negro, is perhaps repugnant
to the white man, because of his features, the color of his skin."
He denied that "the Lord ever intended integration." Stevens
felt that the NAACP was too aggressive and that the South
should be left to settle its own racial problems without interference from federal authorities. The only exception to his negative view of civil rights laws and militant tactics was his willingness to endorse fair employment practices legislation. Stevens'
lack of sophistication was revealed by his total lack of comprehension of the interviewer's questions regarding criteria for
ethical decisions and the importance attributed to right motivation. It was also manifested in his simplistic faith that prayer was
the best hope for a solution to any problem: after testifying
that he had recently acquired a guitar case (at a bargain price!)
through prayer, he exclaimed, "My experience has been, God
is practical, within reason. 'He shall supply all your needs.'"

More sophisticated reasons for opposing the covenant were
articulated by Will Kirby, rector of a large Episcopal church.
An avowed conservative in his social philosophy, Kirby was not
in sympathy with any type of militant action or organization
in the area of race relations, regarding "these so-called civil
rights laws" as an infringement by a tyrannical majority upon
one's constitutional right to be intolerant. Of the NAACP he
said, "I consider this organization a primary example of the
philosophy of Marxism, that the end justifies the means." His
Thomistic theological position led him to believe that the decisive criteria for ethical choice could be inferred from knowledge that "the work of the parish is twofold, and only twofold.
It consists of communicating the gospel . . . and strengthening
the faithful." Thus, although "the housing covenant thing . . .
may very well be part of the *bene esse*" it is "not of the *esse*
of the concerns of the Church." He also placed a very high
valuation upon right motives:

> The evil motivation negates the end. And this has an obverse,
> too; that good means may be employed for a bad end. I think
> it's got to be a three-way coordination here: you've got to have
> proper motivation, proper means, and a justifiable end.

Ted Underwood's reasons for failing to support the cov-enant were less ideological and were by no means a reflection of personal prejudice, political conservatism, or theological skepti-cism about integration as a social objective worthy of Christian action. Underwood labeled himself an integrationist, and he voiced approval of the freedom rides; therefore, even though he refused comment on the NAACP and sit-ins because of in-sufficient knowledge and even though he remarked that the federal government was doing "about all it can" in the area of civil rights, he had no apparent objection in principle to legislation or nonviolent direct action by militant organizations. His attitude toward the covenant was not due to his convictions about proper criteria or the centrality of proper motivation—he had thought out no clear criteria, and he confessed that his seminary training in psychiatry made him dubious about pur-ity of motivation. His lack of enthusiasm was due, rather, to his uneasy feeling that the OHC did not spring from grass roots Christian sentiment, and that its chances for success were almost *nil*:

> I think it's like so many things we do through the Council of Churches. It's like a little Indian war party that separates from the main body of society, from the main tribe, and goes off on little raids here and there, kicking up a small furore around the campfire without getting the whole tribe involved. This is something I've been very much concerned about. The whole Council of Churches—it's ineffective. It's just that the churches are never making decisions on anything: it's always the clergy who are doing the talking and the deciding, and they do it disjointed from the churches, from the congregations—except for the few men who follow through on things more fully than most. Then their people are involved in the particular issue concerned. But most of the things that come up in the Council of Churches, it's purely on the level of the pastors, and maybe a lay delegate, who cannot possibly represent his congregation, because his congregation never had any say in the matter. . . . I'm really in a stew. I want to do something, and I just don't know what to do, realizing that the congregation isn't ready for it. There are an awful lot of strained emotions about this thing. You're not going to mow the lawn with a pair of scis-sors, and until some better ways of tackling these things are discovered, I'd just as soon let them lie.

THE INERT

Three of the white Protestant clergymen gave verbal approval to the open housing covenant, but did nothing to support it. As with its opponents, it is difficult to correlate the inertia of this group of ministers with any single characteristic attitude on race relations, theology, or type of approach in presenting the covenant. On some points, they seem quite liberal; on others, they are clearly conservative.

A near-fundamentalist preacher (he rejected the label "fundamentalist") of a sect-type congregation expressed approval of the open housing covenant, which was strikingly inconsistent with some of his racial and theological views; consequently, his lack of support for the covenant is hardly surprising. The Rev. Tim Miller not only favored the covenant appeal but also predicted substantial success for it: he did not expect "a miracle overnight" but he believed that "in a community such as ours . . . this is going to have an effect on our real estate men, and on anyone who individually sells or buys a home." He assumed recognition on the part of most Newfield residents that "we aren't self-sufficient" and that "our community would never grow if people were individuals"; therefore, he recommended "appealing to their sense of community growth, their community spirit: this would be the way to approach it." Miller felt that "most people know their Christian duty without needing to be reminded of it," and could be counted on to respond to an appeal which touched their desire "to help the fellow who hasn't had the breaks." On the other hand, Miller had a violent antipathy for interracial marriage ("There's nothing that makes me sicker than to see a white man with a black woman, or a white woman with a black man!") that suggested something less than complete acceptance of Negroes as fully equal human beings, and his denunciation of the NAACP was vehement:

> Oh, I don't like them; they're always blowing their own horn. . . . It seems to me that they could accomplish a lot if they went about it by trying to educate the white man as well as the colored man about the problems involved, instead of hollering and shouting and screaming their problems to the world.

We *know* that they've got problems. . . I wouldn't want to associate myself with a hollering, screaming *crowd* that is forever
standing on the street corner saying, "I'm being discriminated
against; nobody's doing anything for me." And this is how they
strike me.

Miller's distaste for militant Negro organizations and for civil
rights laws seemed to be related to his conception of Christian
ethics. He thought that the model for Christian social action
was to be found in the New Testament descriptions of a ministry of mercy to individuals who were poor or sick, and he
thought right motivation essential for right action. Interestingly
enough, it was only in connection with prayer that he mentioned
the importance of collective effort: after asserting that neither
individual prayer nor "a helter-skelter called-together affair to answer a problem" could accomplish very much, he affirmed that
"if all those who are interested in this problem [of discrimina-
tion], if their prayers were united, something would happen."

Another pastor of a sect-type congregation, Jack Quimby,
explained that his willingness to go along with church sponsorship of the covenant had been vetoed by the ruling body of the
congregation, which "felt that right now, they didn't see, except
from the fact that the whole community [would be] saying
the same thing at once, they didn't feel that our church was
necessarily right now at this moment ready to get in on this."
His criticism of another minister's presentation of the covenant showed that he did not doubt the potential effectiveness
of church sponsorship:

It was very much of a facade kind of approach to this matter,
purely on the social—sort of a social expedience level: "This
is what we have to do" and "the problem's right here in our
town." To me, that's not the kind of approach to use. So he
had fourteen people sign the card, fourteen out of 100. Well,
I'm not saying I'm a better preacher than he is, but if I had
fifty people listening to me preach a sermon on this, I'll bet
forty-nine of them would have signed! I know my people better
than he knows his! They think like I think, and I know how
they're thinkin'. And so to me, he didn't meet the problem.

Nor did his failure to support the covenant stem from a high
valuation on pure motivation as a prerequisite for Christian

social action, for he asserted that "motives can be changed . . .
by the Holy Spirit." The decisive factor in his lack of enthusiasm
for the covenant campaign was probably his suspicion of pressure tactics: he disapproved of the NAACP as an organization
which tended to "overmake their point in order to make it,"
and he was opposed to civil rights laws as well as militant direct
action of all kinds. He acknowledged that the covenant was "the
quickest way" to overcome residential discrimination, but he
complained that "this doesn't solve it in the heart":

> I think over a period the more basic thing is to get to the heart
> of it. To convince a man against his will is—it's bypassing the
> more basic problem of the prejudice in the man's heart. And
> we could even cover this up by signing a covenant, and still
> have this within us. So the problem isn't solved. It's just as long
> as I live on the street to the fellow next door to me, that's all.
> But it isn't basically solved in my heart, or in my prejudices, or
> in my family. I think that it could become a matter of prayer
> and preaching and cell groups within our congregation. All of
> our congregations will become the basic discussion, not just
> signing your name, but an opening up of feelings and try to
> tear down some of these walls. Then we're doing something.

Stated approval of the covenant was coupled with strong
reservations and inaction by Louis Dickenson, the only minister
of one of the large "downtown Protestant churches"—so called
by people in Newfield— who chose to do nothing on behalf of
the covenant campaign. He had a number of reservations about
the manner in which the open housing covenant had been conceived and was being carried out. Stating that "the problem is
bigger than finding rents for a few individual families," he
added, "I haven't found the group yet that has taken hold of
the problem on the scale that I think it needs to." He cast asper-
sions on the judgment, the skill, and the integrity of the individual ministers most active in promoting church sponsorship
of the covenant: he accused them of making a mountain out of
a molehill (in regard to an individual case of alleged discrimination); he prophesied limited cooperation by most of the city's
clergymen because of the way the covenant idea had been
"railroaded through"; he objected to "the technique used by the
[Butler Memorial Church Social Action] committee in calling

landlords—I would even go so far as to say they were not
Christians, [because] deception was used." His refusal to participate in the common pulpit emphasis was based on his judgment that this placed a captive audience in a coercive situation.
Dickenson's defensiveness about his failure to support the covenant wholeheartedly can be discerned in his discussion of
"balance" in a church's program as a crucial criterion for ethical
decisions:

> We should try to give a varied diet, so to speak, and over a
> period of years to cover a wide range of things. The urgent
> usually finds a place in the program of the church, and because
> some church or some group of people decides that a particular
> issue is the most urgent now, they can't necessarily expect all
> the churches to feel the same way. Some churches may enter
> this brand new, and may not have done any work in that field
> before, and therefore to them this is it, whereas another church
> may have been working in this for a good many years. It must
> be left up to individuals to define what is urgent.

Another clue to Dickenson's nonparticipation is found in his
remarks on pure motivation, which he considered "extremely
important" [said with great emphasis]. He had come to dis-
like the term "liberal" because of the dogmatism and self-right-
eousness of so many of the self-styled liberals he had known,
and he implied doubts as to their motivation in asserting that
"we must minister to the needs of all the people" and "make
sure we are serving the Lord rather than our own glory or
the needs of one particular group." Dickenson gave qualified
approval to the NAACP and he endorsed civil rights legislation,
but he opposed boycotts and picketing, questioned the value
of freedom rides, and displayed strong negative feelings about
racial intermarriage. His observations pertaining to the probable
failure of the convenant campaign are unusually revealing:

> I think there are a number of reasons. Baldwin last year took
> very little part in things. He was busy studying. Murray Jack-
> son was supposed to be chairman of the Commission on Chris-
> tian Social Concerns [he means the Social Action Committee of
> the Council of Churches], but he didn't do anything. A couple of
> us tried to prod him a little bit, but—just too busy. Harold
> Baldwin got hold of this thing, and he *really* entered in with

full enthusiasm. But as so often happens when you do that, he didn't carry people with him. He pushed through a program. Just the number of meetings—I finally resigned from this committee, because just the pressure of meetings, one right after the other, so it seemed—. And there was really no attempt to carry the other ministers along. He got the program over but he didn't have the ministers with him. This is what I'm afraid of with my congregation; the kind of thing I wouldn't want. The next thing you have to bear in mind is that Peter and his church really started out on this. Uh, ministers are human, very human, and there's always a feeling, "Well, he started it, this is his baby, let him carry it. He's getting all the press—mayor's committee, and so forth." I'm trying to be objective and analyze this thing as best I can. There was also the feeling, "Well, we're not so sure what's going to happen, Peter has stuck his neck out; let's see what happens. And so we'll go along, but not really carry the torch the way he is." We have a group [in the Clergy Fellowship] that are uncooperative generally. You probably know about them. Anything the Council does, they won't do; won't come to meetings, and so forth. Mainly the conservative Lutherans and the very conservative Episcopalians—not St. Thomas, of course. I don't know who might disagree with me on this. We've gone so fast on this that we've never tried to come to grips with it as a Clergy Fellowship. I mean I'm not sure whether we could establish the fact that there's enough security in the group to give an honest expression, anyhow.

The Half-Hearted

Many Newfield clergymen—four white Protestant ministers, and all of the five Roman Catholic priests interviewed—were so half-hearted in their approval of the open housing covenant that their efforts in its behalf were minimal. Despite apparently sound reasons for expecting more from these men and despite apparent differences among them in attitude toward the covenant, they were alike in their neglect of all but the most perfunctory methods of presenting the matter to their congregations.

White Protestants

Among the white Protestant ministers in this group, Dick Ross not only was the most tough-minded, but also had clear reasons for using minimal means of presentation. He was the only

one who did not dilute his endorsement of the NAACP with
qualifications, and he alone was prepared to grant approval
to all forms of nonviolent direct action mentioned in the interview. He regretted the necessity for civil rights laws and organizations employing aggressive tactics, but he acknowledged that
"education won't solve the problem" and concluded that such
structures and such measures are necessary: "I would rather
it be an outgrowth rather than something that is forced upon
us," he mused, "but it just has to be." Ross's ambivalent attitude
toward external imposition of desegregation was paralleled
by his mixed emotions concerning the open housing covenant.
On the one hand, he was quite sanguine about the prospects
for getting a good many signatures for the covenant from Newfield churchmen—and since he considered feasibility a significant criterion for judging the value of social action, he deemed
the covenant worthy of support. On the other hand, he found
it impossible to "look at something like this as being a campaign"
aimed simply at getting signatures. In his view, "such things
should have time to sort of generate in [the people's] lives and
then be a product of their stand more than a product of promotion." His conviction that it would be theologically unsound to
"promote" the open housing covenant led him to confine his presentation of it to the vestibule technique.

Bill Irvin and Don Allen, on the other hand, seem to have
slipped into a half-hearted posture by default. Their reservations about the NAACP and their mixed reaction to civil
rights laws and militant tactics—neither was enthusiastic about
legislation and both were against direct action (except that
Allen endorsed selective patronage and Irvin was willing to
respect protest actions as an expression of conscientious objection to discrimination, though he did not see any objective
value in such actions)—indicate a certain paralyzing fuzzy-mind-
edness that would certainly hamper their efforts to present the
covenant persuasively to resistant parishioners. In addition,
neither had a clearly formulated set of criteria for ethical action which would lead him to place a high priority on combatting racial injustice: Allen's only criterion was the purely
formal one contained in the question, "Is it [a proposed action]

God's will or isn't it?" and Irvin's was simply subjective interest, for he contended that social action should be chosen on the basis of "the thing that appeals to you most, the thing for which you just almost automatically align yourself, your own personal concern." Allen's enthusiasm was dampened further by a dissatisfaction with the lack of cooperation *vis-a-vis* the covenant on the part of the other ministers in his suburb. But the most striking feature of the interview with both these men was the apathy on the housing issue which they attributed to their parishioners, and by which they seemed to have been infected. Irvin confessed that "this problem isn't at the moment for us locally [in a semi-rural community on the periphery of the Newfield area] a *too* relevant issue. . . . We have to do something that at the moment wouldn't have concerned us out here in this community." Allen reported that, because of their isolation from local Negroes, "very few people are really aware of the problem" and "most people feel that it isn't something they personally can do anything about." Both men shared Allen's dour opinion that "the covenant has a rocky road ahead of it," and neither was persuaded that progress along that road was important enough to warrant strenuous effort. As a result, Irvin did nothing more than make the covenant cards available in the vestibule of his church, and Allen buried the matter in an existing study group where he hoped, but doubted, it would get some attention.

For Walter Franklin, the difficulty encountered was more than apathy—it was hostile resistance to the covenant on the part of people who felt very much threatened by it. Preliminary discussion of the covenant with a few leading laymen brought forth "some violent reactions." Noting that there were in his congregation "a couple of people who are living in neighborhoods where Negroes are trying to buy in," he observed:

> They know what's right and yet it's such a—they feel that they've built this house and they've put a lot of money in it, and they think that if one Negro family moves out there they'll ruin it, that the whole thing is going to devaluate, this kind of thing. They don't deny that Negroes have a right to live there, that— they realize this is right, but they just— [breaks off]. And if I tell them that it isn't necessarily true that property values

do decline when Negroes move in, they'll say, "I don't care how many surveys have been done in others parts of the country, this is *my* street."

His moderate racial views, which led him to reject all types of direct action (although he did approve of civil rights laws), and his inability to set priorities for action by reference to well-defined criteria, left him vulnerable in the face of this determined opposition. He mentioned the covenant in a Sunday bulletin, and he discussed it briefly in one meeting of an adult study group, but he did nothing else to make it clear to his congregation that he considered support of the covenant an important expression of Christian concern.

Roman Catholic Priests

The handling of the covenant appeal in the Roman Catholic churches was complicated by a false start which resulted in almost total failure. The reason for the failure of the first attempt to gain signatures in support of the covenant appears to have been a lack of clarity concerning the public climax of the campaign, namely, the publishing of the names of covenant supporters in a newspaper advertisement. In the words of one priest, "The trouble was that this thing was not sufficiently explained to the clergy. It was just sort of left hanging." In accordance with instructions from the bishop's Consultor, the cards were made available to parishioners, but no emphasis was placed on having the signed cards returned; consequently virtually no signed cards were obtained by this initial effort.

Shortly after this, more covenant cards were printed and delivered to the pastor of each parish with instructions to emphasize that signed cards were to be returned to the church on the Sunday following distribution to the laymen. Since the covenant was endorsed by an official representative of the bishop, it was presented in some fashion in each parish; however, unanimous and unqualified endorsement of the open housing covenant campaign was no more to be found among the Roman Catholic clergymen than among the Protestant clergymen. All of the priests approved of the principle underlying the open housing covenant, but two expressed serious reservations about some aspect of the covenant program as it was being conducted in Newfield. One priest felt that it should have been sponsored mainly by civic rather than by religious groups, and that the basis for the appeal should have been "kept more in the civic realm." The objection raised by the other priest was more pragmatic: the presence of some noisy Negro tenants in an apartment house near the rectory of his parish had made it difficult for him to generate very much enthusiasm for the covenant campaign.

Various appraisals of probable lay reaction to the covenant were given. In the opinion of one respondent, the prospect of having Negro neighbors aroused "real fright" in some of the people of his congregation. He reported that the vast majority of his parishioners "are either indifferent [toward the covenant] or else they want no part of it." The pessimism of another pastor was founded on an awareness of his parishioners' concern for family solidarity and property values. He admitted that very few covenant cards had been picked up at his church on the Sunday when they were distributed, and he predicted that "we'll get even fewer back." A third dour appraisal stressed the wariness that laymen felt about signing their name to a card, the final disposition and use of which they did not clearly understand. One priest, although he did not expect a spectacular response to the covenant among his parishioners, emphasized that there was "no radical opposition" to it among his parishioners; furthermore, he denied rumors that some of the people of his parish were moving out of an area where a number of Negroes had recently begun to live.

Each Roman Catholic parish used fundamentally the same approach in distributing the covenant cards to the parishioners. Worshipers were informed of the open housing covenant through a printed announcement in a Sunday service bulletin and/or through a pulpit announcement; they received the cards either by picking one up from a table in the vestibule of the church or by accepting one from an usher as they departed; they were urged to return the signed cards at the worship service on the following Sunday. In one parish, no bulletin is printed for Sunday services; therefore, only through a pulpit announcement did the congregation learn of the covenant. In another, there was a general policy against all pulpit announcements, and no mention was made of the open housing covenant in the bulletin, either; the covenant cards were simply available on a vestibule table for the curious or for those who knew from the newspapers that the cards were to be presented to Roman Catholic parishioners on the last Sunday in April. In four churches—the three which used both pulpit announcement and printed notice to direct attention to the matter of racial justice, plus the one which relied exclusively on the pulpit announcement—cards were handed out by ushers to departing worshipers.

The bulletin used on April 29 in Father Arnold's parish contained this announcement:

> Cards are being passed out in all the Masses today on the Greater Newfield Open Housing Covenant. You are asked to sign and please return next Sunday, May 6th.

A somewhat fuller statement appeared in the bulletin of Father Chapman's church:

> We are asked this morning to take as we leave Church a card indicating that we will accept the policy of the Newfield Open Housing Covenant. Please take one, read it carefully and ask yourself if this is not a statement of the Law of Charity by which we should all live.

Another church noted that "across the country Catholic groups with an active interest in interracial justice are planning special events to mark the May 6 canonization of Blessed Martin de Porres"; however, there was no word about the open housing covenant.

Interviews with the priests—which were held during the week at the end of which all signed covenants cards were to be returned—brought to light no plans for systematic efforts to confront parishioners with the covenant other than announcements made from the pulpit or printed in the bulletin. When the interviewer raised with one priest a question about the letter from the bishop's Consultor, directing the pastors of Newfield churches to participate in the open housing covenant appeal, he received this reply:

> We got a letter from Father Sloan of St. Michael's indicating the way in which it should be done and advising us. It was not an official letter in any way, just a suggestion, and I think it was followed to the letter in each parish. It was pointed out in the letter that it need not be read; in fact, I got the impression it would be wiser if it were not, that one man should not be burdened with this whole thing. I felt that we should each accept it on our own.

The same priest explained the lack of any follow-up action in his parish by saying:

> Well, you see, it doesn't give us an awful lot of time. We've got one week in which it is expected that the cards should be distributed and returned. We just don't have an opportunity to discuss it.

The shortness of time between official presentation of the covenant cards (in the second effort at presenting them) and collection of signed cards was doubtless a partial explanation of the answers given by priests to the question concerning their appraisal of probable lay reaction to the open housing covenant. Father Arnold, who had arrived in his present parish only a few months previously and who had been besieged with one urgent problem after another ever since his arrival, confessed that he could not predict what sort of reaction the covenant appeal would elicit in his congregation because he simply had not had an opportunity to discuss it with them. A similar answer was given by Father Darnell, who reported that his parishioners "have never gone into the matter very much with me." Father Bacon regarded the problem of racial discrimination as "something we haven't been confronted with up here," something which "hasn't been very widely discussed," because "the subject just hasn't come up." Yet Father Bacon's appraisal can hardly be termed neutral. He declared that he was cognizant of "real fright," about the possibility of having Negro neighbors, in the hearts of some parishioners, and he told of a steady exodus of white families from an area of town where Negroes

were moving in.* He also reported that "a lot of people do
not trust the judgment of those who are taking the lead in
pushing this housing covenant. They feel that they have taken
a problem that is really not too great and magnified it out of all
proportion." Resentment as well as mistrust had been fostered
in some members of his parish because of the anguish one
of his parishioners suffered as a result of the testing activities
of the Butler Memorial Social Action Committee: the parishioner concerned was a lady whose "whole life's work was in their
home"; she "almost had a nervous breakdown" because of the
pressure which was exerted on her by the committee members
who "told her she was prejudiced and threatened her with
court action because she didn't want to rent to a Negro family."
Less stormy, but not much more encouraging, was the appraisal of lay sentiment articulated by Father Chapman:

> I don't expect very many people to sign at all. What can you
> tell, though? I don't know. It is the Law of Charity, there's
> no doubt about it, but many people feel that it transcends their
> —it's always someone else. The guy two doors over or in the next
> block, fine, but—. I think that many people feel as I do that it
> could have been left at least in some measure in the civic field.
> Many of the contractors of this town are in this parish . . . and
> I have talked with them, and their sole objection is strictly
> from the practical point of view, that as businessmen they sim-
> ply don't deem it advisable. They have no objection to con-
> structing one of these—er, public housing, provided there could
> be a decent revenue from it.

This unanimous, but uniformly limited, support of the covenant is not altogether surprising in the light of the theological
and social views expressed by the priests. Their understanding
of the authority of the Church, and of the responsibility of the
Church to remind citizens of their moral obligations in regard
to political issues, enabled them to affirm unhesitatingly the
appropriateness of church sponsorship of the covenant. For
Father Arnold, it was "an opportunity for the Church to set
moral standards" in an area of life where laymen needed guid-

*The priest in whose parish this area of town was, denied that the influx
of a few Negro families had anything to do with the decision of some white
families to move to other areas of town.

ance; for Father Chapman it was "an expression of Catholic doctrine . . . an act of fraternal charity." Father Bacon stressed that the Church has a definite responsibilty to "formulate correct thinking in regard to outer space or housing or whatever in accordance with the principles that we know are God-given." Father Ellison and Father Darnell were inclined to supplement their ecclesiastical explanation of the relationship between faith and ethics with more down-to-earth arguments concerning the role of the priest or the inseparability of religion and life. Father Ellison testified that in his experience Roman Catholic laymen expect the priest to "know things from the ground up" when a question of social justice arises, and that "they are disappointed if the priest doesn't set them straight on social problems." For Father Darnell, the heart of the matter was contained in the Great Commandment, which he adduced as proof that "you can't separate religion from all the other segments of life." In directing man to love both God and neighbor, it showed that "you can't have one without the other." The priests were also of one mind concerning the rightness of civil rights legislation; indeed, Father Arnold and Father Darnell voiced impatience with the pace and scope of federal action against racial discrimination.

The comments of the Catholic clergymen on criteria for ethical decision and motivation toward Christian social action were of particular interest. Father Ellison and Father Bacon stressed the sufficiency of reliance on clearly defined rules of moral behavior: concern over purity of motives should not be allowed to obscure the fact that obedience to these rules is obligatory, and clarity on this point is more fundamental than are questions pertaining to motivation. Father Chapman went so far as to assert that having the right end in view serves in some way to make motives good; and he, Father Darnell, and Father Arnold all stressed that one's motive for action can become progressively more pure as one proceeds to perform what he knows to be his moral duty.

The opinions of the Catholic pastors on the subject of race relations shed light on their half-heartedness regarding the open housing covenant. Father Chapman was the only priest who did not qualify his approval of the NAACP and who had a favorable attitude toward nonviolent direct action. Father Arnold approved of the NAACP as a "very conscientious" organization which helps to "educate people," but he explicitly stated that Negroes must "prove themselves" before being worthy of acceptance on an equal basis. Father Darnell was noncommittal regarding the NAACP; Father Bacon was dubious about its worth; Father Ellison was "violently opposed" to the organization. (Father Ellison's disappointment over the failure of NAACP officials to respond to his appeals for charitable assistance to a Negro parishioner in financial and emotional distress prompted him to exclaim, "I would like to see their dissolution in this country!") On the question of direct action, Father Ellison was undecided, stating simply, "They [sit-ins, freedom rides, and boycotts] haven't made much of an impression on me." Father Arnold disapproved of these tactics on prudential rather than on moral grounds: he thought that very little was gained by them, and he feared that the ill-will stimulated by such maneuvers outweighed the advantages. Father Bacon and Father Darnell disapproved of direct action on the ground that it represents a violation of good public order and is therefore a threat to the first prerequisite for a stable common life. Three priests revealed traces of the typical Caucasian bias against Negroes with traits which are "in-group virtues but out-group vices": Father Arnold regretted that some Negroes "push themselves too fast when they get a few privileges" or "try to live out of their class." Father Ellison deplored any efforts to "try to move into a neighborhood they can't keep up with." Father Darnell compared the status of Negroes today with that of Italians when he was a boy. He felt that assimilation had to be gradual and impatience was therefore unreasonable. He even compared the impudence of Negroes moving into a neighborhood they are "not ready for" with that of "shanty Irish trying to live on Park Avenue."

Since none of the Roman Catholic clergymen sought support for the fair housing pledge through any means other than a brief announcement, a discussion of the arguments in favor of it mentioned by them is somewhat academic; nevertheless, these arguments offer some clues as to the lukewarm perform-

ance of the priests in regard to the covenant campaign. Father
Bacon had less to say on this score than any of the rest of his
colleagues. Explaining that he had "never had any serious
reason to give thought to this matter or make decisions regarding it," he said, "I really haven't given it any thought; I have
not reached any definite conclusion." Affirmation of the equality of all men in the sight of God was the argument referred
to most prominently by three priests. Father Arnold repeated
the first article of the Roman Catholic statement appearing
on the back of the open housing covenant card—"that God,
the father, is the Creator of all men and that His Image is
impressed upon the soul of each individual"—as though he
would be willing to rest his appeal on behalf of the covenant
on this one fundamental point. Both Father Ellison and Father
Darnell asserted as a basic Catholic doctrine that "the Negro
is a child of God just like every other man," and Father Darnell
amplified the point by citing the biblical passage which says
that love shown to the least of the brethren is love shown to
Christ himself. These same three priests also reinforced their
arguments by reference to personal conviction or personal experience. Father Arnold testified that he had "always believed
in equal rights." Father Ellison observed "it is only when the
colored person goes off the deep end and gets drunk, and so
on" that he is undesirable, and he maintained that "respectable colored men are respected by whites." His most fervent
statement was the one with which he brought to a conclusion
his answer to the question about persuading others to support
the open housing covenant: lifting his hands in a gesture of
self-evident truth he exclaimed, "How can you be a Catholic
and hate the colored?" Father Darnell told of his resentment
against the "white" and "colored" signs which he had seen while
visiting the South. The most illuminating discussion of favorable arguments was provided by Father Chapman's answer to
this question:

> It [the principle underlying the open housing covenant] cer-
> tainly is within the law of charity. . . . Whether we can also
> stress justice is something that would have to be examined a
> little more, I think. A man has a legal right to dispose of his

property in any way he sees fit. And if he doesn't have the disposition of his own goods, then he's not the owner of that property. That's one reason I say it would be a little more difficult to stress the justice angle rather than the charity angle. . . . In fact, I feel pretty sure we could not make appeal to the people from the point of view of justice. Justice is a *quid pro quo*, and provided it's not entering into the moral field— provided it's not immoral to dispose of one's property in such-and -such a manner—he has a right to do it. Now, for instance, I think it would be immoral to buy a block of houses—er, to turn that house over to ill-repute. That would be a moral problem. Or to sell it to someone he knows will. But this is something where the person owns the home: he has an apartment to rent in it, and I think we cannot say to this person, "In justice you have to rent to that person." However, in *charity* —! You'd have to, in my opinion, you'd have to appeal strictly from the point of view of charity.

THE INEFFECTUAL

A number of Newfield clergymen may be described as well-intentioned but ineffectual in their handling of the open housing covenant. They made more than a perfunctory gesture in support of the appeal, but they stopped short of a thorough effort and they achieved meager results in terms of the number of signatures they were able to gather for the covenant among their parishioners. Included in this group are the pastors of the three Negro churches in the community, five white Protestant ministers who may be described as "sermonizers," and three other clergymen who made some effort to follow up on their participation in the common pulpit emphasis but who nevertheless had little success in persuading members of their congregations to sign the good neighbor pledge.

Negro Pastors

The response of Negro ministers was less wholehearted than one might have expected in view of the importance of the housing problem for Negroes and in view of the ministers' attitudes on the subject of race relations. They were emphatic in their rejection of "moderation" and their espousal of full, prompt desegregation. Luke Archer declared, "I don't believe in segregation in any form. I couldn't preach a true gospel and be a 'moderate.' I don't see how a man can say, 'I don't believe in segregation, *but.* . . .'" Wilbur Chatham agreed that one's opinion on this subject could not be "anything halfway." The only departure from a thorough endorsement of integrationist goals was James Barlow's disapproval of racial intermarriage. Barlow was absolutely firm on this point: he felt that, just as Jews were directed by the Old Testament not to marry outsiders, Negroes ought also "to keep the race pure."

The NAACP was heartily approved of by all three men. Luke Archer stressed that "it isn't an organization to fight for the Negro race, but for any minority group." James Barlow considered the organization "a little too slow in many things." Observing that it had been one hundred years since the Emancipation Proclamation, Wilbur Chatham said, "It couldn't hardly be too fast." Only Chatham had heard of CORE or the Southern Christian Leadership Conference. He maintained that CORE was "moving in the right direction," and he had a favorable opinion of the SCLC, too. Archer and Barlow thought the SCLC was an organization similar to the White Citizens Councils!

On the question of tactics, all three men endorsed boycotts and civil rights laws, but Luke Archer was a good deal more conservative in his tactical views. He felt that the increased hostility generated by sit-ins and freedom rides outweighed their positive value. Archer did not question the legitimacy of these actions—participants in them were acting within their rights; he merely questioned the wisdom of nonviolent direct action "because it's sort of a force; they sort of force those people to do what they don't want to do. And when you force a person, then automatically he becomes hostile." He had particular scorn for "these agitators who came from out of town," for he contended that "they did more harm than good." The logic of his position emerges clearly in his remarks concerning civil rights legislation and government action in the field of civil rights:

> The only way to get things done is through—by laws. But we must be awfully careful. You see, this thing can't be done

overnight. And some people say, "Well, it's been long enough—."
Yes, it's been long enough, but, you see, you have to be awfully
careful how you put your hand in the lion's mouth. And there
are ways to get around this thing. If everybody would get
calm, there are ways.

It [the Federal Government] has done just about as much as
it could do at this point. The South is beginning to come
around. I don't care how many laws you make, if people don't
want to do something, they won't do it.

Archer's preference for the more gradual approach is also exhibited in his preference for the NAACP over the SCLC, a preference which he expressed in criticizing Martin Luther King
when it was explained to him that the SCLC was the organization headed by King. By contrast, Wilbur Chatham felt that
nonviolent direct action was necessitated by the slowness of
the legal approach. Chatham observed, "The law's all right,
but who's going to carry it out?" In applauding the sit-ins and
freedom rides he added, "It would take years to legislate all
this."

Attitudes toward the open housing covenant and toward the
church sponsorship of the covenant campaign were unanimously
favorable among Negro clergymen. Luke Archer spoke for his
colleagues in saying:

I believe that the Church should be inspired by this type of
thing here. We must practice what we preach, and if this kind
of thing is to be arranged, I think it's good for the Church to
take the first initiative, and wage it. I think it's a good thing. I
don't think you can call this an outright politics; this is the
Church's business. We are our brother's keeper. Let's face it, this
is compulsory—for the churches to "meddle" in this thing. Because if we don't, where can we go?

Despite their stand on race relations and their approval of
the OHC, however, the Negro ministers were not strikingly
energetic in soliciting support for the open housing covenant
from their parishioners. None of them took part in the common
pulpit emphasis urged by the Protestant Clergy Fellowship, and
none of them made use of a general mailing to insure that
every member of the congregation had an opportunity to sign
the covenant. Luke Archer had an announcement of the cov-

enant campaign printed in the bulletin for the worship service
of October 22, and for several consecutive Sundays worshipers
were handed a covenant card along with the morning bulletin.
Both James Barlow and Wilbur Chatham announced the covenant from the pulpit, had the cards placed in the vestibule,
and saw to it that the matter was mentioned in meetings of various church organizations. Only Barlow indicated that he had
discussed the covenant with his Church Board. The rightness of
and the need for the goals sought by the covenant were deemed
so self-evident that no arguments designed to persuade people
to sign it were thought to be necessary by these ministers.

Lack of wholehearted support for the covenant on the part
of Negro churchmen can be explained by reference to certain
objective conditions as well as by reference to subjective viewpoints expressed in interviews. It should be remembered, first
of all, that all of the Negro ministers also had another full-time
job; as a result, their ability to carry on a complete ministry
was severely restricted. Since their participation in the Clergy
Fellowship was limited by the 10:00 A.M. weekday meeting
time of that group and since some of the Negro pastors had not
felt entirely welcome in the Clergy Fellowship, it is not surprising that they felt something less than a close sense of identification with the Clergy Fellowship and something less than an
overwhelming desire to join in the common pulpit emphasis
requested by the Fellowship.

Even more important, perhaps, as a factor in the relatively
unenthusiastic response of Negro clergymen were their attitudes
about the nature of church life and the probable effectiveness
of the covenant campaign. They were men of limited educational background and sophistication, being products of a religious ethos which gives prime emphasis to emotional fervor
in the service of worship and particularly in their sermons.
Their espousal of this ethos is evident in their estimation of
the preaching role of the minister as the most important of his
responsibilities, and also in their conception of Christian faith
and discipleship. In responding to questions about the relationship between faith and ethics, the Negro ministers were quite
inarticulate. Their answers were for the most part nothing but

an incoherent jumble of clichés: "Let your conscience be your guide," "First things first," "If you read the Bible and understand it, there wouldn't be any need for anything else," and "The Christian's motto should be the Golden Rule" were typical statements given in reply to questions about criteria, motives, the Bible, and prayer. To anyone whose roots are in this tradition and whose educational opportunities have been few, critical rational analysis seems less appropriate in a sermon than flowery rhetoric and imaginative exposition of colorful biblical narratives, and the minister's role as organizer and strategist in community action does not receive great emphasis.

The Negro clergymen also had considerable skepticism about the likely effectiveness of the covenant appeal. Luke Archer observed that "a whole lot of signing, and nothing concrete materializes from it . . . [means] you're still just stabbing in the dark." He also feared that "a lot of people will say—now don't get me wrong—they'll say, 'Here's something; let me sign it and get it out of my face, and let me just sign it, and let them go on.'" He did not think that the issue could be "forced," and he did not think the housing covenant could "pinpoint people down to these things." Wilbur Chatham complained about a poor response in his congregation, explaining it in terms of a general inability on their part to "take hold and do things." Moreover, he was skeptical of the idea that the churchgoers of Newfield would respond enthusiastically to the covenant appeal, for he pointed out: "Well, almost every homeowner is the member of some church, and you can take it from that. If they were really interested as they should be, they would get more done." James Barlow was more sanguine: he was prepared to believe at least that the other clergymen of the city shared his favorable sentiments toward the covenant. He added, "I don't know whether they're giving it the best they've got, but I think they're doing something on it." No opposition to the covenant was encountered in any of the Negro churches.

It is possible, moreover, and understandable, that Negroes in Newfield may have looked upon the open housing covenant as something intended for white people, not for them: since it was mainly whites who owned real estate, and whites who were responsible for residential exclusion, it was whites who needed to signify their allegiance to fair housing practices.

Sermonizers

Another group of ministers concentrated virtually all of their effort on behalf of the open housing covenant in the sermon which they delivered as a part of the common pulpit emphasis on October 22. Four of these five men were remarkably similar in their views on race relations: they designated themselves as "moderate integrationists," they approved of civil rights laws and the NAACP, but they had qualms about nonviolent direct action. The fifth member of this group differed only in that he was willing to call himself an integrationist, and he approved unequivocally of direct action. All were pessimistic about the covenant's reception among the churchgoers of Newfield, and four reported negative reactions to the covenant on the part of their parishioners.

Larry Oliver had heard members of his church voice the opinion that Negroes want positively favored treatment instead of simply equal opportunities, and Tom Gardner had noted expressions of resentment against both the "pushiness" of Negroes and the zeal of the chairman of the Council of Churches Social Action Committee. The most hopeful appraisal of the covenant's chance of success was the very modest statement on this point made by Byron Thatcher:

> One woman said she would hate to see this happen in her neighborhood, and yet she knew it was the right thing and it was just her upbringing, and so on, that she felt was—uh, at fault. She did want to cooperate, and if it did happen in the neighborhood, she would do all she could to welcome them and make them feel at home. That doesn't say that she would sell to one of them necessarily, but—I think she expressed about as far as most of the congregation would go. Some of them—well, there are one or two who might sell or rent to Negroes if they had the opportunity. I think the most they would do is, if it happened in their neighborhood, they would not panic sell. They would do their best to make the adjustment.

Thatcher admitted that he was actually persuaded to modify his presentation of the covenant cards to his congregation by the negative reaction of his official board when he discussed the matter with them just prior to the worship service on October 22. He explained that "they wanted people to have the right not to sign without—er, losing face." As one parishioner was leaving Thatcher's church after his sermon on the housing problem and the presentation of the covenant, she remarked to him, "Well, you spoiled a lot of Sunday dinners this morning!" In the light of this opposition, it is understandable that Thatcher might have come to feel that "follow-up action would be a waste of time," and that Larry Oliver, in the face of similar opposition, should ask, "Why bother?" when queried about follow-up plans. Perhaps the unarticulated views of the sermonizers were best summed up in the remark of a close friend of Tom Gardner who happened to be present during part of his interview: when the question of lay reaction to the covenant was raised, this person declared (with considerable passion, and with murmurs of assent and nodded acquiescence from Gardner), "These people [in our congregation] are old hidebound Yankees, and we can't in one sermon ram anything down their throats. They'll come around if Tom gives 'em time." Given the rather gloomy appraisal of congregational response to the open housing covenant made by these pastors, it is easy to see why all of them emphasized community pride or the national image in appealing for support.

There were both parallels and differences in the logic of the position adopted by men in this group. Of the three men who were able to comment on the criteria for ethical action which guided them, all stressed either immediacy or the idea of vocation. Byron Thatcher recommended response to "the issue that is being forced on you at the moment," mentioning redevelopment in Newfield as a primary cause of the local churches' interest in minority group housing. For Tom Gardner, the commitments inherent in one's choice of a vocation provided the clearest criterion for moral choice, and he interpreted the calling of the minister in such a way as to emphasize the pastoral role:

If it were a choice between caring for the needs of someone in my parish who was sick, and going to a meeting downtown, such as the one last night [at which Martin Luther King spoke on "Race Relations in America Today"], which I wanted to attend, but couldn't, then I would have to consider calling on the sick person as my primary obligation. My first duty is to them: they rely on me as their minister, and they are the ones who pay me, too.

Carl Morris indicated an awareness of the limitations of using immediacy and one's sense of vocation as criteria:

I think the average individual makes his decision in terms of the local situation, rightly or wrongly. For example, if there is a local problem, this is where he becomes involved. If there is no local problem, then he looks around for a national or world problem. Many times the major problems get by-passed because of this. Again, I think many individuals have talents that might be useful in one area and not be in another, and this has a bearing on one's decision also. In other words, I think what you're seeking is some sort of scale according to which we give time to this or that. I think this scale has to be pretty much within the individual himself, his own convictions, his own faith, or even the call of God, perhaps. And there are many, many incidents, many events, which move an individual to see what can be done and move him to do it. Actually, as a Christian minister, you have to speak to all these problems, to a certain extent, but for example, the Christian minister in Newfield has to speak to the race problem considerably more than the minister in Northern Maine or somewhere where there hasn't been a Negro in twenty-five years.

On the question of proper motivation, Alex Carpenter and Carl Morris showed a healthy awareness of the danger of being inordinately concerned with this quality. Tom Gardner laid greater stress on pure motives; indeed, he avowed that he would "rather have ten people sign the covenant out of genuine, sincere conviction than to have a hundred sign up just because it was the thing to do." Byron Thatcher went even further in his emphasis upon good motives: he implied a correlation between them and effectiveness, because he contended that "the less self-interest enters in, the more successful social action will ordinarily be."

It is easy to say, in retrospect, that men with these views might have been expected to make a token effort in promoting the open housing covenant, but not much more. They acknowledged the importance of the housing problem, they viewed it as a proper concern for Christian social action, they had no objections to strong verbal stands and legal action in civil rights, and thus they supported the covenant. They felt, on the other hand, that their efforts would not bear much fruit, and they did not believe in violating the conscience of parishioners by coercing or manipulating them into signing the fair housing pledge; therefore, they did little more than preach a sermon on the subject. Their prophecies of scanty support proved to be fulfilled, and perhaps self-fulfilling, because very few signatures were obtained from members of the churches pastored by these ministers.

Was there something about the way in which they presented the covenant which contributed to, or virtually insured, a meager response? The answer to that question, in so far as the five sermonizers are concerned, is "Yes." Parishioners in these churches were introduced to the open housing covenant in an impersonal manner involving no strong demand for immediate commitment. All of the sermonizers seemed to share Byron Thatcher's desire that their people should be able "not to sign without—er, losing face," for there was no systematic face-to-face confrontation between minister and laymen, or between convinced laymen and the unconvinced, regarding the moral challenge raised by the covenant. Most of the pastors in this category presented the pledge cards to their congregations by enclosing them in the Sunday morning worship service bulletin. Alex Carpenter and Carl Morris made the disastrous error of recommending a deferred decision on signing: Carpenter announced that the social action committee of the church would handle the collection of signed cards at a later time, and Morris suggested that signed cards be brought by the church office at some time during the following week. As Morris wryly admitted, three weeks after the announcement of the covenant appeal, "This was apparently a mistake, because as yet we have received no cards." In Byron Thatcher's church, distribution

was very haphazard: after a sermon which included the reading of the covenant, he advised the members of his congregation
that "I would have the ushers at the doors to pass them out,
if they wanted to . . . [voice trailed off; sentence remained
unfinished]." Tom Gardner reinforced the inclusion of the cards
in the bulletins by reading the covenant from the pulpit, and
he did follow up on the efforts of October 22 by making additional cards available in the vestibule of his church and by
reminding his parishioners of their availability on two succeeding
Sundays; however, he did not venture beyond these impersonal
modes of presentation.

The Unsuccessful

Three clergymen went a good deal further than any of their
colleagues mentioned so far in following up their initial presentation of the open housing covenant. The situation, thinking,
and methods of presenting the covenant were distinctive in
each case.

Murray Jackson was, because of his membership on the sponsoring Council of Churches Social Action Committee, most
closely identified with the covenant campaign—yet he was, both
theologically and sociologically, the most conservative of these
three clergymen. He objected rather strenuously to the term
"integrationist" on grounds that it was "somewhat aggressive"
and connoted "a person who almost makes a little crusade out
of this." Jackson was willing to endorse the NAACP, but he had
marked reservations about the efficacy of civil rights legislation, and he was not in favor of nonviolent direct action. His
principal argument in support of the covenant was one which fitted in logically with his principal criterion for choosing worth-
while moral activities: the criterion was immediacy, and the
argument was based on empathy. Pointing to the example of
Jesus, who was forced to "change his tactics as he went along"
because "he was so much in demand," and who was "such a com-
passionate person that he couldn't pass anybody by, "Jackson
concluded, "This, I think, is the criterion: you have to meet
. . . what comes along in a cry for help." He illustrated his

point by juxtaposing his own experience as a pastor with the biblical account of the Good Samaritan:

> You can see the mess my desk is in, and it's always in a mess all the time. But one reason I'm in a mess is that the phone is there. And someone says, "My husband is leaving me," or "I'm drunk," or "My father is dying." So all of these things—what are you going to do? You do what you have to do. And you do it because—I mean, you are a Samaritan who's going down the road. He had to *ride.* He had to be in Jericho by 3:45 on important social action business. But gee, this guy is lying there—what do you do? That's the criterion, to meet the need, and then to go on. You don't forget your ultimate purpose, but you do what is presented to you.

In the opinion of Jackson, the strongest arguments for the covenant were an appeal to "fair play" in a democracy and an appeal for each white person to put himself in the place of the Negro. He thought that "unless we seek to defend that right of Negroes to every legitimate privilege as a citizen, then we have a rottenness somewhere and a false front in our nation's freedom." He was convinced that "this is very important and a strong argument. It would appeal to a lot of Yankees who reject the idea that the Church should be involved in this." Jackson's October 22 sermon, in which these themes were stressed, was followed by a mailing urging support of the covenant, and including a covenant card, which was sent to all members of his parish. In view of the fact that this minister showed a clearer awareness than did any of his colleagues of the importance of influencing important citizens in the community to sign the covenant, it is rather surprising that he made no special effort to reach the numerous bankers, realtors, and other high-ranking business and professional men in his congregation.

Sam Hawthorne described himself as a reasonable integrationist. He denied being "one who is all out to break this thing wide open in the present moment"; however, he felt very strongly that "the time has come when we've got to stop being 'moderate.'" Enthusiastic in his approval of the NAACP, he also endorsed sit-ins, boycotts, and freedom rides as justifiable expressions of the conscience of the demonstrator, and he affirmed the necessity for and the desirability of civil rights legislation.

Hawthorne was a staunch believer in the theory that right thinking will surely lead to right action. His stress on the doctrine of justification by faith as the crucial link between theology and ethics led him to assert that "When this doctrine is taken seriously [by Christians], they cannot help but follow through" in a godly, righteous, and sober life. This conviction was paralleled by his firm belief that substantial guidance could be derived from prayer, and by his insistence that pure motives were of the utmost importance. When the question of pure motivation was posed to him in its most extreme form— "If you are contemplating an action which you firmly believe to be good, but regarding which you fear that you yourself may have some unworthy motive, do you think that you should refrain from doing it until you can be sure about your motives?"— Hawthorne replied without hesitation, "Yes, I do."

Given this intellectual orientation, it is not surprising that the Reverend Hawthorne handled the presentation of the covenant in the manner he did. Cognizant of the stubborn opposition to residential integration in his congregation, he nevertheless made persistent efforts to confront his people with their responsibilities in the matter through exhortation and rational discussion. He preached a sermon on the covenant, he repeatedly reminded his parishioners of it in pulpit announcements and in Sunday morning worship service bulletins, and he included a session on racial justice in housing in a Lenten study program later during the year. One of Hawthorne's colleagues felt that he deserved a great deal of credit for pushing the issue as vigorously as he did in a church where so many important laymen were apt to be vexed by his tenacity.

In making his case for the covenant, Hawthorne deemed it wise to "steer clear of the social action implications in the beginning" and to "begin by talking about the survey [on housing conditions among Newfield Negroes], the facts of the matter." He drew on the Anti-Defamation League pamphlet concerning "Myths About Housing" in framing his sermon on "Deceptive Words," a major thrust of which was to persuade his congregation "that as Christians we should stand up to show how false these deceptive words are." The other central point of his message was that "if we are Christians we will act like Christians, and if we do, then we can act in no other way than to regard all men as our brothers." The development of his argument followed these lines: the words through which a man expresses himself are organically related to his very "being," and therefore to all his "doing." One's being lacks integrity if his doing is not in accord with his words. Jeremiah and Jesus were eloquent spokesmen for this truth; both urged men to be "doers of the word, not hearers only." Not only do the prophets of the Bible proclaim this message, but also the great heroes of the Church live according to it. Two examples were given to substantiate this point: that of a young minister who overcame the opposition of cowboys in a frontier town and went on to found the American Sunday School Union, and that of a schoolmaster in the Philippines who allowed himself to be shot by enemy soldiers rather than take down Old Glory from the wall of his schoolroom. Having prepared his listeners by these two stirring illustrations, Hawthorne then issued a ringing challenge to the Christian citizens of Newfield to reconcile their prayers to "Our Father" with their behavior toward Negroes. Considerable emphasis was laid on the fact that the housing covenant program was a community-wide effort, and also on the fact that it was a loving, not a coercive approach to the problem. The sermon ended with a prayer that God would grant all present the strength to live their Christian convictions.

Gus Newton was the most aggressive integrationist among the ineffectuals, and indeed it is quite possible that if he had not been a student pastor with limited experience and time for the performance of his ministerial responsibilities, he could have been a good deal more effective than he was in gaining supporters for the covenant. Newton was familiar with the work of various civil rights organizations and with the tactics being employed in the rights struggle, and he was in favor of militant groups and direct action as well as antidiscrimination legislation. Acknowledging the limits of education and exhortation in combating prejudice, he welcomed laws as a standard to which moralists could appeal in seeking to change behavior, and he felt that is was just for business firms not according equal treatment to Negroes to be subjected to economic pressure which would cut into their profits and force them to alter their policies. Said Newton:

> I guess when you come right down to it economic change is doing more to unlock the doors of discrimination than moral change. This is something the Church ought to be greatly ashamed of. There is the possibility of businesses being ruined through this—and yet, I would say that it is valid for them to be.

Newton's tough-minded practicality was also reflected in his comments on the relationship between Christian faith and social action. In his view, a good deal of the theologizing indulged in by churchmen was a means of evading their obvious responsibilities to "live Christianity!" Each moral decision offers a chance to "decide for or against other human beings," and preoccupation with one's own motives is a snare and a delusion, since "not choosing is itself a choice favoring the status quo." Prayer could furnish guidance, yes—but only if accompanied by hard study and careful thought. No one who understands "the total picture of our New Testament with its basis in the Old . . . could maintain a segregationist doctrine," but understanding it is not simple, and proof-texts provide no automatic answers.

In addition to preaching on the covenant and having covenant cards available in the vestibule of the church at the service on October 22, Newton urged the Commission on Christian Social Concerns of this church to follow through on his sermon by soliciting signatures for the covenant in the manner which seemed best to its leaders. He also planned a series of talks and discussions on race relations for his youth group, and one of the programs in this series was devoted specifically to housing discrimination in Newfield and the logic of the open housing convenant. Newton admitted that follow-up plans needed to include provisions for more face-to-face encounter with parishioners unsympathetic to the covenant, and he allowed that, judging from the reception given his sermon, most of his people "would just as soon forget about the whole thing"—yet he fancied that he had not "run up against as much of a stone wall as is sometimes the case," and he was pleased that "a dozen or so" of his parishioners (from a membership of about 250) had signed the fair housing pledge.

THE EFFECTIVE

Two Newfield clergymen were far more effective than the rest of their colleagues in obtaining support for the open housing covenant. Of all the ministers in the city, they were the ones most closely identified with the battle against discrimination in housing—Peter Everett, pastor of the Butler Memorial Congregational Church, whose Social Action Committee had taken a lead in agitating the issue, and Harold Baldwin, chairman of the Protestant Council of Churches Social Action Committee. Furthermore, they developed a more systematic program for confronting their people with the covenant than did their fellow clergymen. An analysis of their thinking and their methods of presenting the covenant is especially instructive.

Both Everett and Baldwin were aggressive integrationists, giving hearty approval to civil rights organizations, direct action, and legislation barring discrimination. The most notable aspect of their views on race relations, however, is not their willingness to endorse vigorous measures, but their reasons for doing so: unlike most of the other clergymen, who tended to evaluate social action in terms of the intentions of the agents, Everett and Baldwin directed their attention to the consequences of action. The former emphasized the awakening of the national conscience which resulted from sit-ins and freedom rides; the latter was the only minister who explicitly cited the fact that these tactics had effected desegregation of hitherto segregated facilities as his principal reason for favoring them. Baldwin also articulated more clearly than anyone else the primacy of minority group rights over majority group preferences: agreeing that "we want to change attitudes ultimately," he stressed his conviction that "right laws can help to create a framework in which attitudes can be changed," and he declared, "The right of the Negro to equal opportunities or accommodation is far more important than my right to refuse him."

The two most effective clergymen attached central importance to different theological principles as the basis for Christian social action, but they were alike in that they had thought through this issue carefully and could identify cogently the foundation on which they stood. Baldwin's reasoning was quite philosophical: social action was rooted in the nature of God (and of God's redemptive action in Jesus Christ) and the common humanity of all men as creatures of the loving God. Everett's appeal was principally to the biblical theme of sacrificial service to the neighbor—and for him the Bible defines the neighbor as one in need whom we can help. Both men were impatient with concern over purity of motivation: Baldwin doubted the very existence of pure motives, and Everett asserted that ambiguity of motivation "should not keep us from acting." Immediacy was the crucial criterion of moral choice for Everett—"This [housing problem] was right here; this was closer than fallout," he observed, adding, "Actually, we did not choose this, standing back looking at the panorama and asking which was most important, but rather this chose us." Baldwin's answer to the question of criteria, which lays emphasis on the individual's vocation, deserves to be quoted in full:

> The criteria would be (1) readiness, (2) the time available, (3) the *type* of time needed, (4) a viewing of the challenges of the moment as against your understanding of the nature of the gospel and your understanding of the demands that the gospel makes upon you at this particular moment, (5) the individual's abilities, and even his interests. Maybe it's a good thing that everybody in Newfield is not becoming a leader in housing, although I hope that everyone will become at least a follower and do something, although I would be in favor of getting them to do *all* they can—but maybe we're going to need some of these other people who are concerned about gambling or some other area of the Church's witness to take a lead later on, and then the rest of us can be followers.

Both men were aware that no easy solutions could be expected from prayer, but both thought prayer was important in regard to social action. For Everett, it held a promise of "courage to—well, to stand on one's convictions"; for Baldwin, it was related to one's understanding of immediacy and his vocation, because he remarked, "For all I know, the opportunity to be chairman of the Social Action Committee [of the Council of Churches] or to be on the mayor's committee may have been an answer to prayers that God would use me." Baldwin also realized that prayer could become a device for evading one's responsibilities, for when asked what he would say to someone who suggested that the best thing to be done about the housing problem might be to pray about it, Baldwin replied:

> I would say, "Well, I'm glad you're praying about it. But I think God wants you to become a part of the answer to your prayer. Roll up your sleeves and get to work." Of course, I think we can become too pious. This can be an escape.

The arguments for supporting the open housing covenant and involving oneself in the struggle against discrimination in housing were presented by Baldwin and Everett in their October 22 sermons on this theme.

Harold Baldwin entitled his sermon "Love Thy Neighbor" and used as a text James 2:1-10. In his introductory remarks, he moved from the general to the specific by starting with a description of the world situation (in which heretofore oppressed peoples are asserting their right to freedom), passing on to the national scene (where the "good race relations" of the South are being disrupted by bus boycotts, sit-ins and freedom rides), and then pointing to the local situation (where discrimination in housing is a reality which must be faced). After citing the report of the Butler Memorial Congregational Church Social Action Committee as evidence that discrimination in Newfield is no chimera, Baldwin then attempted to explain why the problem existed by articulating—and then refuting—a number of false ideas about "the Negro problem" commonly held: (1) the idea that agitation is bad, since time will solve the problem; (2) the idea that the Negroes ought to be willing to undergo a period of hostility against them, just as various immigrant groups were forced to do; (3) the idea that neutrality is a superior moral posture in regard to this problem; and (4) the idea that a solution is totally the responsibility of Negroes, who could overcome their status if only they tried harder. It was pointed out that: (1) time solves nothing, of itself—time is only a gift from God which man is intended to use in striving to realize His will on earth; (2) two wrongs do not make a right—the ostracism accorded Poles and Irish in an earlier day is no justification for ostracizing Negroes today (and furthermore the assimilation of Negroes is more difficult than was the assimilation of white-skinned Europeans); (3) "being neutral" is the same as siding with the status quo, and is therefore in this particular case the same as siding with injustice; and (4) that Negroes have unequal opportunities for self-advancement (and placing the whole burden of improvement on them is a form of rationalizing).

What is the solution? A paraphrase of the day's text was read in order to show that the Bible urges love for these particular neighbors who happen to be Negroes, and it was emphasized that failure to observe the law in one point is to violate it entirely. An appeal to empathy was followed by an assertion that in this particular case the Christian ethic is crystal clear: all Christians must work actively to overcome discrimination. This injunction was related to the pledge taken two weeks before by all worshipers at a Dedication Service in which the members of the congregation had vowed to bear "costly witness . . . at the busy intersections of life." The covenant card was read and the purpose of the covenant apppeal was explained. Baldwin then attempted to disarm the objection which some persons might have, namely, that they did not want their name to appear in the newspaper as having endorsed the covenant: he cried shame upon such lack of courage, and cited the courage of Christians in Communist lands as a spur to greater zeal. The covenant cards were distributed by the members of the Social Action Committee of the church, followed by a period of silence, a prayer, and then the benediction.

After clearing the air with an opening joke (about a Mississippi Negro who comes to heaven announcing that he has been accepted as a member in a local white church, then suddenly realizes that the last thing he can remember is being totally immersed by the Baptist brethren!), Peter Everett preached a blunt, "come-on-you-guys," no-nonsense sermon entitled "The Negro Will Win." The joke was followed by the relating of four unamusing incidents which had recently occurred in Newfield. The first was designed to arouse empathy for Negroes:

A Negro in our community was asked what he thought about the freedom riders—whether or not he appreciated their gestures—whether or not he was in sympathy with the movement. His comment was, "I've been on a freedom ride all my life. . . ." He drove home the point that though the freedom riders suffered some slight humiliation because of the stand they were willing to take, that he had been humiliated all his life. . . .

The second was designed to arouse pity:

Just a year ago a widowed Negro woman with three small children made valiant efforts to secure housing outside of the ghetto she was living in. After approximately fifty serious efforts, she was worn out, crushed and bitter. Doors had been closed in her face—promises had been made and broken—her hopes had been dashed to pieces. There was nothing for her to do. She was black and that was all there was to it.

The third, a sense of guilt:

This summer I had the frustrating experience of talking with a landlady in our community—a good Protestant woman who had an apartment for rent which was extremely suitable for a Negro family who [sic] I knew. After giving me all kinds of excuses as to why she would not be able to rent to this family, she finally laid the cards on the table and said, "All right, I guess I'm prejudiced."

The fourth, courage and assurance of the rightness of battling against discrimination:

Sometimes there is cloudiness over right and wrong. Sometimes we are all mixed up as to what is good and what is evil. But in this situation we are on the most solid Christian ground—on the most solid Jewish ground—on the most solid humanistic ground that anybody could be on. There is no question but there has been injustice—no question as to the direction we should be going. The fact that the Jews and the Roman Catholics have joined Protestants in formal declarations regarding this situation testifies to the uniformity of the conviction which pours out of the various faiths.

Then the issue was posed: some of us are plainly wrong in our attitudes, and we are going to have to change. How? Partly through empathy; partly through awareness that the myths about Negroes and housing were false. A distinction was made

between fear and anxiety, the latter being "based on illusion."
Asserted Everett:

> If there is honest and sincere fright in all of this, its basis
> is in untruth, and truth will bring freedom. God is color
> blind, and those who harbor racial prejudices are playing with
> something man-made, and I cannot help but feel that the
> only help for the racially prejudiced man is for him to go
> down on his knees and confess it. We Christians ought not to be
> afraid of this procedure anyway.

Immediately upon the heels of this condemnation of the prejudiced was a warning to those who felt that they were not
prejudiced, for

> this does not mean that we are particularly good, or that we
> have no prejudices at all: It only means that in one practical
> area we may have the necessary insight and conviction which
> is now so terribly needed and relevant to the stride toward
> freedom which is being made by our Negro brothers through-
> out the world.

What is the Scriptural basis for this stand? The "story of the
Good Samaritan and the articulation of the Great Command-
ment" (the latter being the text announced for the sermon).
How are these passages relevant?

> We are called not to pass by on the other side. We are close
> to a situation. This is not a Southern problem—it's a community
> problem—it's a Butler Memorial problem. The logic is very sim-
> ple: our neighbor is the one in need whom we are able to
> help—our neighbor, therefore, sometimes becomes the Negro.
> Therefore, we love him, and if we love him we accept him.
> This is not a kind of Sunday morning problem which we solve
> by making a resolution or by claiming in broad generalities
> that we are against sin. Love must be acted out in concrete
> situations where each one of us, in his own way, confronts the
> issues of the day.

The sermon ended with the statement of the prophecy contained in the title—doubtless with the intention that it should
become self-fulfilling through the changed behavior of those
who heard it. Everett informed his parishioners that "the Christian Church . . . can assist or it can ignore the coming of the

inevitable," and he urged them to assist in the acceleration of progress by signing the housing covenant.

The most extensive, and the best administered, follow-up plans were also formulated by Harold Baldwin and Peter Everett. Both of these men, along with Murray Jackson, were members of the Social Action Committee of the Council of Churches, which had sponsored the whole idea of the housing covenant in the Clergy Fellowship. Both of these men had become identified with the Negro housing problem through their service on the Mayor's housing committee. Everett had become even more closely identified with the problem, and various attempts to help solve it, through the work of the Social Action Committee of his church and through his own participation in the NAACP. It is hardly surprising, then, that Baldwin and Everett poured more energy into the covenant appeal than any of the other pastors, and that they achieved greater success, in proportional as well as absolute quantitative terms, than did their colleagues.

Of all the churches with a congregation of more than one hundred persons, none received such a successful response from the covenant program as the Broadway Baptist Church, where Harold Baldwin was pastor. A careful description of the methods of handling the program used in this church should provide some illuminating clues as to how Christian social action of this kind can be carried out effectively.

Systematic study of the Christian's responsibility in the field of race relations did not begin with the housing covenant appeal in the Broadway Baptist Church. The subject was treated in a general way at two meetings of the Adult Forum—the large class which includes all adults who attend Sunday School—in June, 1961. The same subject was picked up when the class resumed its sessions in September (after a two-month vacation period), and it was treated with ever greater specificity each week until early December. Several sessions were devoted specifically to the housing problem, but various other aspects of the field of race relations were covered during this period of time.

The Council of Churches dinner featuring the address by

Dr. Kerr was heavily publicized at Broadway Baptist, and about twenty-eight members of the church attended the affair.

Baldwin's handling of the worship service on October 22, the day agreed upon by the Protestant ministers for their "common pulpit emphasis" on the housing covenant, is noteworthy. As recorded above, his sermon was devoted entirely to the racial problem, and the presentation of the housing covenant was built into the sermon itself. The uniqueness of the mode of presenting the covenant utilized by Baldwin consists in the fact that the covenant cards were distributed to each worshiper by the members of the church's Social Action Committee, who came to the front of the sanctuary to receive the cards from Baldwin and then distributed them silently to the people in the pews. The worshipers had not seen the covenant card before the moment of distribution, and the silence which accompanied the act of distribution created an atmosphere of expectancy for the reading of the covenant by the minister. Of the 162 persons present at the October 22 service, seventy-seven signed the covenant before leaving the church that morning.

For the next several weeks, the members of Broadway Baptist were given a consistent exposure to further facts and moral judgments relating to the housing issue in their weekly parish publication. Several popular misconceptions regarding residence and race were refuted. Several strong affirmations of the rightness of signing the covenant were delivered; for example, one newsletter contained a statement by the pastor to the effect that "Surely we who profess our faith in Christ cannot do otherwise but indicate our support of this [covenant]." Various other items of literature pertaining to the housing question were mailed to the parishioners from time to time.

Especially noteworthy in the Reverend Baldwin's presentation of the OHC was his policy of buttonholing individual parishioners and asking them if they had turned in a signed pledge card. When one of the members of his church refused to sign the covenant on the grounds that "the best people in the congregation" were opposed to it, Baldwin challenged him to name some of the people to whom he was referring. The first two names mentioned were those of men who had in fact signed it. Confronted with this proof of the flimsiness of his excuse for not supporting the OHC, the parishioner readily signed the pledge which Baldwin produced from his coat pocket!

But as the handing out of pledge cards in the worship service of October 22 revealed, the OHC was not something which was being pressed upon the people of the church by the pastor alone. Assisting him in this endeavor was an active social action committee. On October 26, the chairman of the committee, Ralph Hunter, presented the case for the covenant before the men's club of the church. (The film entitled "Crisis in Levittown" was shown on this occasion.) Other members of the committee also went before various church organizations to explain the covenant and urge people to sign it. The committee even made it a point to contact the spouse of everyone who had already signed the covenant in order to see if he or she wanted to add his or her name to the list of signatories. At the beginning of the new year, Hunter sent a letter urging support of the covenant to one hundred and forty-seven church members who in his opinion had for some reason not yet had an adequate opportunity to sign. In February, each committee member agreed to contact five persons who had not yet signed the covenant, and to make one final effort to persuade them to do so.

When the signed cards collected from members of the Broadway Baptist Church were turned over to the Council of Churches Social Action Committee for use in preparation of the newspaper advertisement about the covenant, 111 cards had been collected from the membership of 390 persons, and thirty additional cards had been secured from persons whom Baldwin termed "friends of our church" who were not members of it.

Harold Baldwin's role in the open housing covenant program was more prominent than that played by any other Newfield clergyman. But the minister who was most closely associated with the Negro housing problem in the minds of the public was Peter Everett, whose personal involvement in the issue was well known because of his chairmanship of both the NAACP housing committee and the mayor's special committee on relocation of families displaced by redevelopment. Indeed, the Butler Memorial Congregational Church itself was associated in the public mind with the cause of antidiscrimination in housing, not only because of its minister but also because of the work done by its social action committee under the leadership of Dr. John Wallace.

Butler Memorial's drive to gain signatures for the covenant began when the October issue of the church's *Parish Press* carried a front-page story on the approaching covenant appeal and included a copy of the poster advertising the October 16 Council of Churches dinner. The dinner was billed as an occasion when, "As never before, Newfield's Protestant Churches will be uniting, not just in fellowship, but in deep concern with a problem which plagues their community." The covenant idea was explained, and the particular effort which it represented was placed in context by a warning that "In the months and years ahead extensive work will and must be done before we approach that kind of community in which there will be equal opportunity for all." Sixteen members of Butler Memorial attended the dinner at which the covenant was for the first time officially presented to the people of Newfield.

Everett's presentation of the covenant cards in the worship service of October 22 was less dramatic than Harold Baldwin's. The cards had simply been placed in the bulletin for the morning, and the curious worshiper could have read a part or all of it at any time after being seated. The absence of drama, however, did not keep approximately eighty of the 180 persons in church that morning from signing the covenant then and there.

Follow-up action was limited because of Everett's conviction that everyone in his church had been given ample opportunity to think through his responsibility as a Christian in regard to race relations. Everett felt that there was a danger of placing too much emphasis on the race issue in his church for he had resigned himself to the fact that many of his parishioners simply could not be persuaded to change their way of thinking or living in so far as minority groups were concerned. He felt that the situation called for a minimum of "preaching" about the convenant, combined with a policy of distribution of the convenant cards which gave maximum assurance that everyone in the church received a convenant and was confronted with the opportunity to sign it. With this in mind, he included a copy of the covenant card in the November issue of the *Parish Press*. He also selected the names of about fifty-five members of the congregation who, by the middle of November, had still not signed the covenant, and directed the Social Action Committee to see that these members were contacted individually by persons from the committee. Six committee members divided among themselves the responsibility for this task, and before Christmas they carried it out. Most of the contacts were made by telephone. Only five additional signatures were obtained by this effort.

The total number of persons signing the covenant from the Butler Memorial Congregational Church was 126. The active membership of the church is almost six hundred.

FURTHER DEVELOPMENTS

CHAPTER 5

ON THE MORNING FOLLOWING THE Council of Churches dinner at which the open housing covenant was introduced to the people of Newfield, a front-page article headed "Churchmen Open Attack on Race Bias in Housing" informed the public that a "three-pronged inter-faith [sic] attack on racial bias in housing discrimination was launched last night by the Greater Newfield Council of Churches." The covenant was printed in full, and it was noted that "Mayor Francis H. Fuller was the first person to sign the pledge." Also cited in full were the three endorsements by the Jewish, Roman Catholic, and Protestant clergymen which appeared on the covenant card. Readers of the *Review* were erroneously informed that "The pledges will be distributed to every church in the area by the end of this week."[1]

The fact of the matter was that "every church in the area" was not ready to present the covenant to its parishioners during the week of October 15. As the foregoing chapter disclosed, several Protestant churches did not participate in the covenant program at all, and all of the Roman Catholic churches postponed their participation in the program until much later. The reasons for delayed participation on the part of the Roman Catholic parishes deserve to be described in considerable detail.

In the first place, as noted in previous chapters, liaison between the Roman Catholic clergy of Newfield and the Social Action Committee of the Protestant Council of Churches, which planned the covenant appeal and set the date for its promulgation among Protestant churchgoers, was from the beginning quite precarious. The Protestant leaders made persistent efforts to establish contact with representative leaders of the Roman Catholic community during the summer, but they went ahead with their plans to launch the covenant campaign in October without regard to the success of these efforts to establish contact. From the standpoint of the Catholic clergy, then, the covenant took on the guise of an enterprise concerning which they had some advance notice, but which was presented to them as a *fait accompli*: they were asked to give their endorsement of it without having had a real say in its planning. As one priest quipped, "This was an interfaith housing covenant —interfaith among the Protestants." None of the priests who were interviewed expressed genuine resentment because of this anomalous situation, but all of them were conscious of the fact that the Roman Catholic segment of the Christian community in Newfield had not had an equal voice in determining policy regarding the open housing covenant program.[2]

In the second place, the Catholic churches were in no position to participate in the covenant campaign in October, because of a vitally important fund-raising drive on behalf of parochial schools which was being conducted in Newfield during the fall. According to an appraisal of the situation given by Sean O'Malley in an interview of October 24, it was anticipated that the building fund drive would be concluded about the middle of November, and that Catholic participation in the covenant appeal would commence shortly thereafter. Actually, though, the solicitation of pledges for the school fund did not get underway officially until November 24, and the drive was not terminated until several weeks after Christmas. For obvious reasons, it would have been unrealistic to expect Catholic leaders to divert energy from an undertaking of such scope and magnitude—it involved "a house-to-house solicitation by workers in each of the county's 16 parishes"[3]—in order to support a program of social action which had been initiated and planned almost exclusively by Protestants. Under the circumstances, it is hardly surprising that the covenant was not presented to the Roman Catholics of Newfield until late February.

In the meantime, however, public interest in the housing problems of Negroes was sustained by a series of events which received ample coverage in the *Review*. Ten days after the

Council of Churches dinner, one of the fraternities at the University devoted a session of its monthly forum to a discussion of the housing report of the University Study Committee. The newspaper account of this forum focused attention on the study's finding that although a quarter of the Negro inhabitants of Newfield had at least a high school diploma, there were very few Negro professional and white collar workers in the city. The "plausible hypothesis" drawn from these findings—that discrimination in the form of a "job ceiling" limited the employment opportunities of Negroes in the city—was played up in a front-page headline proclaiming "Negro Job Bias Seen Here." The article pointed out that the absence of Negro stenographers, salesmen and clerks in Newfield business establishments "tends to intensify the stereotype of the Negro as a low occupation worker and to make his opportunities in housing a never-ending problem."[4]

Another event which served to keep the housing problem before the citizenry took place in November. At the suggestion of several men on the University Study Committee (including the Rev. Peter Everett), Mayor Fuller declared November "Fair Housing Practices Month." The mayor's proclamation took note of the fact that the stronger civil rights law on housing had gone into effect in October, and interpreted the passage of this law as an indication "that a majority of the people in [the state] accept the principle of and believe in equality for all under the Constitution." The purpose of the proclamation was to "urge all to help to make our City a strong and vital example of democracy at work by endorsing the cause of nondiscrimination in housing."[5]

On the same day that the mayor's proclamation of November as "Fair Housing Practices Month" was announced, another important piece of information concerning the problem of racial discrimination in housing was made public by the Butler Memorial Congregational Church Social Action Committee. The Rev. Peter Everett issued a press release which declared that "the action group planned to lessen its program of screening Negro applicants for white housing and of knocking on doors in the frustrating search for rentals."[6] Everett reiterated the committee's readiness "to take part in any test case against a landlord charged with housing discrimination," but he said the policy of the committee from now on would be to encourage Negroes to initiate efforts to secure housing without going through the screening process which had been a part of the committee's procedure up until then. Also hinted at, but not explicitly affirmed, in the same article was the fact that the task of encouraging Negroes to make use of the new civil rights law in housing was to be handled by the local branch of the NAACP.

In late January, the NAACP held what was intended to be a very important meeting for the purpose of informing the Negro citizens of the community as to their rights and opportunities under the new civil rights law of the state. The meeting received wide publicity in the Negro community, including the mailing of a flyer to every Negro family in the area. About sixty-five persons (about forty-five of whom were Negroes) attended this meeting, but the officers of the branch were dismayed by the fact that only about a half-dozen new faces appeared. The remainder were the "old faithfuls" who were already familiar with the law and the possibilities which it opened to them. It was recognized, to be sure, that the meeting would serve to reinforce the old faithfuls, but there was great disappointment over the fact that so few new persons had been reached. As a result of this meeting, a new approach was formulated:

> A house-to-house approach (15-20 minute visits with every family in the Negro community) is planned for early February. We will distribute flyers, take housing covenants to sign, and discuss the law with any Negro family that wants to talk about it. We will try to get help from the University Civil Rights Committee [a student group], Butler Memorial people in addition to NAACPers. Hopefully we can use two-person Negro-white teams for all visits. If possible, we'll get Vic Brown of Civil Rights Commission to brief the teams before they go out.[7]

February saw the beginning of an undertaking which was only indirectly related to the open housing covenant but which promised to have some important indirect effects upon the housing opportunities of Newfield's Negro citizens. Under the leadership of the Rev. Peter Everett, an interfaith nonprofit corporation was formed for the purpose of constructing approximately thirty units of middle-income housing. According to a consensus reached at the second meeting of the Committee for Middle-Income Housing, which was in charge of planning construction of the apartments, "the immediate aim of the Committee is not to provide or to cure any lack of housing caused by segregation, but the alleviation of this problem would be one of the secondary effects of the planned housing unit."[8] The committee asserted that "this is to be an integrated project."

By mid-February, the members of the Protestant Council of Churches Social Action Committee were exhibiting signs of acute anxiety over the question of Roman Catholic participation in the covenant program. The Protestant churches had for all practical purposes finished their appeal for signatures, and there was a good deal of impatience among members of the committee to proceed with publication of the newspaper advertisement which was supposed to be the climax of the covenant campaign. Harold Baldwin had made repeated efforts to find out from Sean O'Malley when Catholic participation would begin, but the replies he was able to get were always indefinite. On Sunday, February 18, though, the covenants were presented to the worshipers of some of the Roman Catholic parishes of the city. During the following week O'Malley notified Baldwin that he had been designated by the bishop of the diocese to be the Roman Catholic representative to the Steering Committee which was supposed to plan the advertisement in the newspaper and to determine any subsequent use of the names turned in on the covenant cards.

The first scheduled meeting of the Steering Committee, which was composed of one clergyman and one layman from each faith group, was set for February 26, but the meeting actually did not materialize. O'Malley could not attend the meeting at the scheduled time, and neither could the Catholic clergy representative, because approval of his presence on the committee had not yet been received from the bishop. The Jewish representatives did not appear, either, so Baldwin rescheduled the meeting for two weeks later.

At the second meeting of this group on March 14, the rabbi was present, but again no Roman Catholic representatives were on hand. The principal topic of discussion was how to reach potential signers of the open housing covenant who had not been reached by any of the religious groups in town. Plans were made to have the covenant presented at a number of Newfield civic clubs, and various members of the Interfaith Council were assigned the responsibility for contacting members of the clubs who would be able to make the presentation effectively.

The third meeting of the Steering Committee was set for March 28, but since only the Protestant representatives came the meeting was canceled. At the fourth meeting, April 12, Sean O'Malley was present and (although no Jewish representatives were on hand) some tentative decisions were made regarding ultimate publication of the names of the signers of the open housing covenant. O'Malley reported that the initial presentation of the covenant in some of the Roman Catholic churches had not elicited many signatures and that a decision had been made to make another attempt to reach Catholic parishioners. O'Malley stated that Father Sloan was preparing a statement endorsing the convenant and urging its support, which was to be read at every Mass in all Newfield parishes on Easter Sunday morning. Covenant cards were to be passed out at the door by ushers, and signed cards were to be collected by the following Sunday. An effort would also be made, said O'Malley, to contact leading laymen for the purpose of encouraging them to exert their influence in behalf of the covenant. The Steering Committee made several minor decisions about the format of the advertisement which was to appear in the newspaper to announce the results of the covenant program, but the most significant decision was the setting of May 26 as the tentative date for publication of the advertisement.

Father Sloan decided that Easter Sunday was "not a very good day for distribution of the covenant";[9] therefore, another postponement of final action on the part of the Catholic parishes of Newfield occurred. But on April 18, four days before Easter, a front-page story in the Newfield *Review* quoted Father Sloan and Sean O'Malley as having announced plans for the reading of a pastoral letter inviting signatures for the open housing covenant on the Sunday following Easter. According to this article, Father Sloan had declared "that the principles of the housing covenant accord with Catholic doctrine and . . . that Catholics should be ready to support these principles." He also assured Catholic parishioners that "the invitation to local Catholics to sign the pledge will not carry any persuasion and that the action would be voluntary with the parishioner."

On April 29, six and one-half months after the open housing covenant was first launched, a full-scale effort was made to obtain signatures for the covenant in the Roman Catholic churches of the community. The presentation of the covenant to Catholic parishioners was not carried out with the uniformity and the authority that might have been expected from the *Review's* allusion to a "pastoral letter" that was to be read in all churches, for Father Sloan's letter to the pastors was not read to worshipers from the pulpit. It was simply a directive that each pastor should call the covenant to the attention of his congregation on the Sunday after Easter. But Catholic parishioners were given an opportunity, in one way or another, to sign the covenant, and they were asked to return the signed cards to the church on the first Sunday in May.

A final meeting of the Interfaith Steering Committee was held on May 14. At this meeting it was reported that approximately 750 covenant cards representing almost one thousand persons had been received. These signatures had been verified by telephone calls confirming the signers' willingness to have their names printed in the newspaper advertisement announcing the results of the covenant campaign, and very few withdrawals had resulted from this verification process. The committee decided to include in the advertisement a clipping which could be used by readers to add their names to the list of the supporters of the covenant. Other details concerning the selection of the limited number of names that could be listed and the preparation of a statement describing the purpose of the covenant were left in the hands of individual committee members.

On May 26 the Greater Newfield Interfaith Open Housing Covenant appeal reached a climax with the appearance of a full page advertisement in the Newfield *Review*. Above the endorsements of the covenant signed by a clergyman of each of the three major faiths sponsoring the covenant program appeared these words:

OPEN DOORS?

A community is neither healthy nor free when some of its families cannot rent or purchase homes solely because of their race or religion. Sensitive citizens must awaken to such discrimination. This is a partial listing of those who declare their opposition to housing discrimination and their willingness to welcome people of all races, creeds and national origins to their neighborhoods. They invite the entire town to join them. You may do so by signing the covenant printed in the lower right hand corner of this page and mailing it to the address indicated.

Thirty-seven persons added their names to the list of the covenant's supporters by mailing in the coupon which accompanied the names published in the newspaper. Many of these new signers were persons who lived in outlying areas where the open housing covenant had not been presented at all, but some were residents of Newfield either who had been given no previous opportunity to sign or who had overcome initial reservations or indifference. A few of the new local signers were men with widely recognized political aspirations; one member of the Interfaith Steering Committee conjectured that they might have been impressed by the fact that the first name in the first column of the newspaper advertisement of the covenant was that of the mayor of Newfield! Along with the new signatures for the covenant also came three notices of land or housing which the owners were willing to sell on an unrestricted basis.

In the same edition of the *Review* there was a vigorous

editorial supporting the covenant and inviting those who had not signed it to reconsider their failure to do so, or at least to face the implications of their failure to do so. The editorial applauded "the use of the covenant to bring a moral pressure to bear on people in this city who are doing a bad thing," and the writer expressed his conviction that "the massed use of the names of signers in this city will achieve an important effect in undercutting the thicket of segregation feeling." The value of the covenant appeal was summed up as follows:

> The foremost result of the presentation of the names will be that the non-signers must see that hundreds of their fellow citizens want open housing. Landlords, who fight renting to Negroes on the ground that neighbors will ostracize them and tenants desert, will soon find the ground shifting and then slipping away entirely.

> One achievement of the covenant already is that it has got the leaders and the people of three religious faiths acting in concert to overturn the housing barrier. Only the blindest of bigots will not see that this is a formidable combination and that together it must succeed to win new adherents.

> The other result of the covenant appeal is that signers and non-signers have been confronted with their feelings on the racial issue and on their attitudes to open housing. The cards have made this self-encounter unavoidable. People at last have to see themselves on this critical issue.

CHRISTIAN LAYMEN

CHAPTER *6*

THE FINAL STAGE OF ACTUAL FIELD RE-search as a part of this study was the collection of data concerning the attitudes of Newfield churchgoers toward the open housing covenant (OHC) and related matters. The instrument used for this purpose was a three-page quest-tionnaire which was mailed to a sample of 1,100 parishioners in four churches. A total of 225 completed questionnaires were returned, 157 from signers and sixty-eight from nonsupporters of the OHC (fifty-seven from nonsigners, and eleven from persons who were unaware of the covenant appeal until they heard of it in the letter accompanying the questionnaire).*

CHANNELS OF COMMUNICATION

Two items on the questionnaire were designed to provide an answer to the important question of how people heard about the open housing covenant. Respondents were asked to enum-erate ways used by their church of presenting the covenant to them. Approximately one-third of the signers heard of the OHC through a parish publication, a pulpit presentation, or a church organization. Almost one-fourth of the signers heard of it through the local newspaper. Nonsigners learned of the OHC primarily through the printed word: half of them through the newspaper, and two-fifths through a parish publication. Only one-fourth of the nonsigners were exposed to a sermon on the covenant, and fewer than one-fifth knew of it through a church organization. More than twice as many nonsigners discussed the OHC with friends or neighbors, and the fact that only nine per cent of the signers were reached by this channel of communication implies that informal word-of-mouth

---

*A discussion of methodological considerations pertaining to the ques-tionnaire and other instruments of research used in this study are found in Appendix A.

contacts with neighbors and friends cannot be counted on to produce signatures for an open housing covenant. Emphasis must be laid upon the fact that none of the non-signers reported being contacted personally by either a layman or a clergyman who urged them to support the open housing covenant. It is equally clear that even though the mails may be an effective channel of communication if used in conjunction with other channels, the mails cannot be relied upon as a sufficient approach.

THE DECISION-MAKING PROCESS

Another series of questions probed various aspects of the decision-making process which resulted in a respondent's signing or rejecting the OHC. Respondents were asked to report their initial reaction to the idea of the covenant, the influences which were important in determining their decision to sign or not to sign the covenant, and their most important reason for signing or not signing.

A very high proportion of the signers declared that their decision to support the covenant was immediate: approximately two-thirds said that upon first hearing about the covenant, they "thought it was a fine idea." Similarly, about one-fourth of the nonsupporters registered immediate opposition. One-fourth of the signers felt favorably inclined toward the covenant, but wanted to give some additional thought to the matter before committing themselves; one-tenth of the nonsupporters had an initially unfavorable reaction but were not ready to dismiss the idea of signing the covenant without giving it some further consideration. Only a few respondents initially had a neutral reaction, but more than one-third of the unaware reported "no particular reaction one way or the other" when they first heard about the covenant. Most significant, though, is the discovery that forty-three per cent of the nonsupporters were not opposed to the covenant upon first hearing of it, and thirty-three per cent were favorably disposed initially. If this large proportion of nonsupporters had been urged repeatedly by church representatives to sign the covenant, a large number of them might have done so.

Influences

Many signers (29%) did not need to be convinced that the OHC was worthy of their favor; merely being presented with an opportunity to sign it triggered a previous conviction disposing them to support fair housing principles. Most of the respondents in this category asserted, "No man persuades me" or "Nothing influenced me" or "There was no decision to make," explaining their action regarding the covenant as the result of "personal moral beliefs," "my own conscience," "my own convictions," "my feelings about humanity," etc. Several answers of this kind included an explicit reference to the fact that "This question [was] settled in my own mind long ago": "I have always felt this way," "We have never believed in discrimination," and "I have been a champion of the negro [sic] cause for many years!" are typical of this group of replies. A few respondents cited "family upbringing" or "church influence during childhood" as crucial influences, and a number of respondents used this question as an occasion for stating their understanding of the bearing that Christian faith has upon the social problem which the open housing covenant was intended to alleviate: "My religion," "the Bible," "the gospel of Jesus Christ," "my belief that all men are created equal and that Jesus Christ came to save everyone," and "if one tries to live his religion there is no question" are among the answers of this kind written in by some persons. Two persons spoke of an element of righteous indignation in their convictions on this matter, and one of these linked her decision directly to "front page articles [in the local newspaper] about two fine families able to pay but unable to find housing . . . when forced out of the redevelopment project." One man remarked that the most important influence on his decision had been "the arguments of an associate at work who disagreed with me." Another commented, "I would rather live near, deal with, or work with colored men than Italians."

One-tenth of the signers were influenced by personal experience with Negroes. Some were swayed by "personal friendship with several Negroes," "working with negroes [sic]," or "some wonderful neighbors who are negroes [sic]." Others stressed the empathy for Negroes they had come to feel because of "our experience in selling a house," "contact with Negro children in nursery school, and their parents," "first hand knowledge of the ill effects of housing discrimination," and "just an awakening to what the negro [sic] experienced to get what we whites accept as a matter of course for ourselves." Two expressions of empathy were especially direct: a school teacher declared, "I can see what my colored students have to put up with"; a writer said, "Being of foreign birth, I know full well the problems faced by minority groups."

The most frequently mentioned of all the influences stemming directly from the OHC campaign was that of the respondent's clergyman. Forty-two per cent of the signers checked at least one type of presentation given by their pastor, and eleven per cent checked at least two actions on behalf of the covenant by him. One-third of the signers stated that their decision had been swayed to some extent by a pulpit presentation, the kind of action by clergymen referred to most often by covenant supporters. Other influences cited by one-fourth or more of the signers were the press and the family. "Talking about the matter with associates at work or other friends not living near me" was mentioned by only fourteen per cent of the signers, and neighbors by only eight per cent.

For those who did not sign the open housing covenant, the most important influences were the family and previous conviction: both were mentioned by eighteen per cent of the nonsupporters. The newspaper and associates were each considered influential by thirteen per cent of the nonsupporters, and neighbors were important to ten per cent. All other influences were relatively insignificant. Personal experience also persuaded some persons not to sign the covenant, though: "living the first twenty-one years of my life in the South" or "visiting the South and seeing how the negroes [sic] lived" were cited by a few nonsigners as very influential on their thinking. That not all persons interpret their experience in the same way is shown by the remark of a nonsigner who asserted that his decision regarding the covenant had been most influenced by "serving in World War II with my southern comrades."

It is to be expected, certainly, that nonsupporters would cite the influence of their clergyman infrequently (indeed, one wonders how it happened that the influence of the clergyman is mentioned at all by someone who decided not to sign the open housing covenant!), and it is hardly surprising that they listed family and previous conviction as the most important influences. That so few nonsupporters mentioned the press as a crucial influence leads to an important inference: when news carrying racial overtones is handled responsibly, as it was in this case, even selective perception has difficulty in using this news as a basis for a decision expressing intolerance for the minority group. An even more important inference is suggested by the fact that personal experience was cited more frequently as an influence toward signing than toward not signing the covenant: this finding lends credence to the belief of intergroup relations theorists that contact between individuals of different races (unless it occurs under adverse circumstances) tends to promote tolerant attitudes.[1]

Reasons

Of the reasons for signing the OHC, two are of overwhelming importance: Christian duty and allegiance to democratic ideals. The former was checked by eighty-three per cent of the signers; the latter, by seventy-one per cent. The only other important reason was prudence in international relations, which was checked by merely one-third of the signers. The absence of response on the other suggested items—any of which might have been felt important by a person who ended by deciding to sign the covenant—is striking: only two signers admitted worrying about what their neighbors would think, a like number confessed concern over property values, and only one signer mentioned fear of intermarriage as a factor in his deliberations.

The specific reason for not signing the covenant most often referred to was concern about property values, but this concern was present in the minds of only eighteen per cent of the nonsupporters. The second most important reason reported was anxiety about having one's name published in the newspaper or of giving one's signature for purposes which were not fully understood: fifteen per cent of the nonsupporters gave this reason. Some of the comments registered by this group of respondents are especially interesting.

I did not sign because to have done so would have authorized the publication and use of my name in ways that were not described in any way.

My wife did not approve of the possible publication, as suggested in the covenant, in the local newspaper. I went along with this idea. However, if this item had been eliminated from the covenant, I would have been inclined to have signed in spite of internal opposition.

It is not clear to me who will hold these signed Housing Covenants, or who will have access to them. I have no assurance that my signed Housing Covenant will not be used to my detriment by anyone who might be benefited by it to turn a profit. There-for [sic], I feel that discrimination (to draw a distinction betwene [sic] a desirable prospective nabor [sic] and an undesirable one) has to be made by me at that time in the future when such a decision is required.

A fear that putting one's name on the open housing covenant might obligate one to some future course of action not stated on the card was reflected in a number of statements on this question:

I object to the open housing covenant as I do to any other pledge. It is just another opportunity for some shrewd individual to make his own point or get his own way by using the pledge as a lever in a way that wasn't intended. I want to feel free to judge each situation on its own merits, and not to have to follow a particular course because I've signed a piece of paper.

I do not like to sign blanket statements, but wish to retain the right to judge for myself any individual, whether he is white or colored.

I did not sign because negro [sic] or white applicants for any rental I might have would be accepted or rejected on my determination of their suitability as tenants. . . . I prefer to decide their suitability rather than giving a blanket statement I would accept them—white or negro. [sic]

It is probable, therefore, that some nonsupporters of the covenant were actually opposed to discrimination in housing, but did not sign because, unclear about the use to be made of the OHC cards, they feared the possible misuse of their pledge. It is also likely that some persons failed to support the OHC because they did not understand the importance of collecting as many signatures as possible to demonstrate strong integrationist sentiment. One nonsupporter declared, "I felt that my signature would be meaningless since everybody in town knows that I am running an integrated housing situation already."

A concern for neighbors or family is apparent in the remarks of a few respondents:

> In the development in which we live, my neighbors cannot afford to have to sell their homes at a loss nor can we. I feel I am responsible to my neighbors, too. If I signed the covenant, I would feel obligated to sell to a negro [sic] if one applied.

> I do not wish that my feelings would tend to force someone else to do something against their wishes. Unless a person lives in a multiple apartment unit or owns the same, they [sic] should have no say in this matter. Furthermore, this whole racial issue has gotten completely out of hand and the stresses are showing in our teenagers and those who are mentally and morally deficient.

> It is not a question of color. Other nationalities are as bad or worse in many instances. . . . I would like to live as I know I should (act Christianity) but I believe also that I must help myself or God will not help me. If I lived by this "covenant" my family could be in the same situation as negroes [sic] are at present. It is hard enough to care for my family (food, clothes, etc.) now without trying to help someone who does not want to help himself.

Approximately one-eighth of the nonsupporters expressed fear of intermarriage; approximately one-tenth voiced fear of what their neighbors would think if they signed the open housing covenant. Among the miscellaneous reasons given for not signing the covenant are these:

> I am not a property owner.

> Did not own property in the locality.

The Negro is not entitled to more consideration than others. I would not object to negroes [sic] as neighbors who are of good character.

Integration will come about best through education. To gain acceptance and respect a person must earn that respect. Forced integration cannot bring this about.

I have the feeling that we are tending to push too hard on this issue. I feel that we can accomplish more by less spectacular means.

One of the most significant findings in regard to the non-supporters of the covenant is that more than one-third of them gave no reason at all for their decision. One might plausibly infer that failure to give a reason for not signing indicates either the absence of a rationally defensible argument or lack of clarity in the thinking of the respondent. For example, the infrequent mention of fear of intermarriage could mean simply that respondents were unwilling to admit the importance of this reason in their own minds. On the other hand, it may mean that this fear, which is so often alluded to in the popular lore on residence and race that is passed on from generation to generation of homeowners, is less prevalent than conventional wisdom decrees. Perhaps concern about racial intermarriage is a paper tiger on which less ammunition should be wasted.

THE PROBLEM AND THE ROLE OF THE CHURCHES

A third major series of questions posed to lay respondents dealt with substantive issues raised by the problem of housing for Negroes and church sponsorship of the open housing covenant campaign. Laymen were asked whether or not they recognized the existence of discrimination and the inadequacy of housing for Negroes in Newfield. They were also asked their opinion concerning the appropriateness of the covenant as a social action concern of the city's churches, and of sermons on the subject of the covenant. Finally, they were asked to indicate approval or disapproval of a series of actions often suggested as remedies for the problem of racial injustice in this country.

A large majority of the respondents acknowledged the reality of the problems which the open housing covenant was intended to help solve and they granted that the churches have a responsibility to help solve them. Only four per cent of the signers were hesitant about endorsing church sponsorship of the covenant, but twenty-seven per cent of the nonsupporters had doubts about the propriety of religious sponsorship and nineteen per cent flatly opposed it. The figures on willingness to endorse the preaching of sermons on the open housing covenant were almost identical: ninety-two per cent of the signers favored sermons on the issue, but only fifty-six per cent of the nonsupporters did.

Among signers as well as nonsupporters, acknowledgment of the inferiority of existing housing for Negroes was far from unanimous, much less so than acknowledgment of discrimination against Negro homeseekers. Only about three-fourths of the signers and five-eighths of the nonsupporters acquiesced to the proposition that "A majority of Negro families in Newfield live in housing that is inadequate," whereas nine-tenths of the signers and five-sixths of the nonsupporters admitted the reality of housing discrimination. Only three nonsupporters (4%) denied this; only eight (12%) claimed to have no opinion on this question. It is clear, then, that although they were comparatively unwilling to grant that the churches of the community had a legitimate interest in sponsoring the OHC, even nonsupporters were compelled to concede the existence of the housing problem for Negroes.

SOLUTIONS

Five methods of dealing with the problem were suggested to the respondents; they were asked to check all methods of which they approved, to indicate which method they deemed most important, and to name any methods of which they disapproved. It is instructive to note which methods were most strongly rejected by signers and nonsupporters, as well as which methods were most highly favored.

The two methods endorsed by the vast majority of the respondents were education of Negroes "to have higher standards" and education of white people "so that they become more favorable to integrated neighborhoods and apartments." About nine-tenths of the signers approved education of whites; about seven-tenths approved education of Negroes. Preference for these two methods was reversed among nonsupporters: almost three-fourths endorsed teaching higher standards to Negroes, but only about one-half endorsed teaching whites more favorable sentiments toward residential integration. Thus more signers than nonsupporters see the attitudes of white people as a critical source of the problem.

More than one-third of the signers, but slightly less than one-third of the nonsupporters, endorsed construction of "good housing for Negroes in a nice part of town." Both groups showed very little enthusiasm for nonviolent direct action: this method was endorsed by fourteen signers (9%) and two nonsupporters (3%). The greatest difference between the two groups appeared on the question of the desirability of "additional civil rights legislation": only seven nonsupporters approved this method; sixty signers (38%) checked it.

The preference for educational methods of dealing with the problem of discrimination was also reflected in the fact that only two respondents asserted their opposition to education of Negroes and only four persons (all nonsigners) opposed education of whites. Thirty per cent of the signers and forty-one per cent of the nonsupporters of the covenant objected to nonviolent direct action. Thirty-one per cent of the signers and twenty-seven per cent of the nonsupporters signified disapproval of building housing for Negroes. Eight per cent of the signers and twenty-seven per cent of the nonsupporters were against stronger legal provisions for civil rights. It should be emphasized that repudiation of stronger legal protection for civil rights was much stronger among nonsupporters of the covenant than among supporters, and that among signers rejection of building housing for Negroes was just as great as rejection of direct nonviolent action. Many signers doubtless interpreted the proposal for construction of "good housing for Negroes" as a perpetuation of segregation which should be rejected.

Several important implications may be discerned here. In

the first place, it is apparent that the people of Newfield regard education as the most fruitful way of getting at the problem. With signers, emphasis is placed upon educating whites to be more tolerant; with nonsupporters, the emphasis is on "educating Negroes to have higher standards"—but the faith of both groups of respondents rests overwhelmingly with education rather than with law or direct action. Secondly, though, it must be observed that the stress on education is not accompanied by a strong rejection of civil rights legislation and nonviolent direct action; the former method was specifically opposed by only fourteen per cent of the total sample, and the latter tactic was opposed by only thirty-four per cent of all respondents. It seems safe to conclude that the small proportion of residents who favor nonviolent direct action would meet with less than massive resistance should they decide to initiate such action, and that the sizable group of persons who favor additional civil rights legislation could count on outnumbering their diehard opponents.

DEMOGRAPHIC FACTORS

In an attempt to learn more precisely the reason for the opinions of certain segments of the sample, we analyzed answers given by subgroups of respondents according to religious affiliation, education, and occupation. No single variable emerges as determinative of attitude toward the open housing covenant, but a number of useful insights regarding likely reactions from various kinds of persons can be suggested.

Roman Catholics and Protestants

Protestant signers were more willing than Catholic respondents to admit that a majority of the Negro families of Newfield lived in inadequate and restricted housing. A possible explanation for this finding is to be seen in the fact that Catholic respondents, having a lower proportion of highly educated persons and persons of professional status, probably have a higher proportion of persons who live in modest circumstances themselves and who therefore define adequate housing in modest terms. Contrary

to much popular lore concerning the independence of Protestants and the subservience of Catholics to the Church, the
supposedly more individualistic Protestant respondents were
slightly more liberal than were Catholics on the question of
church sponsorship of the open housing covenant and the
propriety of sermons on this subject.

Roman Catholic signers were less liberal than were Protestants on the matter of civil rights legislation as a means of
attacking the housing problem: this method was mentioned
by only twenty-seven per cent of the Roman Catholics, but
by forty-one per cent of the Protestants. On the other hand,
fifty per cent of the Roman Catholic signers named construction
of housing for Negroes as an important means of dealing with
the problem, whereas only thirty-one per cent of the non-
Catholic signers checked this item. When asked which methods
they opposed, Roman Catholic signers mentioned additional
civil rights legislation about as often as did all Protestant
signers; they mentioned construction of housing for Negroes
less frequently (23% as against 33%), and they opposed direct
nonviolent action twice as emphatically (50% as opposed to
26%).

There are no striking differences between the patterns of
response of Protestants and Catholics on questions having to
do with reason for signing the covenant and influences affecting the decision.[2]

Education

The findings derived from the lay questionnaire support
the widely held assumption that high educational attainment
is correlated with awareness of the prophetic role of religious
institutions and with sensitivity to social injustice.[3] The respondents with the most education were consistently more
liberal than were other respondents in acknowledging the
housing problem and the Church's role in combating it, and
respondents with the least education were consistently the most
conservative on these questions.

High educational attainment is also correlated, however, with
stronger opposition to civil rights laws and direct action. The

fact that a higher percentage of college trained persons were wary about construction of housing for Negroes is congruent with the assumption that education enlightens its recipients regarding the injustice of segregation; nevertheless, the high proportion of college graduates opposing civil rights legislation and nonviolent protest raises doubts about the scope of the supposed liberalizing influences of higher education.[4]

The analysis of reasons for signing or not signing the OHC according to educational attainment of respondents contains three noteworthy findings. The first is that fear of intermarriage is correlated with low educational attainment. Another is that virtually all of the concern over property values and the opinion of one's neighbors was registered by respondents with a relatively high education. The last is that awareness of the international repercussions of discrimination was shown by a smaller proportion of those with more than a college education than by any other group of respondents.

The tendency of less educated persons to fear intermarriage is merely suggested, not established, by a pattern of opinion based on so few responses; nevertheless, this finding fits in with, and confirms, the assumption that this fear rests in large measure on ignorance. The high concern of the well educated for property values, although it reflects ignorance of well-established facts, can be explained by the likelihood that respondents in this group are more apt to be homeowners. It is more difficult, however, to explain their lack of concern about the damaging effects of discrimination upon American prestige abroad. Perhaps they felt that prudence in international relations was a relatively ignoble reason for signing the covenant, and therefore did not care to give this reason when answering the questionnaire.

The importance of various influences which might possibly affect decisions regarding the OHC varied according to education. A pulpit presentation by the minister was reported to be the most important influence on respondents with less than a high school education, and this influence was tied for first place or was in second place among those with less than a college degree. With college graduates and postgraduates,

though, the influence of the minister was rated as less important, and previous conviction was at the top of the list. The
implication here is that the least educated persons are most
open to persuasion by their minister, whereas the highly educated are most likely to base their decision on prior opinion.
It is significant that the press and discussion with one's family
were considered at least moderately important by all groups,
and that only among the most highly educated group were
the mass media other than the newspaper more important than
the press and the family. This finding suggests that for the
great majority of citizens general discussions of a social problem, such as discrimination, in magazines and on television
are of less moment than discussions of local issues in the home-
town newspaper or with the family.

Occupation

On questions regarding acknowledgment of the problem and
religious sponsorship of the OHC, blue collar workers were
consistently the most conservative and professional persons
were consistently the most liberal. The same is true on the question of methods for attacking the housing problem: blue collar workers were among the most paternalistic groups in regard
to the construction of housing for Negroes, and they were the
least liberal on civil rights legislation and direct nonviolent
action; professionals were the most aware and the most liberal on these points.

No significant variations of opinion according to occupational status are apparent in regard to reasons given for signing
the open housing covenant, but several interesting variations
are evident in regard to influences affecting respondent's decisions about the convenant. Blue collar workers were influenced
more by pulpit pronouncements than by anything else except the
press, and previous conviction was far less important to them
than it was to other groups of respondents. This finding reinforces the interpretation placed upon the findings concerning
important influences on persons with relatively little education:
persons at the lower end of the scale on education and occupa-

tion were most likely to have their decisions formed by what the minister says. These two influences received an equal number of votes from professional people, indicating that although many members of this group based their decisions on opinion that had already been formed, there were just as many who were influenced by the minister. Pulpit presentations were tied for second place with family discussion among housewives, but previous conviction was the most significant influence for this group. White collar workers seemed to be least amenable to persuasion from their minister; the press, family discussion, and previous conviction were more important to respondents of this category. The fact that family discussion was at least moderately, if not crucially, important as an influence on each group of respondents is, from the point of view of the churches, encouraging: if the church is successful in one of its primary tasks—the strengthening of family life and the promotion of dialogue among family members in the context of commitment to Christian discipleship—then it may be able to reach many individuals who are not greatly influenced by contacts with the minister.

Summary

The sample of lay opinion reached by the questionnaire was not large enough or representative enough to provide con-clusive findings regarding the probable reaction of Christian laymen to an OHC or similar forms of social action. A number of tentative insights can be derived from the data, though, and these may prove instructive to religious and civic leaders who wish to engage their communities in similar programs.

A variety of approaches was used by the churches involved in this study, and the results of the questionnaire indicate that a variety of channels of communication was successful in reaching prospective signers of the open housing covenant. The importance of what the minister says in the pulpit was evident from the frequency with which this approach was mentioned as both a channel of communication and an influence affecting the decision of the respondent. The importance of an extensive follow-up effort after initial announcements in pulpit or parish publication is suggested by the fact that many nonsupporters were initially favorably disposed toward the covenant: had they been offered other opportunities to sign it while still in this favorable frame of mind, many additional signatures might have been obtained.

Several significant findings emerge in connection with influences on respondents' decisions and respondents' reasons for supporting or not supporting the covenant. There was a very large reservoir of latent support for the covenant among Newfield churchgoers: a large proportion of the signers declared that previous conviction was decisive in persuading them to sign, and an even larger number looked upon the covenant as something which ought to be supported on the basis of Christian as well as American ideals. The two "moral arguments" for the covenant were considered far more important than any prudential arguments, and concern for property values and intermarriage was not registered by a large proportion of even the nonsupporters.

A majority of all respondents acknowledged both the inadequacy of housing for Negroes and the pattern of restrictive policies toward Negroes in search of housing in Newfield; indeed, an overwhelming majority of even the nonsupporters admitted that discrimination was a reality in their community. Nonsupporters were less willing to approve the propriety of church sponsorship of the open housing covenant and sermons on the covenant than they were to admit the existence of the problem, but approval of the churches' role in seeking a solution was virtually unanimous among signers.

Education of Negroes to higher standards and of whites to less prejudiced attitudes were the preferred means of attacking the housing problem. Civil rights legislation and the construction of "good housing for Negroes in a nice part of town" were endorsed by a sizable number of respondents, but nonviolent direct action had few advocates. None of these tactics was condemned by more than about one-third of the total sample, and disapproval of either educational approach was voiced by almost none of the respondents.

None of the special variables tested suggested the hypothesis that support for or rejection of the open housing covenant can be located in any particular segment of the population. Except for the fact that very few Roman Catholic nonsupporters were willing to return the questionnaire, there were no striking differences between Catholic and Protestant respondents. Highly educated professional persons (especially women) who had not lived in the community for as long as forty years were most likely to be liberal in their definition of the situation from which the covenant campaign arose and in their endorsement of supraeducational methods for changing the situation. Relatively less educated persons of blue collar occupational status were most likely to have their decision regarding the covenant molded by the minister rather than by previous conviction. But the most significant single finding of the analysis of special variables which was performed is that efforts to promote a nondiscriminatory climate of opinion must be directed to all segments of a population, for there are no dramatic parallels between any of the indices tested and either a consistently liberal or a consistently conservative mentality.

ON TECHNICAL AND
MORAL WISDOM

CHAPTER 7 INTELLIGENT CHRISTIAN SOCIAL ACTION requires both moral and technical wisdom. Moral wisdom is a clear perception of the Good—in the universe, for society, and for particular men—and of the proximate goods that ought to be sought in concrete situations. Technical wisdom is knowledge of how to achieve these specific goods in man's individual and common life; it requires sophistication in strategy and tactics. Both types of wisdom are necessary, because knowledge of the Good is irrelevant unless accompanied by knowledge of how to approximate it in society, and technical wisdom is wasted or even dangerous unless directed toward good ends.

The meaning of these two concepts, and the intimate connection between them, can best be illustrated by stating, and then comparing, a cardinal tenet of each kind of wisdom. It is an axiom of moral wisdom that justice, rather than order or love, is the most relevant norm in social ethics. A corresponding axiom of technical wisdom in the field of race relations is that prejudiced behavior, rather than prejudice, is the crucial front in the battle against racial injustice, and that this is the point where attacks can be most fruitfully unleashed.

Order is the most basic requirement of man's common life, for without it life would in fact be the "war of all against all" which Hobbes declared the condition of pre-political man to be. Love is the loftiest ideal for human relationships, and even an initially just calculation of rights and duties is apt to deteriorate into injustice unless calculation is tempered with love. But order maintained at the expense of injustice is not an acceptable norm by which to measure the moral stature of a society, and love as a basis for society is more than can be expected of sinful creatures whose selfishness, bad enough in personal relationships, is compounded in the political, economic, and social structures of collective existence.[1] Social relations cannot be adequately governed by love in its pure form devoid of all calculations of rights and duties. A focus on justice is necessary, in the words of the noted Protestant theologian Reinhold Niebuhr,

> to extend the sense of obligation towards the other, (a) from an immediately felt obligation, prompted by obvious need, to a continued obligation expressed in fixed principles of mutual support; (b) from a simple relation between a self and one "other" to the complex relations of the self and the "others"; and (c) finally from the obligations, discerned by the individual self, to the wider obligations which the community defines from its more impartial perspective.[2]

Justice provides an element of rationality without which love may become nothing but spasmodic pity, shortsighted devotion to one other person, or parochial loyalty to a small in-group. As Niebuhr observes,

> A relation between the self and one other may be partly ecstatic; and in any case the calculation of relative interests may be reduced to a minimum. But as soon as a third person is introduced into the relation even the most perfect love requires a rational estimate of conflicting needs and interests.[3]

Thus justice, which refuses to allow the denial of essential rights, yet demands the surrender of many privileges so that all men may have their due as human beings, is the most important moral point of reference for those who seek to define the good society realistically and build it effectively.

The implications of this axiom for contemporary American Christians are clear. Rejection of nonviolent direct action as a tactic in the civil rights struggle may represent a sincere concern for social order. Faith in education may reflect an idealism about the nobility of human reason, and insistence upon the necessity for purity of motivation may reflect a faith in the potentialities of the redeemed heart, that are valuable ingredients in the Church's social thought. But the claims of justice are so important that a temporary disturbance of order is worth risking, and the possibilities of eliminating all prejudice through appeals to reason or love are too remote to warrant postponing the fight for justice. What Reinhold Niebuhr had to say in 1932 about the preservation of moral values in politics is still true today:

> A rational society will probably place a greater emphasis upon the ends and purposes for which coercion is used than upon the elimination of coercion and conflict. It will justify coercion if it is obviously in the service of a rationally acceptable social end, and condemn its use when it is in the service of momentary passions. The conclusion which has been forced upon us again and again . . . is that equality, or to be a little more qualified, that equal justice is the most rational ultimate objective for society. If that conclusion is correct, a social conflict which aims at greater equality has a moral justification which must be denied to efforts which aim at the perpetuation of privilege.[4]

It is extremely important for every Christian to examine his preference for order or love in society to see whether it may not represent the shadow of an ideological taint. Property rights, for example, are a useful device for the preservation of order and the rewarding of initiative and diligence; as such, they are pragmatically justifiable in a Christian social philosophy. When property rights are used to justify the oppression and exclusion of a whole group of one's neighbors, though, the moral legitimacy of the concept becomes dubious.[5] Objections to civil rights laws on housing (or even to the "interference" of public opinion as registered by an open housing covenant) based on the latter type of reasoning are expressions of moral insensitivity. The same may be said of inordinate preoccupation with pure motives: of all temptations, the worst is not "to do the right thing for the wrong reason," as T. S. Eliot maintains;[6] it is *not to do the right thing*, even for the right reason.

Closely related to the axiom of moral wisdom just discussed is the proposition that prejudiced behavior, rather than prejudice, is the most important aspect of the problem of racial injustice. Social scientists agree that "general attitudes of prejudice do not necessarily predetermine prejudiced behavior," for "a specific attitude at one moment does not predetermine the act that will eventuate at another moment."[7] After discussing exclusion of Negroes from fraternities where prejudice was far from universal, from factories where employers had many different sentiments regarding Negroes, and from restaurants on one side of the street (the American side only) in Panama, Earl Raab and Seymour Lipset declare:

> Whether in the fraternities of Ann Arbor, the factories of Texas, or the streets of Panama, it is not the prejudiced attitude which is itself important to the social problem of prejudice. It is *the act of excluding* Negroes . . . that makes prejudice a problem for society. The attitudes are important only insofar as they cause these acts [emphasis added].[8]

A few examples will elucidate the meaning of this important principle. Consider the Northerner—the genuinely unprejudiced Northerner who attended integrated schools, lived in an interracial neighborhood, and attended interracial parties all his life—who comes to the South and refuses to mingle with Negroes for fear of being ostracized by his white friends. Are this man's actions any less cruel to Negroes than those of the racist? Consider the employer who would like to adopt a merit employment pattern but does not do so for fear of what his customers or his Caucasian employees might do. Is his policy any less restrictive toward potential Negro employees than the policy of an ardent segregationist? Consider the homeowner who refuses to rent or sell to Negroes, not because of prejudice in his own heart, but simply because of the expected prejudice of his neighbors in whose eyes he does not want to lose favor. Is his behavior any more kind to the Negro family in search of housing?

In every one of these cases discrimination and a denial of the right of Negroes to have equal advantages in our society exist independently of whether or not the white persons concerned are guilty of stereotyped thinking regarding Negroes. From the standpoint of the dispossessed minority group member, there is no difference between the actions of this unprejudiced Northerner and this unprejudiced employer and this unprejudiced homeowner and the actions of a rabid segregationist in the same social roles. From the standpoint of social ethics, the conformist is just as vicious as the bigot.

Furthermore, there are many indications that prejudiced behavior is apt to create prejudiced attitudes even where they did not previously exist. The Yankee who adopts the Southern way of life may soon find himself participating also in the mind of the South: the more he becomes used to accepting deference from Negroes without using the conventional courteous forms of address to them; the more he laughs at clubroom jokes which belittle Negroes and uses racial epithets himself in order to fit in with his Southern friends—the more he will actually come to accept prevailing Southern notions about the inferiority of Negroes and the legitimacy of "keeping them in their place." The employer who never hires Negroes may rationalize his timidity by coming to believe that no qualified Negroes ever apply or that Negroes really aren't fitted to that type of work, anyhow. The homeowner who doesn't have the courage to rent to Negroes will find reasons for believing that he acted in the only right way, after all, considering the fact that most Negroes really are pretty sloppy and lazy and apt to give the neighborhood a bad name by having wild parties every Saturday night.

Not only is prejudiced behavior independent of prejudiced attitudes; continued prejudiced behavior may actually lead to the holding of prejudiced attitudes. To give the biblical adage a new twist, it might be said that, "As a man is in his actions, so will he come to think in his heart." But fortunately the principle works both ways, as numerous studies have shown:[9] initially prejudiced workers come to accept Negroes who can do the jobs, initially prejudiced residents come to welcome Negro neighbors, and initially prejudiced churchgoers come to regard Negro parishioners as full-fledged members of their congregation.

The most important item of technical wisdom in the area of race relations runs parallel to and reinforces one of the most central insights of moral wisdom. Prejudice can be altered by changing prejudiced behavioral patterns directly. A measure of love will follow the establishment of justice, whereas justice in society may never come if we insist that love must first come in the hearts of men. That is why the necessity for the exercise of various forms of power is a corollary of the axiom about justice, and that is why the necessity for civil rights legislation and bold initiative on the part of various public and private "gatekeepers" is a corollary of the axiom about prejudiced behavior. Rights must be granted regardless of acceptance—and the best way to foster acceptance is to grant rights immediately.

A NORMATIVE MODEL FOR ACTION AGAINST DISCRIMINATION IN HOUSING

CHAPTER *8*

MANY PRAISEWORTHY VENTURES IN community action fail because their initiators have failed to formulate with precision a model of action which clarifies exactly what they are doing and how it may best be accomplished. The only way to state in systematic form the judgments and recommendations about action against discrimination in housing arising from this study is to present them within the framework of such a model.

Every instance of social action has four main stages: the decision to act, planning, execution, and consolidation. In the decision phase, the fundamental prerequisite is, of course, alertness to social needs. This phase also demands realistic calculation of resources for meeting the needs (and of obstacles to be overcome). Planning is essentially the formulation of strategy. It involves the setting of priorities for action according to considerations of timing and feasibility, and this requires the specifying of proximate goals to be striven for, of the "targets" to be attacked (that is, the persons, groups or institutions which must be induced to perform certain deeds or adopt certain attitudes necessary to the attainment of goals), and of the tactics to be used in bringing about the desired results. The execution phase pertains to the effective implementation of planned tactics, and here the ingenuity and skill of the individuals involved are crucial. Consolidation requires publicity about the gains registered, and full exploitation of the new conditions and opportunities created. Naturally, the new problems encountered in this phase may lead to a whole new cycle of action.[1]

An OHC campaign is only one step in the much more complicated and comprehensive battle against discrimination in housing, and if the problem is rightly perceived in all of its dimensions, planning of the covenant appeal will include provisions for follow-up action in which other steps are taken. The covenant itself is designed to affect directly only one phase of the problem; its targets are limited and must in addition be defined with precision and attacked with appropriate tactics. Its beneficial effects will be largely lost unless the publicity given to the covenant is abundant and favorable. Using data gathered and ideas developed in Newfield and other American communities, we shall sketch now a model for an OHC campaign and present recommendations for follow-up action aimed at securing improvement in all dimensions of the housing problem of minority group families.

THE DECISION PHASE

The conditions which encourage sensitivity to the problem of discrimination in housing in many communities across the country today are in themselves a major resource to be taken into consideration during the decision phase of an OHC program. The story of the covenant in Newfield shows how national trends and state or local events can lead to interest in the minority group housing issue and create a situation in which a substantial measure of support for residential integration can be elicited.

Four developments in national life were of great importance in the gestation of the Newfield OHC. Discrimination in housing was just as much a reality in Newfield in 1940 or 1950 as it was in 1960; but without the doubling of the Negro population which occurred in the decade before the last census as a result of Negro migration from the South, the problem of residential exclusion might not have assumed proportions large enough to attract serious attention from community leaders. Moreover, the problem might not have prompted remedial action except for the increased political and moral pressure for the elimination of undemocratic practices that resulted from independence movements in former colonial territories and civil rights agitation in the United States.[2] Federal government programs in public housing and urban renewal provided an added stimulus to recognition of the problem, and the "organizational revolution" of the past century,[3] which created numerous agencies, both public and private, having a stake in democratic human relations, insured that organized action on behalf of equal opportunity in housing would take place.

These national trends had manifested themselves in Newfield itself and the state where it is located. The action taken by the Butler Memorial Church Social Action Committee leading to the open housing covenant campaign would not have been possible but for the passage of a state fair housing law. Community attention was centered on the problem of residential discrimination because of the necessity of relocating citizens (many of them Negroes) displaced by the local urban renewal program. Awareness of the problem was intensified further by the press coverage given to the University Study Committee's report on the housing conditions of Newfield Negroes. Denominational officials of all major religious faiths represented in Newfield provided a stimulus to action by their heightened emphasis on the church's responsibility in the fight against racial injustice, and resources for carrying out social action in this area of concern were furnished by denominational literature and denominational staff officials who traveled about urging local religious leaders to do something to improve race relations in their communities.[4] Voluntary groups such as the NAACP and public agencies such as the State Commission on Civil Rights also supplied information, advice, and encouragement to local groups evincing an interest in action on the race issue.

The ripeness of the moment for an attack upon discrimination in housing was further enhanced by several other factors which exemplify irregular national trends, and which exhibit distinctive features in the Newfield situation. The mayor of Newfield was more than willing to identify himself with efforts to promote a nondiscriminatory climate of opinion by declaring November "Fair Housing Month," for he was aware that Negro voters constituted a potential balance of political power in Newfield. According to a political science professor at the University, the city's Negro voters were considered especially important by local politicians because, despite the fact that the number of Negro voters was small compared to other ethnic blocs, they were an unaffiliated segment of the electorate, a segment which might be won almost *en masse* by the party which could establish itself as defender of their interests. Party leaders reasoned that if they could once attract Negro support on a dramatic "race" issue, then they could create a pattern of party allegiance which would yield increasingly important rewards in the future.[5] As the equivocal statements of both candidates in the mayoralty race of 1961 revealed, this desire to woo the Negro vote was counterbalanced by a desire not to alienate white voters through the advocacy of "extreme" action regarding housing;[6] nevertheless, that the mayor was willing to issue a proclamation favoring fair housing was an important indication that Newfield was ready for the launching of an open housing covenant appeal.

Especially significant as a straw in the wind pointing to the desirability of the covenant campaign was the University Study Committee's report that many Negro household heads wanted, and could afford, better housing for their families. Since it could be argued that these families were prevented from obtaining more desirable housing only by the barrier of discrimination, the existence of this effective demand for better housing in the hands of a fairly large number of Negro homeseekers was an asset to sponsors of the OHC in gaining support from other clergymen and community leaders. One Protestant clergyman felt that the report on housing was respected (even by people who disliked the University and resented the report) as both reliable and important simply because it emanated from the University.[7]

The point is obvious: circumstances which make the time ripe for action on the housing issue constitute an important resource favorable to the initiation of action. If in a community with urban renewal or a rapidly expanding nonwhite population, a tolerably alert press can be counted on to keep the public aware of the freedom movement in the world, the civil rights movement in the nation, and the housing difficulties faced by Negro families, particularly relocation problems caused by urban redevelopment; if, moreover, there is a state fair housing law and local efforts to make use of it—the time for action is ripe, and the burden of proof is on those who counsel delay.

But the calculation of resources which is so crucial in the decision phase must reckon with unfavorable as well as favorable conditions. Again, as with the positive resources, the obstacles present in the Newfield situation are the kind that might be expected to exist in many American communities at the present time. It will be covenient to discuss these under two categories: those which influenced the minority community and those which influenced the majority community.

The Minority Community

As the University Study of Housing Conditions for Negroes in Newfield showed, the adult portion of the Negro community of the city is made up almost entirely of persons who were born in the South and who are now employed in working-class occupations. Thus the pool of potential Negro leadership in Newfield is not large, and this leadership does not have a very broad base of upwardly mobile Negroes with which to work. An explanation of this state of affairs is afforded by two important concepts now current in the literature of social science, which are especially applicable to Negroes of Southern provenance and low socio-economic status who have recently arrived in the North.

One partial explanation is found in the concept of "relative deprivation," which is considered by contemporary sociologists to be an important principle for the understanding of reference group behavior and attitudes.[8] According to the positive corollary of this concept, "relative status" is enjoyed by a person who from the standpoint of general cultural expectations is not well off, because he may nevertheless consider himself relatively fortunate when he compares his lot to that of friends or relatives who are worse off than he is. For example, the ex-tenant farmer who is working at an unskilled job that pays him $50 per week, and who is living in a home with certain conveniences which none of the folks back on the farm ever

enjoyed, is apt to feel, in a certain sense, "satisfied." As demonstrated in Chapter Three, Negroes in Newfield are better off
economically than are Negroes in the South, and virtually all
of the families contacted live in houses equipped with refrigerator, flush toilet, electricity, running water, and other conveniences which are quite often missing from the homes of
Southern Negroes. It is to be expected, then, that many respondents recently arrived from the South would express less dissatisfaction with their housing situation than would a person who
identifies himself with a less deprived reference group and
who evaluates his circumstances according to expectations less
conditioned by past deprivation.

Another partial explanation suggested by the Southern background of so many Newfield Negroes is that they are following
the pattern of "avoidance" which serves as a protective device
for a considerable segment of the Negro population, especially
Negroes in the South. As various studies have shown, Southern Negroes are apt to be more distrustful of white persons
than are Negroes who have not lived in the South—the accumulated experience of generations of Negroes in the South has
taught them to avoid contact with whites outside the well-
defined role-situations where they know what is expected of
them.[9] Furthermore, they have learned to avoid showing their
true feelings to white men: in the South, it would often be dangerous to do so. It it possible, then, that many of the respondents
involved in the study of housing conditions failed to mention
experience or anticipation of discrimination simply because
they were unwilling to admit such feelings to a white interviewer unknown to them. It is also possible that some respondents were unwilling to voice complaints about the policies of the
landlords for similar reasons. (Several respondents did in fact
express uneasiness lest their complaints against the landlord
should reach his ears.) Another manifestation of this behavior
pattern of avoidance is to be seen in the fact that so many
Newfield Negroes search for a place to live through friends
rather than through the newspapers or realtors.

The poor housing conditions of Negroes in Newfield are also
related to the fact that so few white collar jobs are held by

Negro citizens of the community. The findings reveal that a remarkably small number of Negroes in this city are engaged in clerical, sales, or professional occupations. This is true in spite of the fact that over one-fourth of the respondents have graduated from high school or had some education beyond high school. The low occupational status of Newfield Negroes is related to their housing problem because, in the first place, white collar jobs offer more opportunity for advancement and therefore more opportunity for eventual bargaining power in the housing market. Occupational status affects housing, secondly, because the absence of Negroes from visible white collar jobs reinforces the widespread misconception that Negroes are somehow not interested in or fitted for anything but blue collar jobs. Such stereotyped thinking would be mitigated by the presence of Negro stenographers, clerks, salesmen, and professional men in the offices and stores of the city.

The importance of relative status and avoidance as negative factors is confirmed by the fact that the leadership of the Newfield NAACP was composed of a mere handful of individuals, many of them whites. It cannot be said, of course, that the leadership of such an organization should be composed of Negroes; nevertheless, this fact is indicative of a scarcity of able Negro leaders. This interpretation of the state of affairs in the Newfield NAACP is confirmed by several items of circumstantial evidence. Two of the men who had served as president of the branch in recent years were obviously men of very meager leadership ability.[10] Only four of the Negro professional persons in the city took any kind of active part in the work of the branch. It is also noteworthy that the enthusiasm of Negro citizens for NAACP activities was much greater in regard to recreational affairs than it was in regard to agitation on behalf of civil rights.[11]

The Majority Community

Of the negative influences which tended to operate on the white citizens of Newfield, four are especially important: the general antipathy toward residential integration on the part of white persons in the state where Newfield is located; the specific ethnic make-up of the city's population; the fact that interest in the housing problem was popularly regarded as having been "stirred up" by people who did not have a large stake in the community and who were not, for the most part, property owners; and the absence of close rapport between religious and secular leaders of the desegregation efforts in the community.

The State Commission on Civil Rights study on statewide racial attitudes, which was published in 1961, found that only one-third of the white residents were favorably disposed toward residential desegregation.[12] Even more important, though, was the fact that such a large proportion of Newfield's population was made up of second- and third-generation immigrant families with a very strong sense of ethnic identification. The negative influence of this factor was compounded by the fact that for the largest of these ethnic groups real estate holdings had exceptional symbolic value as proof of Americanism and the achievement of middle-class status.[13] Since a very high percentage of the rental units economically accessible to Newfield Negroes were in the hands of Italian families who were especially jealous of the financial and symbolic value of their property in land and houses, the dimensions of the problem were enlarged considerably.[14] It is partly because of the ethnic factor that the support of the covenant by Roman Catholics was relatively insignificant. Evidence for this inference is to be seen in the fact that no signed covenant cards were obtained from one of the national parishes of Newfield, and only three from the other one.

Another important factor present in the Newfield situation was the feeling on the part of many of its inhabitants that "we have no problem here" and that the persons responsible for the University Study and the open housing covenant appeal were "making a mountain out of a molehill." It is difficult to assess the strength of this factor, but it was manifested in numerous remarks made to members of the University Study Committee by local friends. For example, a reliable informant reported to one committee member that "people in town think this whole thing has been stirred up by the nonproperty-owning liberals on the hill [where the University is located]." The presence of this sentiment is also attested by some of the comments made on the questionnaire for laymen:

> I don't like the pressure put on the whites by the sit-ins, the freedom rides, the [University] professors, the NAACP always being in the newspapers. . . . I used to like the few Negroes we had in Newfield; a few years ago they were not as conspicuous. But now there are to [sic] many for the size of our town. . . .

> I object that outsiders come into a community and try to stir up sentiment for some particular cause. The city of Newfield was getting along very well with the colored people and most [sic] all of them were happy. Then along comes a fly by night preacher who sticks his nose in where it doesn't belong. The city started a redevelopment project and everything was going well, but when the people who lived in this neighborhood moved out the commission rented the places to negroes [sic] who came in from the south and other places. Now this element of NAACP which includes both races are trying to force this rifraf [sic] on a good clean neighborhood. . . . The negro [sic] or white man who thinks for himself and tries to make something of himself does not ask for or seek all this commotion. I also do not know why you in [the nearby city in which the researcher lived] have anything to say about Newfield. Stay in your own backyard and let the people of Newfield take care of themselves.

> I do not believe the white people should try to run the Negroes and I believe they have stirred them up, making them discontented and causing a great deal of trouble and unhappiness.

> I have the feeling that we are tending to push too hard on this issue. I feel that we can accomplish more by less spectacular means.

A final negative factor which might be mentioned, even though it failed to assume serious proportions, was the tension existing among some of the individuals who were most instrumental in sparking civil rights action in Newfield. Many of the top leaders within the local NAACP (most of whom were also on the University Study Committee) were hostile to the Church, and they felt that much of what was done by the religious groups interested in civil rights was futile or ineptly carried out. There were even some doubts as to the motives and perseverance of the Church people involved in these reform efforts. For their part, some of the individuals who played leadership roles in the Christian social action described here felt that their contribution was aggravatingly snubbed by the University Study Committee, and they regretted the lack of full cooperation which they thought characterized the endeavors of their secular counterparts. As stated above, these tensions never caused a serious breakdown in communication between the two groups, nor did they prevent either faction from at least trying in apparent good faith to cooperate with the other faction. It is indubitably true, nonetheless, that a fuller measure of rapport would have led to better results from the open housing covenant campaign as well as from some of the related civil rights activities originated by nonchurch sources.

THE PLANNING PHASE

One of the lessons to be learned from Newfield is that even the most elementary and the most obvious prerequisites for intelligent planning can be overlooked although they are verbally acknowledged. To plan community action that is supposedly under joint sponsorship without the participation, from the earliest stages of planning, of one or more of the putative sponsors is to court at least a mild form of disaster. A conflict with some previously planned project of the omitted sponsors is a dangerous possibility, and lack of enthusiasm (not to speak of lack of cooperation or downright resistance) is a virtual certainty under these circumstances. Unless requirements of timing make immediate action imperative, and unless the joint sponsorship is desired only for symbolic purposes and can be counted on without the danger of hurt feelings, the initiators of an action program should avoid making arrangements (particularly setting dates) without the participation of other sponsors.

Before priorities can be assigned to different ends and goals in a rational manner, it is necessary then in the planning phase to specify in very precise terms exactly what objectives (that is, proximate goals) are to be sought in the contemplated action. An open housing covenant is a device intended to contribute to the end of racial equality through the achievement of the goal of a changed climate of community opinion, but the specific objectives of the covenant appeal must be thought of more precisely, and in clarifying objectives the targets of the action will also become clearer. One objective is greater willingness on the part of white residents to welcome Negro neighbors; one of the targets, therefore, is the white population in general, but especially the whites who have a large emotional investment in the lily-whiteness of their residential neighborhood, and most especially the housewives who set the tone of the "neighboring" activities in a residential area. But even the most liberal whites will have no opportunity to welcome Negroes unless the "gate-keepers" who control housing opportunities let Negroes through the racial barrier; another objective, then, is changed policies on the part of realtors, landlords, and potential sellers of privately owned homes, and these persons comprise another target with special characteristics. A third objective is greater willingness on the part of Negroes to seek interracial housing accommodations; consequently, that portion of the Negro community which can afford higher rents or home purchase and is sufficiently acculturated to desire a different sort of home environment constitutes another (and extraordinarily crucial) target of the covenant.

Another essential ingredient in the planning phase is the clarification of goals, the recognition of possible conflicts among them, and the setting of priorities according to the importance of different goals and the feasibility of attaining them. The dilemma confronted by those who are interested in better housing for Negroes is a striking illustration of this point. In this case, the conflict is between *welfare values*—better housing in the sense of decent, safe, and sanitary living quarters instead of filthy, hazardous, crowded slums—and *status values*—better housing in the sense of an environment where one's family is free of the stigma of being segregated into an all-Negro ghetto. This conflict occurs most painfully in connection with bargaining among politicians over the question of the location of public housing projects in large cities where Negroes make up a high percentage of the population. Political representatives from the white suburbs will agree to vote for the construction of low-income housing if Negro politicians will agree to accept building sites that for all practical purposes make *de facto* segregation a certainty. Negro civic leaders—officials of the NAACP and the Urban League, ministers of middle-class and upper-class churches, Negro professional people, etc.—insist that additional public housing should be built in areas where integration can be maintained. Negro politicians are under pressure from their constituents to insure their basic welfare by providing new opportunities for adequate housing for families which are living in miserable conditions; Negro civic leaders are under pressure from civil rights liberals to insure that the vicious circle that perpetuates prejudice is broken by opposing segregation in every form.[15]

In connection with the setting of priorities among different goals, the conflict between welfare and status values must be faced because in some cases it may be necessary to channel most of one's limited resources into an effort to attain one type of goal rather than the other. In Newfield, for example, a frank recognition of the conflict between welfare and status goals, plus awareness of the greater numbers and more pressing needs of the lower-class Negroes of the city, might have led to greater stress on challenging the benign quota in public housing (or specifically the very low tipping point observed by the manager of public housing in Newfield) and less stress on the construction of new housing (albeit integrated housing) for middle-income families. It might be argued, on the other hand, that the very reason which makes housing such a critical item on the social action agenda dictates insistence on integrated housing, not just decent but *de facto* segregated housing. As noted in Chapter One, residential discrimination is the hardest nut of all to crack because it touches on the whole self-image (particularly the sense of status) of whites. But by virtue of this very fact, integration in housing may offer very rich dividends in terms of newly learned lack of prejudice against Negroes on the part of white people.

The significance of housing in determining one's whole attitude toward himself is also a factor which highlights its significance in changing attitudes about other persons. Several studies have been done of the effects of interracial housing on the attitudes of individuals toward members of another racial group. One of the most important investigations of this kind was performed by Morton Deutsch and Mary Evans Collins, whose book *Interracial Housing: A Psychological Evaluation of a Social Experiment* is a classic in the literature on intergroup relations.[16] Deutsch and Collins found a number of important differentials between the attitudes of people who had lived in integrated housing projects and the attitudes of those who had lived in segregated projects:[17]

(1) There were many more instances of "friendly, neighborly contacts between members of the different races" in the integrated developments.

(2) "The integrated projects were characterized by a friendlier, more cohesive social atmosphere." Not only did white housewives have closer relations with Negro housewives, but they also had closer relations among themselves. Moreover, "there was no evidence to indicate that this gain in social cohesion of the integrated project resulted in or from an over-all loss of friendships with people outside the project."

(3) Housewives in the integrated projects became "more favorably disposed toward the Negro people in general, as well as toward the Negroes in their projects."

It might also be pointed out that integration in previously lily-white suburbs may be of unique value because so many of the key policy-makers in government and industry live in such suburbs. If the stereotyped notions about Negroes, or about the reaction of whites to Negroes, in the minds of these policy-makers can be altered, the dividends reaped in corporations and government agencies could be enormous.[18]

The implication of the Deutsch and Collins study, and of those like it, is that a lowering of the racial bar in housing will lower the general level of prejudice in the white community by providing whites with an opportunity to become acquainted with Negroes and learn that they are not, after all, such a strange and fearful breed. The evidence of these studies does not promise that *all* white persons will develop a more favorable attitude toward Negroes, nor does it promise that the

growth of sociable relations and friendly feelings will automatically accompany a decline in stereotyped thinking about
Negroes. But it does suggest that a new situation of interracial
contacts does, in a majority of cases, result in more open attitudes and more civil behavior.

THE EXECUTION PHASE

The tactics appropriate for dealing with each target will vary
so greatly according to the unique circumstances of locale, per-
sonality, and power configurations that few general principles
can be laid down *a priori*. The arguments which sway one man
will leave another man cold, and others will be so utterly im-
pervious to any and all arguments that some sort of leverage
other than mere persuasion will have to be used with them.
The same agent who is effective in persuading or manipulating
one target may be totally ineffective with another, and the logic
of both his success and his failure may remain obscure. But
a few maxims about presenting the open housing covenant may
be stated on the basis of lessons learned in Newfield and several
other cities.

Channels of Communication

The findings of this study lead to the conclusion that although
"multitudinist" techniques of communication—that is, techniques
which attempt to "touch the maximal number of people in the
community through minimal means"[19]—are certainly not a sufficient approach, they may be quite useful in publicizing an
open housing covenant. The fact that so many laymen reported
learning about the covenant through a variety of channels indicates that impersonal methods of communication do repay a
not inconsiderable dividend in terms of signatures for the covenant. But face-to-face contact is even more effective, as the
experience of OHC workers in the Washington, D.C., area
makes clear:

> In Bannockburn, where canvassers went from door to door,
> signatures were secured from 67% of the 268 families in the
> neighborhood. The return would have been higher if all of the
> houses had been contacted as there were few direct refusals.[20]

The importance of utilizing multiple channels of communication to publicize an open housing covenant, and of face-to-face contact in soliciting signatures, is highlighted by the fact that a large number of eventual nonsupporters of the Newfield convenant were initially undecided about or even favorably inclined toward signing it. Repeated exposure to appeals on behalf of the covenant may well prove crucial in gaining the support of individuals who have no strong feelings about it one way or the other. Parishioners who are not fully persuaded by one or two exposures, or by any one type of exposure, may be persuaded by the cumulative effect of a number of invitations to sign the covenant from a number of different sources. This interpretation of the findings points also to the importance of reinforcing the appeals of the minister with urging from laymen: a variety of approaches by the minister alone may come to seem worrisome and resistance to his prodding may be rationalized on the grounds that he is "fanatical" on the subject; if, however, there are a group of respected laymen who obviously share the minister's zeal in the matter, many fence-straddlers may be won over.

Another comment on channels of communication concerns the importance of favorable press coverage. Since the fundamental purpose of a covenant program is to change the climate of opinion in a community, this factor is vital to the success of the endeavor. If press treatment of a city's housing situation is infrequent or complacent, public awareness of housing problems may remain so low that the very existence of these problems is not acknowledged. If good coverage and editorial support are not given to the open housing covenant—either during the time that efforts to obtain signatures are being made or at the time when the names of signers are published—it may fail dismally in securing signatures, or the impact of even a goodly number of signatures may be lost on the community. That a majority of nonsupporters of the convenant in Newfield were nevertheless willing to admit the existence of both poor housing conditions among Negro families and discrimination against them is due in no small measure to the excellent reporting and the frequent editorials on this state of affairs found in the

Newfield *Review.* The "softening up" effect of being forced to acknowledge the existence of the housing problem is important in lowering the resistance of prejudiced persons to attacks upon the problem by others.

The experience of Newfield church leaders is also instructive in regard to the desirability of linking communication about the covenant with an opportunity to sign it immediately. Large groups of persons signed the covenant at the Council of Churches banquet, where the covenants were presented for signature immediately following speeches on its behalf, and at those church services where distribution of the covenant cards was built into the worship service. The advisability of on-the-spot collection is emphasized by the failure of churches where distribution occurred before or after the service, or where collection of the cards occurred at some later time.

Influences

Despite the skepticism of cynics, many churchgoers do pay attention to what their pastors have to say on behalf of social action. That the influence of one's clergyman was found to be more important than any other influence named by signers of the Newfield open housing covenant is testimony that the influence of clergymen is still great with numbers of their parishioners. But it should be noted that it is not the authority of his office that is decisive: very few respondents, including Catholics, declared that they supported the covenant because they felt their pastor wanted them to. It is of the utmost importance, therefore, that a minister do more than simply register his approval of an open housing covenant: he must state the case for the covenant persuasively in a sermon, a pulpit announcement, a letter in a parish publication, a talk before a church group, or in personal conversation. It is what he says or does in connection with the covenant that counts, not the mere fact that he urges his parishioners to sign.

This is not to say, however, that the influence of the minister operates in the same fashion with all types of parishioners. Many relatively highly educated persons may have strong latent sympathies for the aims of a covenant, and they may need only a little urging to recognize in themselves previous convictions which incline them to support it. The influence of previous conviction may be least, and the influence of the minister strongest, among persons of relatively low educational and occupational standing. This is a significant finding, for it means that where the resources of a church for publicizing a covenant are limited, it would be wise to concentrate those resources on convincing the less educated and the blue collar workers in a congregation. In other words, the return on a given expenditure of energy by the minister and the Social Action Committee is likely to be highest among this segment of the church's membership.

Although the findings of this study suggest that, when combined with other efforts, the sermon is an important instrument for stimulating the consciences of parishioners, they do not encourage the belief of most Protestant ministers that the preaching role is the most important part of the clergyman's vocation.[21] The Newfield ministers who relied almost exclusively upon the sermon as a means of eliciting support for the open housing covenant did not succeed in reaching many of their parishioners—and this was true even in those cases where they preached rather forceful sermons on the subject.

Another significant conclusion which may be drawn from the findings is that special efforts must be made by church leaders to achieve an effective influence on behalf of the covenant from informal conversation among families, neighbors, and friends. It cannot simply be assumed that the favorable sentiment generated by various "spectator influences" (such as sermons, the newspaper, or the mass media) will automatically filter down to a large number of other persons through conversation. The emphasis placed on individual decision by many clergymen had perhaps too great an impact upon churchgoers, for most decisions to support the covenant seem to have been made in isolation from other members of the church, neighbors, and associates. It is also clear that the family—an institution supposedly strengthened and invigorated by the Church—was not crucial as a source of guidance in the making of moral decisions for Newfield Christians.

An ingenious device used in the Williamstown, Massachusetts, fair housing drive merits special mention. The value of face-to-face contact in presentation of the covenant was given an added dimension in this small college town by the use of teen-agers. An attempt was made to see to it that every home in the community was visited by a two-man team composed of one adult and one high school youth. The sponsors of the Williamstown OHC felt that a special moral force would be exerted on prospective signers by the presence of a young person at the time when the pledge was explained to him: they reasoned that it is more difficult to exhibit cynicism or even mere hesitancy about assumed cultural values—in this case, equal opportunity for all American citizens—when a supposedly unspoiled, idealistic youngster is watching. There are many reasons why one might expect a large percentage of the citizens of such a town to support the covenant, but the extraordinarily high figure of seventy-five per cent signers obtained in Williamstown was doubtless due in no small measure to this clever tactic.[22] And of course the additional value of a more memorable confrontation with the moral issue embodied in the OHC goes far beyond the fact that more signatures are secured: getting as many signatures as possible is an intrinsically important goal of the covenant campaign, but it is even better to get them in such a way that the signer realizes the full significance of committing himself to the moral meaning of the convenant and commits himself to it wholeheartedly.

Reasons

The findings of this study regarding why people sign, or do not sign, an open housing covenant suggest three useful guidelines for action:

(1) Many signatures will be lost if the purpose and the limits of the fair housing pledge are not very carefully explained to prospective signers;

(2) It is strategically advantageous to explain the covenant as an educational device; and

(3) Some of the issues generally considered most weighty

in the minds of white residents of a community facing integration may not be quite so important as is commonly thought.

The purpose of an open housing covenant must be clearly explained to the people of a community by its sponsors; otherwise, many signatures are apt to be lost in the resulting confusion. If prospective signers do not understand that the names of most signers will be published in a newspaper advertisement as an educational device to display the strength of pro-equality sentiment in the city, they may neglect to add their names to the list. The covenant should be presented to the public as an educational device; it will then be regarded with interest at least by the many persons who disavow "radical" means of dealing with civil rights problems, but who have great faith in the benefits that can be expected from education.

It is also essential for the success of the covenant appeal that citizens be advised of the precise limits of the obligations they agree to assume in signing the covenant, and of the final disposition of the signed cards. It is probably wise to include on the card a statement specifying that the signer's name will not be used for any purpose without his permission. The verification of signatures prior to publication of the newspaper advertisement is also an important part of the whole procedure of a covenant campaign, for inclusion of the names of any persons who do not want their names to appear can cause embarrassing retractions which will diminish the impact of the advertisement.

The widespread acceptance of "education" as a method of overcoming discrimination reflected in the response of laymen in Newfield leads to the inference that the covenant should be explained to community residents as an educational device. It can be argued with great plausibility that the collection of a large number of signatures will, by demonstrating widespread support for equality of opportunity in the purchase of a home, educate all of the people of good will in the city who would like to rent or sell housing without discrimination but have heretofore been afraid to do so because of their mistaken notion that "other people would object." If this interpretation of the purpose of the OHC campaign is emphasized, the resentments of those who see it as a coercive mechanism may be allayed, and the good will accorded to anything billed as educational may accrue to the fair housing pledge.

It is easier to predict what kinds of reasons for signing will be counted important by supporters of a covenant than it is to say what kinds of reasoning might sway nonsupporters. Appeals to religious and democratic values were both effective in Newfield, and they probably will be with many persons in most American communities. Fear of declining property values or intermarriage does not appear to be nearly so important as is generally thought; therefore, it might be safe to devote very little attention to arguments intended to refute these fears when seeking to win supporters for an open housing covenant.

THE PUBLICITY PHASE

The publicity phase of an OHC campaign is actually not separate from the planning and presentation phases, but runs concurrently with them, for the newspaper stories announcing the covenant and describing plans for distributing fair housing pledge cards among the townspeople are also important ways of publicizing the liberal sentiments that will hopefully change the climate of community opinion. The climax of a covenant campaign is the publication of the names of the signers, together with the text of the fair housing pledge and the endorsements of it made by religious and civic leaders. The details of this final dramatic gesture deserve to be considered carefully, for unless it is delivered effectively the fruits of all the labor spent in gathering signatures may be in large measure lost.

The first step in the process of designing the ad is the selection and verification of the names which will appear in it. Since a full-page ad is large enough to include several hundred names, selection of these from the list of all signers seldom poses much of a problem, and the principles governing selection are fairly obvious: names of all sorts and conditions of men should be included so as to impress upon readers the fact that people of various classes, ethnic backgrounds, and religious persuasions are among the supporters of the covenant. A special effort should be made to make certain that all prominent citizens, particularly those commonly regarded as spokesmen for various segments of the population, are listed. In Newfield, obedience to this principle meant that no Roman Catholic signers were omitted in the ad, and that names clearly identifiable as Irish, Polish, Italian, and Jewish were placed where they would have the greatest chance of being noted by anyone who scanned the ad rather hurriedly.

All names being listed must be verified by a letter or phone call to the person concerned, asking if he is willing for his name to appear in the ad. In theory, verification is not necessary, because the covenant card should contain a statement advising signers that their signature will be interpreted as consent to make use of their names in publicizing the results of the appeal —but in practice it is wise to double check before the ad is composed. Verification is necessary, not only because some names may have been sent in fraudulently by some person other than the one whose name is given (either as a prank or with malicious intent), but also because some signers may have changed their minds since putting their signature on the pledge or may not have understood that consent to publish was implied as granted with the signature. Some of the names are invariably eliminated as a result of this step, but it is far better to lose the name of even an influential person than to have a complaint about unwarranted use of names after the ad is published. Just a few such complaints, or even one publicized complaint from an important person, can badly damage the impact of the covenant on local citizens. This rather tedious chore was in the hands of an exceptionally capable woman in Newfield, and it was performed to perfection: not a single complaint about misuse of a name was registered with sponsors of the covenant.

Composition of the ad also requires careful thought. The general rules of clarity, emphasis, and attractiveness which apply to the arrangement of words in any newspaper ad must of course be followed, and in Newfield the sponsors were fortunate in having the advice of an experienced journalist. Their ad included a coupon which a reader could use to add his name to the list of signers, and the explanatory statement at the top of the page urged readers to make use of this coupon. That the thirty-seven additional names received on coupons included several men with known political aspirations may indeed prove the effectiveness of the strategic placing of the mayor's name at the top of the first column of names in the ad. Unfortunately, however, the absence of the names of realtors, bankers, and other men of high standing in the business community of the city detracted from the influence exerted by the ad. As interviews with Newfield realtors several months after the covenant program showed, they were able to dismiss the ad by citing the omission of the names of such persons and by claiming that many of the signers were not property owners or for various other reasons had no real stake in Newfield as their permanent home.[23]

The publicity phase reaches a climax in the ad listing signers, but this does not need to be the only component of the climactic moment, nor does it need to be the final act of publicizing the covenant. As noted above, the Newfield sponsors were fortunate in having a favorable press, and they were wise in persuading a leading editorialist to comment on the significance of the covenant in his column appearing on the same day. It might be argued that the editorial was dangerous in so far as its laudatory remarks reinforced a tendency to regard the covenant as an end in itself apart from follow-up activities, but certainly the editorial enhanced the message of the ad in a very valuable way, and it illustrates one of the possibilities for making the most of the covenant that is open to sponsors in any community where the sympathies of an editorial writer are with them.

Subsequent publicity did not appear in Newfield, but a word can be said about this aspect of the publicity phase in other cities. One of the most effective devices of this kind is that used by the fair housing group in Pasadena, California. It is a spot map, showing residential areas of the city where support for the covenant was widespread. This graphic presentation of the results of an OHC campaign has the advantage of showing at a glance those parts of a city where a prospective Negro

homebuyer can expect to find friendly sentiments. It also fortifies, in a way that no listing of names and addresses can do,
the impression that support is extensive, for the areas on a
map where a large cluster of dots representing signers appears
is a forceful and memorable way of saying, "Look how many
persons in favor of residential integration live in these neighborhoods!" (The use of a spot map would of course not be advis-
able if there were not enough signatures to create an impression
of strong pro-integration sentiments, or if the signers were too
tightly concentrated in just a few areas.)

Follow-Up Action

In line with the author's conviction that an open housing
covenant program cannot be maximally effective unless it is
accompanied by many other types of follow-up action aimed
at other aspects of the problem of minority group housing, the
entire following section of this chapter is devoted to an outline
of other measures which might profitably be undertaken. Several of the actions proposed here are exceedingly ambitious:
not every community has the resources to begin such action
immediately, and in such cases the mobilization of resources
must be accomplished before the recommended steps can be
taken; furthermore, some of the actions require the joint efforts
of many local groups in securing legislation or administrative
decisions at the state or national level. But the thinking of
citizens who are seriously interested in helping to put an end
to discrimination in housing should not be limited to short-
range goals or that which is immediately possible: the horizons
of their thought must extend to the outermost boundaries of the
field for action. And any of the recommendations set forth in
the following pages could be carried out if sufficient support
for them were developed, community by community, throughout the nation.

Attacking the Internal Roots of the Problem

A thoughtful examination of the dimensions of the housing
problem for Negroes suggests that remedial action may be most
fruitfully considered under three headings: attacking the internal

roots of discrimination, attacking its external roots, and over-coming the inadequacy of housing available to Negroes. If the difficulties arising from the behavior pattern of avoidance dis-cussed earlier in this chapter may be viewed as a special type of insufficient acculturation deserving separate treatment, then vulnerability to economic barriers, limited acculturation, and avoidance may be designated the principal internal roots of discrimination.

It is all too easy for a white person or for a middle-class Negro to admonish lower-class Negroes about the importance of education and diligence in taking advantage of every op-portunity for job training and advancement. Relatively privi-leged persons have never been troubled with, or have succeeded in overcoming, job barriers and job ceilings, so naturally they believe in the efficacy of the drive to self-improvement. Noting that eighty-six per cent of the Negro wage-earners in Newfield had never sought advancement through additional education or training, they might regard the problem as one which could be solved with a good pep talk. But such advice provides cold com-fort to the man who has perhaps bruised his head against these barriers and has given up. One's misgivings about such advice are increased in light of Professor Conant's report that the rate of unemployment among graduates of many city high schools is almost as high as the rate among drop-outs, and in light of the statistics on unemployment throughout the nation.[24] There may not be enough jobs to go around for a long time to come, and part of the acculturation process that the entire populace of technologically advanced nations may have to go through involves learning to live with this fact as a more or less perma-nent feature of existence in the modern world. We may have to develop more equanimity about having large numbers of persons on public welfare all the time, and we may have to readjust our notions about man's need for and duty to work, so that the stigma of being without a job is eliminated.

Nevertheless, one of the most important lines of attack upon the housing problem is an attack upon school drop-outs and a full-scale campaign of encouragement directed at Negro wage-earners and Negro youth to develop to the fullest extent their own economic capabilities. The success of these efforts depends in large measure, of course, upon their coordination with efforts to remove discrimination in employment. But there is certainly a lot of room for improvement in the vocational training and the motivation for self-development imparted to youngsters by parents and teachers, and this is a basic line of attack which deserves to be thought out with all the ingenuity that can be mustered. Some authorities estimate that only one per cent of the Negro boys in vocational schools in certain large American cities are receiving training which fits them for jobs which will be immediately available to them upon graduation.[25] Others contend that this estimate is grotesquely misleading, maintaining that modern vocational training should develop the capacity to learn new skills rather than teach certain limited skills that may be obsolete in five years.[26] Be that as it may, all experts agree that a good high school education is more important than ever before, most especially for Negro youth. Other observers stress the importance of providing training for young men and women in relatively unskilled jobs, such as domestic service: they admit that this approach is offensive to many Negroes, but they insist that it can provide a source of income and a means to greater self-respect for thousands who are willing to take advantage of it in a situation of slack employment.[27] Even more important, perhaps, is the elimination of textbooks, especially in the fields of history and literature, which perpetuate derogatory stereotypes of Negroes or fail to do justice to the contribution of Negroes to the development of American greatness.[28]

Another attack upon vulnerability to economic barriers is the establishment of credit unions. Credit unions are important, in the first place, because they provide a refuge from the loan sharks and "easy-credit installment-purchase" salesmen who so often victimize unsophisticated people.[29] They are important, secondly, because they provide a context for effective counseling of slum dwellers who might resent and resist advice from social workers or ministers. Saul Alinsky, prime mover of the Back of the Yards community organization in Chicago, points out that no one likes to be asked about his financial condition or told by a social worker that he is a fool for spending his money in such-and-such a way—but if he comes to a community credit union for a loan, he realizes that questions and advice are in order, and he is willing to listen because he feels it was his idea to seek out assistance.[30]

To speak of credit unions is to speak of consumer education, and this touches on the question of acculturation. Social workers and ministers in urban centers find that a great number of the persons with whom they deal do not have even a rudimentary knowledge of sound budgeting practices or sound methods of transacting business. They need to be taught to demand receipts for all payments; they need to be taught the advantages of shopping in large chain stores instead of at corner markets, etc. What they need, in short, is a course in "urban orientation." Fortunately, the need for a systematic approach to this problem has now been recognized, and several cities are now in the process of carrying out experimental programs that may set a pattern for the entire country. The Washington Urban League has recently instituted a "Newcomers" program in which an effort will be made to initiate recent in-migrants into the ways of city living. This program will be implemented in part by having experienced urban families "adopt" newcomer families for a short period of time, for the purpose of teaching them in informal ways the lore of getting along in an urban environment. In Pittsburgh, ACTION-Housing is acting in cooperation with the city government (and the Ford Foundation) to sponsor "urban extension agents" whose job it will to be to go into the homes of unsophisticated people and operate in much the same fashion that rural extension agents have been operating for years. The Relocation Officer of urban renewal in another large Eastern city is of the opinion that the acculturation which should result from such measures will have far-reaching consequences: in his efforts to relocate families displaced by redevelopment, he has found that many landlords, though somewhat skeptical, are willing to take a chance on their first Negro tenant. If the landlord's housekeeping standards are met, the good word spreads, and it is possible to locate other Negro tenants in that neighborhood. Whenever the landlord's stand-

ards are not met, though, the effects upon neighborhood sentiment are disasterous.[31] Urban orientation training could be a
powerful instrument in overcoming white skepticism and thus
opening up more housing opportunities for Negroes. The use
of public housing projects for training in acculturation is also
a promising device: in one Connecticut city, underprivileged
persons have been allowed to live in public housing for a short
period of time, during which they were given instruction and
experience in the housekeeping practices which would be expected of them by private landlords.[32]

Given the fact that economic capabilities are not going to
expand miraculously overnight, the majority of Negro slum
dwellers must face the prospect of living where they are for
some time to come. Their lot could be greatly improved if the
acculturation process included concentrated efforts at "unslumming" deteriorated neighborhoods. Many communities have
found that the "block club" approach is an effective device for
achieving this end. A block club is simply an organization of
people dedicated to the purpose of making their homes
more attractive and more livable. A city bureaucrat may
not respond when one person in a slum area phones and asks
for trash removal, but when he is informed by a clergyman (or
some other person with enough status to kick up something
of a fuss through newspapers or official channels) that all of
the people in a certain block have prepared all their trash for
collection, he may sit up and take notice. The landlord may
be reluctant to have his house fixed up, but if he and all the
other landlords on a block are notified that a collective effort
at cleaning and painting is underway, and that the tenants are
willing to furnish the labor if the landlords will furnish the
materials, the paint and lumber may be forthcoming.[33]

A final line of attack which might be considered a remedy
for economic vulnerability as well as an item of acculturation
is the systematic propagation of birth control information and
materials to slum dwellers. This is not simply a technical problem which can be solved as soon as a better pill is perfected;
it is a problem involving the low-income person's whole worldview of despair.[34] The difficulties presented by the lower-class

mentality are very great, but even greater is the importance of population control among families that cannot provide adequately for additional children.

Avoidance can be dealt with in three ways: disseminating information, giving reassurance, and providing experience in contacts with whites. The provisions of civil rights laws which insure a measure of equal housing opportunity to Negroes should be published and explained throughout the Negro community in every locality where such laws exist. Information about the local availability of the more than 40,000 dwellings repossessed by FHA should be disseminated, because racial discrimination is prohibited in the disposal of all these units of housing, and many of them fall into a price range that Negroes can reach. An effort should also be made to convince prospective Negro homeowners and apartment seekers that die-hard resistance to them is actually confined to a very small minority of whites, and that in any event violence is unlikely should they move into a predominantly white neighborhood.[35] The willing buyer–willing seller agency is a valuable device for overcoming avoidance. Most important of all the measures that might be taken to combat avoidance is casual contact between whites and Negroes of equal status. Friendly, informal equal-status contact is needed to communicate the feeling as well as the knowledge that integration is possible to persons who have had little opportunity for association with members of other races and who are suspicious of them. Promotion of equal-status contact is a line of attack which also helps to eliminate the external barriers to housing opportunities, of course, and it is a method of ameliorating the problem that serves to point up the importance of racially inclusive churches.[36]

Attacking the External Roots of the Problem

Since the basic cause of residential exclusion is located in the white population rather than the Negro population, attacks upon the external roots of the problem are even more essential than attacks upon its internal roots. The four principal categories to be considered are educational, economic, legal, and nonviolent direct action.

The educational approach is of course typified in the OHC and in neighborhood stabilization; it is sometimes included as well in state laws setting up a Civil Rights Commission. A propaganda campaign on behalf of open occupancy is often allowed or required by such laws.[37] Groups of private citizens can also implement the educational approach through a neighborhood or apartment house opinion poll to discover how many people really would move out if Negro tenants moved in. If a large majority of the tenants or homeowners have no objections to Negro neighbors, then the ground is cut out from under the argument that the landlord or home seller can't afford to deal with Negroes lest a mass exodus of whites should result. This tactic is not recommended, though, except in places where a favorable poll can be accurately predicted in advance, for advance notice often causes fears that might not have been thought of if Negroes simply arrived without warning.[38]

A second approach to the problem of exclusion is that of increasing the total supply of housing available in a given area. The availability of a larger number of housing opportunities tends to lower rents by making the housing market more competitive, and it also reduces congestion. One of the most notable undertakings in this category is the construction of planned interracial housing developments. Morris Milgram is perhaps the best-known builder of such housing—it is his firm that was involved in the Deerfield case—but his is not the only one, nor the largest one, and there are likely to be more and more contractors building for open occupancy as time goes on.[39] One of the most significant things about privately developed interracial housing so far is that the people who live in developments of this kind are not intellectuals or beatniks or anybody with a special stake in being liberal. The homes which have been sold to whites in private interracial housing have been sold because they were good homes for the price charged. This proves that the racial factor is not necessarily an overriding consideration, and that other benefits will beguile average people with average prejudice into more desirable patterns of behavior.[40]

The legal approach is perhaps the most fruitful of all the methods of attacking the external roots of the problem. It is heartening that sixteen states and quite a few cities have passed civil rights legislation affecting housing. But there are numerous loopholes in most of these laws, and enforcement is not always effective, thus efforts to improve the administration of existing laws are almost as vital as attempts to secure legislation in states not covered. An exhaustive survey of "Administrative Enforcement of Antidiscrimination Legislation" published recently in the *Harvard Law Review* ended by declaring, "It seems necessary for the commissions to take more of an initiatory role than has been the rule."[41] The effect of a policy of reliance upon individual complaints has been "to leave wide gaps in enforcement, especially in areas where individuals are generally reluctant to act."[42] The authors concluded that "commission activity should . . . be in the area of uncovering discriminatory practices and taking coercive action to eliminate them systematically."[43] There are no states in which it is possibile to "freeze" an apartment which is allegedly denied to a Negro applicant because of his race until the legitimacy of his complaint is established by the State Civil Rights Commission and the landlord is either persuaded or ordered to rent to him.[44] This means that an enterprising landlord can always evade the order by seeing to it that he has no vacancies left when the case is settled. A promise by the landlord that he will not discriminate the next time a vacancy comes up is not a very satisfying victory for the Negro applicant. (The situation here is comparable to that in school desegregation suits where the rights of the plaintiff are supposedly satisfied by having other Negro children admitted to a white school after his own children have already graduated from the school into which admittance was sought. This state of affairs caused Thurgood Marshall to suggest that the only way a parent could be sure of having the rights of his own children protected would be to file a suit for admittance when the child was born!)[45] Present enforcement policies also call for extraordinary patience on the part of Negro applicants, because informal conciliation is the rule in most states, and public hearings are exceedingly rare. In the first ten years of the New York State Commission Against Discrimination, for example, only four of 3,150 cases reached the stage of a public hearing.[46] As the authors of the *Harvard Law Review* essay assert:

> The most serious flaw in the enforcement process is the [Fair Housing] commissions' general inability to provide an adequate remedy for the particular complaints. If the respondent insists on his procedural rights, it will ordinarily take the commission three to five months to follow a case through from the initiation of the complaint to the issuance of the final order by the hearing panel. . . . In states in which the commissions rely heavily on counciliation, organized interest groups have criticized their hesitancy and delay in securing enforceable orders at public hearings. Such dissatisfaction may lead to disdain for the remedies offered by the commissions, and so diminish the number of complaints, upon which commissions are to a large extent dependent for the initiation of their activities. Thus, by delaying the enforcement process, commissions to some extent choke off the source of their regulatory power.[47]

Even when the public hearing is held, there is no guarantee that its effect or consequences will be favorable: in the field of housing, "a reputation for discrimination may even enhance the reputation of a broker or a builder."[48] The teeth embodied in a fair housing law, therefore, should consist of something more than supposedly adverse publicity: conviction on a charge of discrimination should bring about "a commitment by the [party convicted] to obey the letter and spirit of the antidiscrimination law, and an undertaking to display prominently the notices published by the commission to inform the public of the existence of the law."[49]

To speak of the provisions which ought to be included in a fair housing law raises the whole question of new legislation needed in the field of residence and race. One of the most promising proposals made along this line is that calling for a new provision in the laws governing urban renewal which would make it impossible for a contractor who refuses applications from Negroes for his apartment buildings and private homes in the suburbs to qualify for the lucrative construction opportunities arising from urban redevelopment programs. In order to get a contract for building in the area covered by urban

renewal, a firm would have to guarantee a policy of open occupancy in all of its other enterprises.[50] Another opening for
the use of economic leverage by the government arises in connection with the placement of large federal facilities: "In lo-
cating government installations there should be a requirement
that housing be as fairly available to employees of the institution
as is employment."[51] The political and business leaders of most
communities would be willing to reconsider their fear of de-
segregated housing if they knew that a government payroll of
several million dollars per year depended upon their willingness
to guarantee equal housing opportunities in their locality!

The fourth possible way of attacking the external roots of
discrimination is nonviolent direct action. Some of the difficulties of protest actions in the field of housing have been
admirably articulated by James Q. Wilson in his article on "The
Strategy of Protest" in the September, 1961, issue of *The Journal
of Conflict Resolution*:

> (1) There is disagreement among influential Negroes as to
> the source of the problem, what ought to be done about it,
> and what can be done under the circumstances. There is con-
> siderable uncertainty as to what Negroes should protest *for*—
> liberalized mortgage requirements, more police protection in
> changing neighborhoods, the ending of restrictive real estate
> practices, legislation barring discrimination in sales and rentals,
> or some combination of all these. . . .
> (2) The targets of protest action have become unclear or
> ambiguous. . . . What is the target for protest aimed at "equal
> opportunity in housing"? One cannot picket, or boycott, or send
> deputations to all the real estate brokers, all the mortage bankers,
> all the neighborhood improvement associations, or all the com-
> munity newspapers. If one selects a single target—one house
> or one block in a certain neighborhood—one may gain con-
> cessions, but these concessions will be limited to the specific
> case and will represent no change in policy. . . .
> (3) Some of the goals now being sought by Negroes are
> least applicable to those groups of Negroes most suited to
> protest action. . . . Even when the goal can be made specific,
> it becomes difficult to mobilize the masses when (a) the end
> sought clearly benefits, at least immediately, only middle- and
> upper-class Negroes and (b) no general, principled rationale
> can be developed which will relate the specific goal to the
> aspirations or needs of the rank-and-file. . . .

(4) Many specific goals toward which action can be directed occur in situations that place a negative value on protest. . . . Inducing whites to accept one Negro family is difficult; inducing them to accept a family which the whites believe was "planted" by the NAACP and is, thus, the vanguard of a host of Negro families is much more difficult. . . .[52]

Despite these difficulties, however, direct action has achieved tangible results in many communities. Concessions "limited to the specific case" are not to be dismissed lightly, as any family in quest of housing will testify. In New York, San Francisco and several other localities, picketing and sit-ins in the office of a realtor or at the site of a housing development have resulted in acquisition of a dwelling by a Negro applicant. In some cases, there is a carry-over value in terms of a changed attitude on the part of the real estate man concerned: Eunice Grier tells the amusing story of a realtor who once sneaked out the back door of a demonstration home in a housing development and climbed over a wall in order to avoid Negro applicants, but who was so struck by the indignity and incongruity of his action that he made up his mind never to resort to such evasion again![53]

In view of the possibility of securing specific gains, and in view of the possibility that more far-reaching changes of attitude and policy may sometimes accompany specific concessions, direct action should not be ruled out as a fruitful tactic in housing. The smallness of return on energy expended in this manner gives force to Wilson's contention that the best approach in several areas characterized by discrimination, particularly housing, is what he calls "secondary strategy," which is an attempt "to create the possibility of meaningful bargaining on a whole range of issues by being able to offer other parties the compensation of ending a protest campaign."[54] The model for this type of action is as follows: Protest organization A campaigns against target B in an effort to obtain goal C. At the same time, bargainers X are dickering with target Y for goal Z. Assuming that there is bargaining linkage between the two targets, and enough irritation on the part of target B to want to put an end to the protest demonstrations against his good name, he might be prevailed upon to use his good offices with target Y to make concessions to bargainers X. In return for the favors received X would agree to persuade protesters A to end their campaign of protest demonstrations. Wilson cites the following example of secondary strategy:

> Obtaining more middle-income public housing units might be the goal, but the the target would be an urban renewal program which would displace Negroes. The campaign against urban renewal would be reduced if the goal [of more public housing units] were granted. The bargaining linkage here might be [with] the Negro association which induces the backer of the urban renewal project to prevail upon the city housing authority to construct the housing project.[55]

The three principal obstacles that must be overcome before this model can be approximated are as follows: (1) There must be sufficient congruence between the goals of the middle and lower classes to make mass support possible, and the goals must be sufficiently specific to interest the masses; (2) The means used in building mass support must not limit unduly the flexibility of the bargainer—for example, if the speeches that rally the masses attribute a too "moral or sacrosanct quality" to the specific goals being sought, the bargainer may fear being called a traitor if he compromises on these goals, and settlement may be impeded; (3) This strategy "places a great premium on coordination among Negro leaders and organizations," and this is "rarely easy to obtain."[56]

As Wilson's model of secondary strategy implies, direct action is likely to be most effective when used in combination with other tactics involving other targets. And this conclusion is simply a reiteration of the same principle at stake in the assertion that any OHC campaign must be accompanied by varied follow-up action: the war cannot be won unless all kinds of troops are attacking with all kinds of appropriate weapons at many places along the front.

Overcoming Inadequacy

The fight against discrimination is only one part of the picture. If the housing problem of Negroes is to be solved, the inadequacy of their present housing conditions as well as the restrictions on their choice of homes must be dealt with. Perhaps the basic need here is for good housing codes, codes that do not permit overcrowding, the existence of hazards to health and safety, or exorbitant rents. This would of course require a more general public acceptance that housing is just as much in the public domain as restaurants are, and that society has just as much right to demand certain minimal standards in housing as it does in restaurants. To attain public acceptance of this principle ought to be a prime goal of anti-discrimination education, for surely the influence of housing conditions upon the health of society is at least as important as the influence of public eating places upon the physical health of diners.

Unfortunately, a housing code is only so good as the enforcement policies that back it up; consequently, citizens groups will have to work for firm enforcement just as diligently as they do for the drafting of good codes. But landlords who make improvements in their property want to raise the rent— or if they can't raise the rent, they don't want to make the improvements. And when poverty-stricken tenants think that a campaign for stricter enforcement of the housing code is going to mean either higher rents or condemnation of the property, they are often persuaded that the evil they know is to be preferred over the unknown evils of having to find another place to live for the little money they can afford to pay. So the tenants are not enthusiastic, oftentimes, about filing complaints of housing code violations, or having them filed by someone else. The answer to this dilemma might be a combination of rent controls and a repossession law which would allow the city to take over operation of property a landlord refused to bring up to standards, to make the needed improvements, and to collect the rents until the improvements had been paid for.[57] Or the problem might be solved by widespread adoption of the precedent established by the New York courts which have ruled that landlords are not entitled to collect rent on substandard apartments.[58] Recent experience in Baltimore proves that judges who really want to see housing codes enforced can do so: landlords adjudged guilty of violations there have been required to begin improvements on the property in a matter of hours.[59]

Another encouraging finding emerges from the experience of Indianapolis, where tenants who initially opposed rehabilitation for fear that it would lead to higher rents later came to feel that the improved standards were worth a reasonable additional charge.[60]

An economic approach to the problem of inadequate housing would involve either the expansion of demand through improvement of employment opportunities for Negroes, or the expansion of supply through publicly or privately financed housing for low-income and middle-income families. Serious attention should be given to Jane Jacob's proposal that subsidies be provided to enable low-income families to stay in neighborhoods which have appreciated in value instead of being forced by higher rents to move away.[61] A side benefit of this proposal would be the preservation (or the creation) of neighborhoods not segregated according to income. The same benefit would result from James Rouse's similar proposal that families in public housing be allowed to stay there even if their income rises above the level set for admittance simply by paying more rent.[62] Decreasing the rapid turnover of tenants and the enforced exodus of families who indicate superior leadership abilities through earning a raise in pay is especially to be desired in low-income public housing projects.

Two other points of particular interest in connection with an economic approach to the problem are loan-blacklisting and the benign quota. Financial institutions make slums—or, to be more precise, they prevent unslumming—by refusing to make loans for rehabilitation in certain areas of most cities.[63] Loosening credit for improvement of residential buildings would go a long way toward improving the lot of Negroes who live in slums, especially if loans can be made available in neighborhoods where the block club approach has created new incentives toward healthier and more attractive homes. As for the benign quota, it may be questioned on several grounds. It raises the theoretical issue of whether or not a quota is by definition a denial of individual opportunity which, regardless of intent, cannot be tolerated in a democratic society. For the pragmatic thinker, this objection is not compelling: if he can be shown that the actual consequences of a quota are on the whole beneficial to society in the long run, he will not boggle at the alleged violation of principle. A more pertinent objection is that the benign quota requires great faith in its long-range good effects, because its immediate effects are so undesirable. It often causes many desperately needed apartments to be left vacant because white tenants for them have not appeared, yet Negroes are not being admitted because of concern over the tipping point. After lengthy reflection on the moral, political and legal aspects of the benign quota, a Connecticut lawyer named Peter Marcuse reached the conclusion that is was a justifiable device if used to promote interracial contact that would eventually lower prejudice and discrimination—but only if the individuals excluded by the benign quota were willing to make the sacrifice of their immediate interests for the sake of the attainment of long-range racial and societal goals! Mr. Marcuse writes:[64]

> The distinction that we are drawing between permissible and impermissible uses of benign quotas is the distinction between the voluntary and involuntary use of such quotas. It may well be that there is a logical inconsistency in saying that a given policy is desirable as substantially advantageous for a large group, although detrimental to a few individuals, as long as none of those individuals objects, but saying that if any one of such individuals should object, the policy becomes undesirable if insisted upon. Nevertheless, this happens to be the result of one of the basic premises on which our constitutional rights are predicated. Such rights, in American jurisprudence, are individual rights and not group rights. These individual rights are held sacred against any government interference, no matter how well motivated it may be, and our courts are protecting them also against more and more forms of private interference.

Having said that, the author adds, "The one argument in this area that is not only irrelevant but even by now harmful, and should be finally rejected for good, is the argument that governmental action should be 'colorblind.' "[65] Given a society in which Negroes are socially defined as "different," it is folly not to acknowledge that existing difference in an effort to alter the unjust conditions resulting from this erroneous definition of the situation. The ideal of color blindness is "a statement of an aspiration, not a fact" in contemporary American society—"and to make the aspiration become fact it must first be recognized that there is still a difference," for "to ignore the existence of inequalities, discrimination and prejudice does not help to erase them."[66]

IMPLICATIONS FOR
CHRISTIAN SOCIAL ACTION

CHAPTER *9* THE TWO GREAT DEVELOPMENTS IN Christian social action in this country during the present century are two movements usually known as the Social Gospel and Christian Realism. The former represented a recognition on the part of the Church of her responsibility to "Christianize the social order": that is, to improve conditions in society as well as to redeem individuals from sin in their personal lives. The latter represented a more temperate assessment of the possibilities and impossibilities of social reform on the basis of second thoughts about the nature of man and the structures of society. The Social Gospel was a mighty surge forward in the Church's pilgrimage toward moral wisdom; Christian realism, although it included highly significant advances in moral wisdom, was even more important as a forward thrust along the path to technical wisdom. Our analysis of the OHC campaign in Newfield offers much food for thought concerning the degree to which the lessons embodied in these two movements have in fact been learned by rank-and-file church members and lower-echelon church leaders.

AWARENESS

The evidence furnished by an analysis of the Newfield OHC campaign is not altogether discouraging, for it suggests a relatively high level of awareness of Christian responsibility in public affairs. If one assumes that support of the covenant was a minimal act of good will which every Christian person should have been willing to take, and if one judges the response of Newfield churchmen according to this absolute standard, then the response must be termed dismal. Some clergymen opposed the OHC, and others were lukewarm (or worse) in their efforts to promote it. Of the more than ten thousand adult church members in the Newfield area less than ten per cent signed the covenant; furthermore, one of the national parishes containing almost one thousand families had no signers whatsoever, and another national parish with well over one thousand families had only three. Only two churches elicited the support of more than ten per cent of their parishioners for the covenant.

In the light of relative standards, however—that is, in comparison with similar programs conducted by church and civic groups in other American cities—the populace of Newfield responded in very respectable numbers. Covenant appeals in Hartford, Connecticut (a city of 187,000) and New Haven, Connecticut (a city of 152,000) produced less than one thousand signatures in each place, and an appeal in Des Moines, Iowa (a city of 209,000) produced only two thousand signatures.[1] Many communities have had less vigorous leadership from their churches, and of course most comparable cities have had no OHC appeal at all. Thus discouragement over the absolute shortcomings of the Newfield covenant campaign should not prevent one's recognizing its relative success and the positive factors contributing to it.

More encouraging still is the extent to which the church people of Newfield acknowledged the inadequacy of housing for Negroes and the reality of discrimination against them. That a majority of even the nonsupporters of the covenant admitted the existence of these problems is a sign of hope. To be sure, the familiar rationalizations of the status quo were sometimes reiterated by clergymen and laymen alike; however, comments of this kind were very infrequent.

These findings are especially interesting when one compares them with figures from other studies. Only a decade or so previously, Kenneth W. Underwood discovered that the Roman Catholic pastors of Paper City* regarded "the following areas

---

*A predominantly Catholic city in New England which is the locale of his celebrated study, *Protestant and Catholic* (Boston: Beacon Press, 1957).

in the public life of the city as presenting no moral issues of concern to the Church:

> housing for low-income people; tax policies and welfare expenditures of the local government; collective bargaining of labor and management in the city; extension of union activity; expansion of political participation in the community; reform or change of the political and governmental structure of the city; [and] economic instability of an inflationary nature in the community.[2]

As one of the priests observed, "We certainly decry poor housing, but housing is a material concern, and the priest's first aim is to remedy things of a moral nature." In the words of two other priests, "Better housing and higher wages are political issues, not moral," and "The Church cannot press for such things as better housing [because] the Church's task is to prepare men for life in the hereafter through living a spiritual, clean life now."[3] The scope of Christian social concern was defined in similarly restricted terms by most of the Protestant ministers of the same city, who tended to "interpret the relation of Christianity and politics in private or personal terms" and "to portray public life in terms of a series of unrelated, unpatterned events, overshadowed by private and family concerns."[4] These tendencies are "most starkly illustrated" in the annual report of a minister who, in summarizing events in the life of his church between 1930 and 1939—a period in which the depression wrought havoc in the community, "devoted only three lines to the economic depression and the experience of unemployment for laymen."[5]

The absence of widespread fears regarding racial intermarriage—or, at any rate, a disinclination to admit such fears—is noteworthy, because one's attitude toward intermarriage is a telling index of the degree to which one truly accepts members of another race as full-fledged human beings. Newfield's record on this point is better than that in many other cities. In suburban New Jersey, thirty-six per cent of a sample of 112 respondents feared that "residential integration would lead inevitably to intermarriage. . . ."[6] In Minneapolis, one-fourth of the whites contacted in an opinion survey expressed fear of intermarriage.[7]

It is a further sign of hope that most of the laymen contacted in this study approved religious sponsorship of the OHC and sermons devoted to the issue. Only a very few respondents "protest[ed] the use of the Church and its worship services for inciting hatred, rabble rousing, and forcing the wilful desires of a few on the many," or conceived of "church on Sunday as a 'Spiritual Bath,'" or professed to "believe ministers should preach the 'Word of God' . . . and not stoop to dabbling in politics." That many respondents regarded their decision to sign the covenant as a fruit of previous Christian conviction rather than a result of any influences brought to bear during the covenant campaign is a welcome indication that many laymen need only to be presented with an opportunity for concrete social action in order to become active participants.

Indeed, Newfield laymen appear to be more liberal on this point than laymen who were asked about the appropriateness of church pronouncements on social issues in two other studies. Lenski found that only forty-six per cent of Catholic laymen and only forty-two per cent of the white Protestant laymen in Detroit thought ministers should take a stand on controversies relating to racial integration.[8] Glock and Ringer, in a survey of opinion among a national sample of Episcopalians, discovered that only about three-fifths were willing to endorse a policy of public stands on political issues by their church.[9]

Most encouraging of all, perhaps, was the presence in Newfield of a small but highly capable and seriously committed group of churchmen who were willing to devote a great deal of their time to the OHC appeal. The two ministers who played leading roles in the venture did so in the knowledge that they were incurring the wrath (and the withdrawal of financial support) of many parishioners. It is surely no accident that the two churches led by these pastors were the ones with the most vigorous social action committees—and also the two churches which were incomparably more successful than any other churches in gaining support for the open housing covenant. It is significant, moreover, that the membership and the leadership of these two committees were composed of different types of persons. One committee functioned largely through the efforts of faculty personnel from the University or other individuals of relatively high educational and occupational status; the other depended on persons of average educational and occupational standing.

But even though the picture of Christian response in Newfield is not entirely dark, it offers abundant evidence that American churchmen have not learned well the lessons of the Social Gospel and Christian Realism. Acknowledgment of the existence of community problems and of the responsibility of the Church regarding these problems is commendable. But little comfort can be derived from mere acknowledgment of a reality which can no longer be ignored so long as understanding of the dimensions and the urgency of the problem remains minimal, and appreciation of the scope of remedial action required remains dim. The poverty of response beyond the level of acknowledgment of social ills and Christian responsibility in principle displayed in Newfield is unfortunately typical of a national tendency. A recent nationwide survey of Methodists showed, for example, that more than ninety per cent of the members of this denomination consider social change a key responsibility of the Church, and forty-six per cent of the respondents contacted in this survey considered social change at least as important as, or more important than, the salvation of individuals[10]—yet the Methodist Church has been spectacularly dilatory in eliminating segregation and discrimination in its own organizational structure and in community life in those areas of the country where it is numerically strongest.

The insensitivity apparent here is a result of both deficient technical wisdom and deficient moral wisdom. The most basic defect in technical wisdom is plain lack of information and the clear thinking that information nourishes. Thirty-five years ago, the authors of *Middletown,* a study of a Midwestern city of about the same size as Newfield, reported that the six clergymen of the community who were interviewed had very little time for reading:

> The reading of these six men is all done "on the run." "My only chance is late at night before I drop off asleep," said one of the most energetic of the six. "It's not really reading, I'm

too tired, and then, too, I read *for* sermon material rather than giving myself up to what the author has to say."[11]

The study suggested, furthermore, that parishioners did not recognize the importance of continual replenishment of the mind to a minister. One pastor complained that "it may be another generation or so before the general level [of education] will be high enough so that people will expect a minister to have time and energy for study if he is to be worth shucks as a minister."[12]

A generation has passed, but the present study still leaves room for doubt concerning the degree to which the importance of serious reading to clergymen or laymen is recognized. One of the most striking findings of the study is that the sources of information relied on by the Newfield clergymen for their knowledge of an area of social concern as important as race relations were so limited. Perhaps we judge these busy pastors in the light of unrealistic expectations: if a minister or priest reads the daily newspaper, one or two religious journals, and a popular news magazine, this is possibly all that can be expected of him. There are occasional articles of high quality in denominational magazines and secular periodicals such as *Life*, *Time* and *Look*. But the clergyman who does not go beyond the material which is made available to him in these sources is not likely to be equipped with a very high degree of sophistication concerning the social problems that demand intelligent comment from him. That only two clergy respondents reported even cursory familiarity with any of the professional journals in the social sciences is disappointing; that none reported regular reading of the public affairs periodicals, through which specialized knowledge filters down to influentials at the community level, is alarming. Theories concerning prejudice and discrimination, and strategies for dealing with them, have undergone significant modifications during recent years, and it is of the utmost importance that clergymen should be aware of them. And if the clergymen of Newfield do not read professional journals and the best public affairs periodicals, or even the best denominational publications on matters pertaining to social ethics, it it not very likely that many of their parishioners have a better record on this important point. Evidence from other records of the reading habits of Americans indicates that the people of Newfield are not atypical in their neglect of the important sources of technical wisdom. Some sample circulation figures speak for themselves. According to N. W. Ayer and Sons' *Directory of Newspapers and Periodicals for 1962*, more than 13,000,000 families subscribe to *Readers' Digest* and almost 7,000,000 subscribers are reached by *Life* and *Look*. By contrast, *The Reporter* has only 170,156 subscribers; *Foreign Affairs*, 45,503; and *The New Republic*, 40,278.

A second example of a lack of technical wisdom is at the same time a result of the first. It is a failure to realize clearly that the primary point of attack in the struggle to overcome racial injustice is prejudiced behavior rather than prejudice. Many comments made by clergymen in response to a variety of questions reflected the common assumption that attitudes must be changed before behavior can be altered. Some pastors acquiesced to the myth of Social Darwinism that moral behavior in society cannot be legislated against prevailing folkways and hostile citizens, or they warned that more time was needed to prepare people for integration, or they discounted any method of attack so artificial as the open housing covenant, because this approach did not "get to the heart of the problem," or because it involved "pressure from the outside." To say that segregation (unjustified denial of one's right to *belong*) and discrimination (unjustified denial of one's right to *have*) should be the primary points of attack is not to deny the seriousness of stereotyping (unjustified denial of one's right to *be*).[13] It is simply to say that assigning priority to an attack on prejudice rather than prejudiced behavior is putting the cart before the horse. It is to say that attitudes are more likely to change along with changing behavioral patterns than behavior is to be transformed by attitudes transformed in isolation from behavior in particular social contexts (if indeed that feat can be accomplished at all on a broad scale), and that behavior is more accessible to direct attack—through law, aroused public opinion, or economic pressure—than attitudes are.

The relationship between technical and moral wisdom is very close at this point. Faulty moral wisdom is displayed in the tendency of most Newfield clergymen to regard love rather than justice as the relevant ideal for social ethics. Now, it is certainly true that a minister would be unfaithful to his calling if he neglected his responsibility to promote love in the hearts of men, and it is true that the parishioners of his church are his special responsibility in this regard. But in the special branch of the Christian life known as social ethics, and in the special branch of Christian discipleship known as social action, the primary goal is the promotion of justice in the affairs of men. The open housing covenant hopefully did serve as the occasion for many churchgoers to reappraise their attitude toward Negroes and to repent for the prejudice in their hearts—but the fundamental purpose of it was to alter the behavior of a substantial number of people in the community by demonstrating that discrimination in housing was unfashionable, unnecessary, and wrong. The primary aim of the covenant appeal was frustrated, therefore, in so far as the confrontation of the Christian people of the community with the covenant resulted only in repentance and reappraisal of attitudes but not in changed behavior toward Negro renters, buyers, and neighbors. The interviews with the clergymen give good reasons for believing that they did not clearly realize that this was the case. The comments of several ministers reveal a kind of theological romanticism which takes it too much for granted that the preaching of justification by faith, or devotion to the *esse* of the concerns of the Church, will automatically lead to right action. The comments of several other ministers exhibit a naive assumption that knowledge of the housing problem through newspaper accounts of it, or reflections upon the principles of democracy and wholesome community life, will automatically lead to nondiscriminatory behavior in regard to Negroes.

It is difficult to avoid the conclusion that there was not enough "goal-direction" in the thinking of Newfield clergymen: they were so preoccupied with the ideal of social reform as inwardly moral (that is, voluntary) that they did not give sufficient attention to the moral pressure which needed to be brought to bear on their people in order that the desired reform might take place. They were so obsessed with the importance of leaving the decision about signing the covenant up to each individual that they did not "speak with authority" in urging their people to sign the covenant. In sum, by failing to plan an intensive follow-up program to drive home the message made in an initial announcement or pulpit presentation of the covenant—by failing to set up discussion groups which could probe the fears and illuminate the values of parishioners, and by failing to engage influential persons in dialogue on the issue —most clergymen left some doubt as to whether or not they "meant business" in supporting the covenant.

Signs of a lack of goal-direction were also evident in many remarks concerning race relations or the relationship between faith and action. The most striking illustration of this tendency was the fact that only two clergymen evaluated freedom rides on the basis of desirable goals achieved in comparison with undesirable effects created. Instead, most respondents evaluated freedom rides in terms of the motivation of the participants or the antagonism between Negroes and whites in the South that were brought to light by the rides. But an intelligent assessment of the merits of the freedom rides must begin with the recognition that they were instrumental in bringing about an order from the Interstate Commerce Commission barring all segregation in public facilities connected with interstate transportation.* If it can be shown that negative results stemming from the rides outweigh the vast implications for good of the ICC ruling, then the freedom rides can be judged wrong, because the point would then be established that the goal accomplished was not worth the price paid. The same could be

---

*At a meeting of the University Study Committee on January 22, 1962, Martin Luther King drew a causal link between the rides and the ICC ruling. A reliable informant who has been in frequent contact with officials of the United State Justice Department also declared that one of these officials told him the ruling would never have come about but for the freedom rides.

said of the process of evaluating any kind of social action: if the good of one's neighbors is the goal of ethical activity, then the fundamental criterion for evaluating concrete options should be the probability of increasing the welfare of one's neighbors (without canceling out the achievement of this goal by creating too many other results which are bad for the same or other neighbors). The criterion is in any case not the degree of purity of the moral agent's motivation. Other manifestations of a lack of goal-directedness are present in the disapproval of "outside agitators" voiced by several clergymen, and in the answers to the direct question regarding the importance of purity of motivation given by some men.

Another manifestation of deficient moral wisdom is the failure of so many Newfield churchmen to appreciate the urgency of the housing problem for Negroes. Included in this category are not only the laymen who refused to support the OHC and the clergymen who flatly rejected participation in the covenant appeal but also those who paid lip service to the appropriateness of the OHC but neglected to support it actively. Also implied is an indictment of the majority of the remaining clergymen who did such a poor job of presenting the covenant that they were actually doing little more than going through the motions. There is a curious and disquieting discrepancy between the unanimous affirmation by Newfield clergymen of the right, even the obligation of the Church to take public stands on important social issues, and the less than vigorous effort on behalf of the open housing covenant which was all that was forthcoming from most of them. To be sure, this was not a case of Christians in racial crisis—the housing problem in Newfield was not of the same magnitude as the school desegregation problem in Little Rock. But for this very reason the rather lukewarm response of most Newfield clergymen is all the more disturbing: most community problems, and most programs of social action designed to ameliorate them, are ambiguous; they can be shunted aside by rationalizations based on the fact that no compelling crisis exists. If the typical reaction of Christians in racial normalcy is a half-hearted gesture in the direction of "good will" rather than an aggressive attack on an unjust status quo, that is a sad commentary on the vitality of the Church's prophetic witness in the world.

This criticism of the moral insensitivity of many Newfield clergymen touches upon another aspect of their definition of the situation confronting them which reveals a lack of moral wisdom. Few pastors demonstrated a lively awareness of the seriousness of the housing problem *for the Church*. The integrity of the Christian Church is at stake every time it is confronted with an important social problem demanding ameliorative action, for every such challenge to which the Christian community fails to respond is an indication that the Christian gospel has not been comprehended in its fullness. Despite the admirable lack of compartmentalization that characterized their understanding of the relationship between Christian faith and social action, most of the Newfield pastors appeared to view action concerning the housing problem as an optional matter. They seemed to view it as a regrettable sore on the skin of the body politic, but they did not communicate to the interviewer a sense of their awareness that this sore was both a source and a symptom of infection in the Body of Christ.

In defense of these pastors it might be said that nonparticipation in the open housing covenant program does not necessarily indicate hardness of heart toward Negroes or dullness of spirit in regard to the Church's mission in society. Nonparticipation might simply be the result of a calculated decision that in one's fulfillment of his vocation as a pastor other items of concern were more important. That is why the question of criteria for making ethical decisions is of such significance. The fact that the very question about criteria was puzzling to several respondents and the fact that it received a very inarticulate reply from the majority of them suggest neglect of one of the most important areas of ethical reflection. As for some of the criteria that were stressed—immediacy, subjective interest, and balance—they reveal an understanding of the Christian's responsibility in society which is open to serious question.

Consider the criterion of immediacy. It is a valid criterion in the sense that it warns one against becoming so devoted to abstract principles or cold-blooded calculation that the faces of the individual neighbors whom one wishes to love are lost sight of. But it is a faulty criterion in so far as it expresses a pietistic, paternalistic, or "privatized" notion of Christian social responsibility. It is true, as one of the ministers said in an interview, that the Christian is a Samaritan who can never be callous about the man set upon by thieves, who bleeds in a ditch by the side of the road. But it is likewise true, as Martin Luther King has observed, that the most intelligent thing to do in a situation where individuals are constantly being attacked "on the road to Jericho" is to establish a "Jericho Road Improvement Association" to see to it that police protection is provided on the road at all times.[14] It is better, in other words, to prevent evil by collective action than it is to bind up wounds individually after evil has been allowed to occur. There is a grave risk of using limited resources inefficiently and fruitlessly if the criterion of immediacy is not subordinated to an analytical overview which identifies the most important issues and determines the division of responsibility which is most rational for a group of men with varied talents and particular callings.

Another criterion frequently cited by Newfield clergymen was that of "subjective interest." To state the criterion in these terms is to obscure and cheapen what ought to be a very important criterion for the Christian; namely, the criterion of one's own vocation. But the concept of the Christian's vocation in society is objective: it is defined in terms of the abilities which God has given a man plus the needs of the society in which God has placed him. Thus, to say that "what appeals to you," or "what you are interested in," is a criterion for responsible decisions regarding participation in social action is at the very least misleading, and it may be downright irresponsible if "appeals to" and "interested in" are defined by subjective whim rather than by an objective appraisal of talents and inadequacies in a man.

A deficiency in both technical and moral wisdom is exemplified in the individualism that characterizes much that was said and done by the clergymen of Newfield. This individualism is apparent to some extent in the premium placed upon changing prejudiced ideas in the minds of individuals; it is even more apparent in the methods used by clergymen to present the open housing covenant to their parishioners. In the first place, the approach used by almost all of the Newfield clergymen was marked by a striking absence of references to denominational pronouncements favoring desegregation in general and integrated housing in particular. The covenant was presented to many laymen of the city, including Roman Catholics, as a purely local matter and as a purely individual decision, rather than as an expression of a moral witness on a significant public issue which had been endorsed in principle by official bodies or authorities in every denomination. Thus the moral authority of the particular community of faith to which churchgoers supposedly had a loyalty was not brought to bear. In the second place, very little in the way of a coordinated program for making the covenant campaign as effective as possible was worked out among the clergymen involved, either among the different faiths sponsoring the campaign or among pastors of the same faith. There may have been valid reasons for this, but many drawbacks are also obvious: for example, the lack of a coordinated program meant that nonchurchgoers of Newfield were not likely to have been presented with an opportunity to sign the covenant.[15] Even within Protestant parishes, very few ministers reported consulting with congregational leaders about the manner in which the covenant could be most effectively explained to their people. Finally, the important task of persuading individuals to take a more liberal point of view was entrusted to exhortation or exposition of facts through a lecture technique that did not encourage the group catharsis or group learning process which many experts deem so essential to education in new attitudes and values.[16] Nor was there any evidence that the clergymen appreciated the enormous importance of contact between racially different persons of equal status in reducing intergroup tensions and stereotyped thinking about minorities.

The hardness of heart and the individualism of Newfield Christians lend some credence to the theory of certain social analysts concerning the privatization of religion in present-day

America. According to Gibson Winter, "religious faith and practice have become a private sphere of American life—a sphere preoccupied with the emotional balance of the membership, the nurture of children, and the preservation of a harmonious residential milieu."[17] Church membership having become primarily a means of securing some sense of "belonging" in a highly mobile society where one family in five moves each year (and where many religiously affiliated people in metropolitan areas move far more frequently), and interest in religious faith having become primarily a means of obtaining self-confidence through "the power of positive thinking" and the learning of "techniques of spiritual mastery," social irresponsibility on the part of such churchgoers is inevitable. In these circumstances, religion has become what Peter Berger declares it to be in contemporary America—an instrument of symbolic integration which ratifies the legitimacy of one's social roles and satisfies one's thirst for reassurance that he lives in "an O.K. world." Then Berger's charge approaches the truth: the social function of religious institutions is precisely their irrelevancy in regard to the significant public issues of the day.[18]

Exaggerated deference to the principle of individualism is a trait deeply rooted in the American character and in American church life. The emphasis upon individual decision regarding the OHC in its presentation by so many Newfield ministers echoes the sentiments expressed by the typical Protestants of Paper City, who believe that "the sum of Christian ethics is that each man respect his own conscience" and that one should "make his moral decisions by 'thinking over what the minister says in church, praying, and [concluding that] what I receive is final for me.'"[19] The absence of shared convictions and cooperation among the clergymen of Newfield repeats the pattern discerned in Paper City, where "each minister pursues highly individual interests of his own . . . or devotes his time entirely to the operation of the traditional services of his church":

> The highest level of co-ordinated action achieved by the [ministerial association of Paper City] has been to develop a policy that individual ministers will not make controversial public

statements on social or religious issues separately, but will make them all together. Such statements have been made only on a few social issues—gambling and transportation of parochial students in public buses. The co-ordination ended when effective opposition developed to statements.[20]

EFFECTIVENESS

The Newfield story indicates that the lessons regarding effectiveness in social action strategy to be learned from Christian Realism have been apprehended even less surely than those regarding awareness of the Church's responsibility. It is true that some churchmen of the city worked for passage of a stronger civil rights law when it was being considered by the state legislature, and a few churchmen were active in publicizing the law, encouraging Negroes to make use of it, and cooperating with those who did so. Several Protestant leaders showed admirable shrewdness in dealing with newspapermen and the mayor. But many of the worst shortcomings of Newfield churchmen as strategists and tacticians of social action are also apparent in churches throughout the country.

Even when the degree of privatization is insufficient to result in social irresponsibility, individualism is one of the prime causes of the effectiveness of Christian social action. This ineffectiveness has two main ingredients: "pseudo-transformationism"[21] (the notion that the changed hearts of individuals must inevitably and automatically lead to a society in which evil has vanished) and a virtual phobia against the use of power in dealing with people. According to Will Herberg, Protestantism has never forgotten a principle assumed in the days of the frontier, namely, that "social justice would naturally follow . . . individualistic piety, in which right living by the individual was stressed."[22] In the belief that a truly moral man would make all of his decisions and take action in a manner transcending the pressures and conflicts that plague ordinary men, pietists hoped that society would be saved if enough individuals were saved. This confidence that "personal conviction and purity of motive can overcome limits imposed by group interests and institutional structures"[23] had clear implications for the political realm. The Christian voter's attention should be centered, "not upon the consequences of public policies and upon those who support or oppose those policies, but upon the estimation of the relative personal piety of the candidates":

> The "good" and the "evil" men are known by their personal virtues and vices—virtues such as church participation, regard for family, honesty; vices such as irreligion, sensuality, alcoholic intemperance, dishonesty, profligate expenditure of public funds for personal gain. These corruptions require personal salvation, not "political solutions."[24]

It is this kind of mentality, strongest among Protestant sectarians, perhaps, but not confined to their circles, which lead to "uneasiness about collective action and mass movements, and a tendency to avoid involvement in political issues that are interpreted by politicians in such terms."[25] Thus many of the Christian people of Newfield did not appreciate the necessary role of militant civil rights organizations and direct action. Reflected in many of the comments recorded on questionnaires from laymen and in interviews with ministers was the assumption that normalcy in progress toward racial justice consists of an inching gradualism that never moves farther or more rapidly than the voluntary consent of the majority group allows. Expressions such as "This thing can't be done overnight" or "It's going to take a long, long time" were subtly transmuted from realistic assertions of a distasteful truth about the pace of social change into arguments against the use of any method which might arouse antagonism among substantial numbers of respectable citizens. Many nonsupporters of the OHC resorted to familiar rationalizations about the inferiority of Negroes or the need for long-suffering patience:

> The Negro in Newfield has every opportunity to prove himself. Ninety per cent of the Negroes in Newfield are irresponsable [sic].

> It [difficulty in securing housing] is not a question of color but a question of irresponsibility.

> I feel that the Negro as a race must make a much greater effort to prove that he is willing to accept a responsible place in society than he has to date. Those individuals that are re-

sponsible persons usually find suitable housing, even though the sledding is tough. The balance are irresponsible; they are looking for the free ride, the handout.

Some people are always looking for outside help but do nothing for ther selves [sic]. People nowadays [sic] are leaning on the goverment [sic] for just about everything. I think negro [sic] problem must be done little by little.

In Newfield the law-abiding, self-respecting, ambitious Negro is few and far between. I don't believe the majority are interested in integration. We're putting the cart before the horse. The Negro *must be reached first* [Italics in the original].

Some [Negroes live in housing that is inadequate], but the majority are living as they like to.

The NAACP, although it is approved as a necessary "extreme," comes to be regarded as a radical organization. One finds it easy to be suspicious of the ideological allegiance of protest groups such as the NAACP or CORE. Civil rights legislation may be frowned upon on the theory that morality cannot be legislated—or even if such legislation is approved, approval is given with the idea that its function is purely symbolic, and vigorous enforcement of the legislation, or social action based upon it, is regarded as "pushing too hard." Inordinate signifi-cance is attached to the antagonisms aroused by direct non-violent action, and insufficient attention is directed to the hitherto hidden antagonism of which such action is the expres-sion (and to the justification for the latter kind of antagonism). In short, the burden of proof comes always to be laid upon aggressive tactics and the impatient mentality—and pessimism about vigorous attacks upon the status quo becomes a self-fulfilling prophecy because it inhibits resolve and action. This syndrome contributes to and is frequently reinforced by bound-less faith in the power of education, or simply the passage of time, to effect both improved attitudes and improved behavior.

Another sign of lack of sophistication regarding strategy is the lack of follow-up action after the OHC campaign. On two different occasions an outside speaker attempted to make it clear to a gathering of Protestant leaders that the covenant appeal could not be maximally effective if it were not a part

of a continuing program designed to combat discrimination.[26]
Despite these warnings that a change in the community's climate
of opinion—which the open housing covenant was supposed
to promote—would probably be transitory unless accompanied
by changed structures of community interaction, the covenant
seems to have been looked upon by many clergymen as a
"project" that could be quickly carried out and quickly forgotten. The fact that many congregations never heard about
the covenant except at one service or in one parish publication
(or in pulpit announcements and bulletin notices covering a
period of only three or four weeks) is a typical illustration
of the tendency of Protestants "to conduct spontaneous, spasmodic 'one shot' crusades on a variety of unrelated issues."[27]

It appears that the attitude toward political power held by
Protestant clergymen in Paper City is still all too prevalent.
They were "anxious to see good done in politics," but they
lacked "concrete knowledge of the relevant alternatives of action available to them."[28] They were "eager to counsel laymen
on religious and ethical problems in politics," but only rarely
did they know "the party affiliation of the leading laymen or
the extent of their political activity."[29] Even when they tried
to accomplish something requiring power, they were inept:

> When the moral stand taken by the Protestant clergy called
> for a fight, the ministers, with few exceptions, knew little about
> the methods of political influence available to them. They wished
> to operate only in their traditional role as preachers, with
> statements to the public.[30]

Their action in regard to public issues was limited to "frenzied
crusades to remove some social problem by a 'one shot' solution," and they themselves were reduced to nothing more than
"cheerleaders in the great game of politics, encouraging men
to fight for such general and universal goals as brotherhood
and justice."[31] Small wonder that one of these ministers, re-
coiling from the frustration of an unsuccessful attempt to exert
political influence in the community, concluded that "I and
other clergymen ought to concentrate in the future upon personal counseling."[32]

Even Church social action agencies on the national level continue to operate in terms of a model of the political process which is highly unrealistic. William J. Cook, Field Director for the Council on Religion and International Affairs, presents the following caricature of the model inferred from the practices of Church agencies:

> (1) There is a mass public which, properly "educated" and organized by the agencies, can make its voice heard in Washington. Then, evil policies will be abandoned and Christian policies pursued. The program implication is that more effort, more speeches to more people about a Christian position on issues in international affairs will turn the trick.
>
> (2) The second part of this two-part model concerns Washington. In Washington are the levers of power. The levers are controlled by men who are either evil or ignorant of the moral nature of their policies. If the evil ones could be removed, and by lobbying the ignorant moved, then Christian policies will be pursued.[33]

Mr. Cook arrives at this definition of the model used by Church groups by reflecting on the assumptions underlying the three types of program activity given highest priority by these agencies: "(1) resolution-producing and accompanying 'educational activities' directed at church and public audiences; (2) subtle electioneering through publishing voting records . . . ; and (3) lobbying and testifying before Congressional committees. . . ." He notes that "a common element in all of these agency programs is the rigidity induced by a 'position of the Church' fixation," which "does not permit necessary flexibility for developing either legislation or broad policy in a pluralistic society."[34]

It appears, then, that the critique of Social Gospel naïveté voiced by the leading prophet of Christian Realism thirty years ago still needs to be uttered. To an astonishing degree it is still true that "the unvarying refrain of the liberal Church in its treatment of politics is that love and cooperation are superior to conflict and coercion, and that therefore they must and will be established." The proclamation of this ideal is still "regarded as a sufficient guarantee of its ultimate realization." Christianity is still, for too many pastors, "interpreted as the preaching of a moral ideal, which men do not follow, but which they ought to," and the counsel of these pastors is still that "the Church must continue to hope for something that has never happened."[35] There is still too little appreciation of the need for "a pragmatic ethic in which power and self-interest are used, beguiled, harnessed and deflected for the ultimate end of establishing the highest and most inclusive possible community of justice and order."[36] Far too few Christians are yet willing to admit that "the terrible Jesuitical maxim which all good people must abhor"—that the end justifies the means—is a principle in which "all good people are involved,"[37] or that "if good men wish to help create a better world, they [must] support methods they themselves might not, as good men, otherwise choose."[38]

One final example of the ineffectiveness of most Christian social action is to be found in the techniques of communication employed by many Newfield clergymen. Those who laid great stress upon the individual parishioner's right to decide for himself whether or not to support the covenant, and those who based their approval of the OHC on vague appeals to abstract principles, were duplicating the errors described by Campbell and Pettigrew in their study of the ministers of Little Rock during the school desegregation crisis there. A preacher is practicing evasion through the "every-man-a-priest" technique when he prefaces the substantive remarks of his sermon with a statement of this kind:

> "I am going to state my own opinions. We believe in freedom of opinion in our church, and you, also possessing free access to knowledge of God's will, may hold a different opinion, which I assure you I shall respect." Each listener is encouraged to seek his own answer, and the minister does not argue that his answers are the right ones. [39]

As the authors of *Christians in Racial Crisis* observe, this posture is doubtless welcomed by many listeners, "since there is no condemnation of the opposing views which the listener holds," and since the clergyman has undercut his preaching by "removing any special moral force from what he says."[40] In the "deeper issues" approach, the minister attacks sin in general without attacking specific sins in the lives of his parishioners and calling upon them to change their ways of living in this or that particular area of life. So long as a pastor merely "states the principle, or at most poses the question, but does not provide the answer," parishioners can well afford to affirm the freedom of the pulpit.[41] Another faulty technique of communication utilized by a few Newfield ministers is what Schneider and Dornbusch, in their superb study of religious best-sellers, *Popular Religion,* call "counter-suggestion cues."[42] This term refers to a mode of expression which arouses in the listener a sentiment opposite to the meaning conveyed by the literal content of what is said. If, for example, one speaks of God as a "heavenly dynamo" that one should "plug into" in order to get spiritual power, the vulgar metaphor destroys an attitude of reverence for the holy God of righteousness. Similarly, the argument that support of the OHC is dictated by "community pride" arouses sentiments that militate against the aims of the covenant: since one normally thinks of his "community" in terms that are defined by common class values and customs, and since "pride" (or "self-respect") is usually gauged by allegiance to these values, acceptance of Negro neighbors will be an unattractive prospect if the operational values and customs of one's residential community are thought to be hostile to Negroes.

Ineffective communication is a particularly striking illustration of the intimate relationship between technical and moral wisdom. Inability to communicate may be due to lack of knowledge or insufficiently developed skills, but these in turn may be the result of a half-hearted desire to communicate—or the failure may in fact be the result of great shrewdness (conscious or unconscious) in the art of delivering one message ostensibly while making sure that a message less offensive to the audience can easily be read between the lines. There is probably an element of bad faith* as well as ignorance and ineptitude in most sermons, and both moral and technical deficiencies are an expression, as well as a reinforcement, of each other. As

---

*For an explanation of this term, see footnote 18 for this chapter, p. 245.

Peter Berger observes, preachers find it difficult to admit openly that most sermons do not influence many parishioners in a significant way and they bolster their self-esteem by declaring the preaching role more important than any other ministerial role.[43] In moments of candid self-appraisal they admit to themselves, however, that few lives are radically altered by their sermons. So they find it easier to rationalize inadequate reading and sloppy sermon preparation, thus contributing to the pulpit ineffectiveness they fear. The same could be said for pseudo-transformationism, the phobia about power, and the penchant for futile "one shot" crusades: all of these characteristics may be the result of either naïveté or bad faith, and in most cases are to some extent a product of both.

INTROVERSION IN THE ORGANIZATION CHURCH

Evaluation of the awareness and effectiveness of the Christian social action carried out in Newfield must focus, finally, on the local parish church as the unit of analysis. Numerous critics of the local church are so convinced of its worthlessness that they would cheerfully see it supplanted by new institutional forms.[44] Others, though acknowledging the symptoms of desuetude, are persuaded that signs of renewal are promising enough to warrant continued investment of resources in the parish form of organization.[45] The remainder of this chapter is devoted to a discussion of some of the shortcomings of the local church revealed in Newfield and other places, and to some recommendations as to how its social action may be invigorated.

The political ineffectiveness that stems from individualistic pietism is related to and expressed in the pattern of parish life typical in many local churches throughout the United States. One of the features of what Gibson Winter calls the "introversion" of the "organization church" is its distorted view of itself and its own potentialities. Because the moral influence of religion is seldom felt in the political realm as church officials would like to see it felt, they are in a position of being able to attribute the continuing existence of evil to the fact that

"Christianity has never been tried." They are able, furthermore, to make the most absurd claims regarding the Church's monopoly on true worldly wisdom. The *Catholic Mirror* of Paper City informed its readers just after World War II that "every wholesome pronouncement on faith, morals, on Christian education, on the family, on social reconstruction during the last decade has come from her [the Church]."[46] In the midst of the depression, Protestant ministers in the same city announced that no secular social program—communism, fascism, socialism, or capitalism—could contribute to the fashioning of a good society, and that is was "to Christianity and to it alone we must look to lead us out of the dilemma" confronting the nation.[47] This exaggerated confidence in the all-sufficiency of right faith and right intention was accompanied by "a withdrawal from the concrete, specialized activities of society as too 'temporal' or 'technical' to be interpreted by moral and religious insight," and "this led to ministerial concentration upon more narrowly defined 'church issues.'"[48] Flashes of this complacent narrowmindedness were evident in comments of Newfield clergymen to the effect that truly important concerns always find a place in the work of the Church, or that the united prayers of the faithful are bound to bring beneficial results, or that ethical endeavor should simply be allowed to "grow" out of faith instead of being "promoted."

The dominant characteristic of the introverted organization church is its concentration on institutional rather than ultimate ends. The functioning of the machinery of the church—the denomination or the local parish—is valued more highly than the accomplishment of the ends for which the institution supposedly exists. The consequences of this value preference are evident in the way different churches relate to each other as well as in the way the life of each parish is carried out.

The "covert competition" and "antagonistic cooperation" now prevalent in American life are also typically present in relationships existing between faiths, denominations and local congregations.[49] The veiled hostility, the lack of communication, and the petty rivalries apparent in Newfield have been noted by observers of church life in other communities, too. Ecumen-

icity is a golden word among many church leaders, both
Protestant and Catholic, nowadays, and many currents, both
secular and religious, are flowing in the direction of church
unity. It is still true, nevertheless, that the clergymen and laymen of even those denominations which comprise "common-
core Protestantism" think of the church primarily in terms of
their own parish and its pressing concerns:

> The usual church member experiences no organizational life
> beyond the local church. He is aware of no over-all Protestant
> programs for influencing or interpreting American culture in
> which his church or denomination is to take part. He reads
> none of the literature produced by the top-level interdenom-
> inational agencies expressing an emerging "open-ended" con-
> sensus among Protestant leaders on the relation of theology
> to various areas of society or vocational groupings. And this
> literature is only occasionally processed and meagerly summa-
> rized for lay reading in the denominational literature most
> widely circulated in the churches and through which the ecu-
> menical agencies have their chief access to local congregations.[50]

If the upstate New York village described in Vidich and Bensman's penetrating study of *Small Town in Mass Society* is typical, a silent war for members and influence goes on behind the
façade of interdenominational agreement in most similar communities throughout the nation.[51] The battle for land in "high
potential areas" in the suburbs is a major factor in the abandonment of the inner city by Protestantism,[52] and young men
in a hurry to mount the ladder of denominational prestige are
not unaware that all other ministers in their community, and
all other ministers of their denomination in a geographical
area, must be looked upon as competitors and treated as rivals.

Within each parish, the organization church has "substituted
survival for ministry."[53] The clearest illustration of this in Newfield was the discrepancy between the effort expended on the
"every member canvass" for funds and the gesture toward the
OHC in most churches. Members are typically swept up in a
round of ceaseless activities designed to strengthen the institution by increasing the size of the membership and the loyalty
of members to the local church. Increased loyalty on the part
of the members derives, says Gibson Winter, from two latent

functions of the round of activities in which they are immersed: they are blessed with a glow of "belongingness" because of their participation in group activities, and with a feeling that their sins have been atoned for by the penance of drudgery![54] (Winter is careful to note that it is not activism *per se*, so often attacked by intellectual critics of American life, to which he objects; it is the content of the activities which renders them relatively useless from the standpoint of the ultimate ends of the Church.)[55] The primacy of institutional ends is also evident in the management of parish affairs by the laymen charged with this responsibility:

> Leaders of Protestant congregations who labored to preserve public worship and Christian instruction defined faith as right disposition, devout individual attitudes, and conventional moral observation; in their view social, political and economic structures would be altered only when men had achieved the proper disposition. Churches were voluntary associations in which men and women gathered for the inculcation of the proper dispositions. . . . The leaders of these voluntary associations exercised responsibility by protecting the property and financial interests of the religious group so that the preaching and teaching might continue. In their terms, if a neighborhood became undesirable, it would be irresponsible to stay there; if admission of Negroes threatened to disrupt the voluntary fellowship, then better that a few should suffer than all be destroyed.

> The exodus [of the Protestant churches from cities into their "suburban captivity"] was an inevitable consequence of this view of Christian faith and church ministry—a view which conceived the church as a private institution devoted to the ennoblement of private life and to the amelioration of the ills of the society through individuals.[56]

A preference for institutional rather than ultimate ends is manifested, too, in the program planning of many churches. The compulsion to keep the church calendar always chock full of a variety of events designed to appeal to all kinds of folks for all kinds of reasons comes to exercise a kind of tyranny over parish leaders. The annual report of congregational activities must demonstrate that parishioners have had an opportunity to "cover" every important interest during the course of the year. Thus a "balanced program" comes to seem more important than a persistent attack on one important problem. The criterion of balance has it merits, of course—an obsession with any one social need to the exclusion of all others would be stupid if practiced on a community level. But the question is whether or not the requirements of "balance" have not become so extreme that anything more than a one shot flirtation with any one item of social reform is condemned as extremism. The policy of tipping one's hat to every conceivable interest of the membership or every social issue is self-defeating—yet many comparatively worthless parish activities or irrelevant social action ventures have been established by force of habit as one of the things that simply must be done at a given time each year. The practice of having a yearly observance of "Race Relations Sunday" is frequently cited as an example of just this sort of mandatory yet meaningless flourish. In Newfield, the October 22 presentation of the OHC was for many churches just such an instance of a ritual occasion, accompanied by very little follow-up action and having very little effect.

This critique of balance as a helpful criterion may also be related to the criticism of excessive individualism voiced above, and both may be interpreted in the context of the need for a richer understanding of the doctrine of vocation on the part of the ministers of Newfield. If they had had a lively sense of the normative primacy of ultimate over institutional ends and, consequently, of the importance of teamwork among themselves and among their churches, they might have been less wedded to the notion of balance in the total program of individual churches and individual ministers. Perhaps the single most plausible explanation of the failure of Newfield clergymen to support the OHC is to be found in their tendency to put the concerns of their own congregation above all other considerations. In the case of the Roman Catholic priests there were, of course, specific institutional reasons for lack of cooperation: their exclusion from the initial planning stages of the OHC campaign was one, but even more important was the conflict with their plans for parochial school construction. To press the OHC appeal vigorously in a locality where so many landlords and realtors affected by it were Roman Catholic parishioners would have been to jeopardize the building of the school—for more than ninety per cent of the money raised for this purpose had been merely pledged, not yet donated, by the same parishioners who might become quite disgruntled at being urged seriously to participate in what many Catholics viewed as a Protestant-initiated "do good" scheme inimical to their economic and ethnic interests. Aside from the Protestant pastors who plainly opposed the OHC for theological or strategic reasons, the inertia, the half-heartedness, and the ineffectiveness displayed by many clergymen seem to have been a function of low priority assigned to a "program" which was peripheral to the interests of their congregations. In the weight-shifting, chair-squirming uneasiness displayed by many ministers as they discussed the OHC, the interviewer could not help sensing a strong feeling of ambivalence. The respondent's attitude on most aspects of race relations and on the relationship between Christian faith and social action prompted him to feel that the covenant deserved his backing, and the reference group pressures emanating from denominational superiors and professional colleagues dictated at least *pro forma* cooperation with the covenant campaign. But as Ted Underwood perceived*— and even though one may disagree with his decision to ignore the OHC, one must give him credit for seeing a great weakness in its inception—the covenant campaign was, in the eyes of many ministers, just "a program" of the Protestant Council of Churches (or of a couple of friends in the Clergy Fellowship). As such, it represented just another rather irksome demand upon their time, another program item which had to be "fitted in" somewhere so that later it could be said, "We participated, didn't we?" or "We were sympathetic to what was being attempted, although we didn't have time to do much with it." Many clergymen were apparently oblivious to what they were doing, of how they were in fact reacting to the OHC. The reasons given for not supporting the covenant vigorously are often legitimate enough, granted certain presuppositions—but the pastors who did little because of their aversion to

*See above, p. 75.

"promoting" Christian social action, or because they wanted to avoid encroaching upon the right of each parishioner to "decide for himself" did not seem to be willing to face up to the implications of their presuppositions and of an approach based upon them. The clergymen who were obviously shoving the matter aside were either unaware that this was what they were doing, or else they were too disingenuous to admit it to another person. They needed to hear these words from a report on OHC campaigns in California:

> The goal of an integrated community will not be achieved by developing a perfect program (if there is one) but by *starting now,* possibly with an open housing covenant campaign, improving techniques, expanding objectives, and recruiting dedicated leaders.[57]

The preference of the Protestant ministers in Newfield for their preaching and pastoral roles and their low valuation of the role of community leader are typical of the viewpoints of pastors all over the country. A major study of role expectations and role conflicts in the Protestant ministry completed a few years ago revealed that forty per cent of the minister's professional working day of about ten hours was devoted to the work of parish administration (which an average of sixty-four minutes per day being spent on "stenographic work," such as the writing of letters, the preparation and printing of stencils for mimeographed materials, etc.), twenty-five per cent to pastoral duties, and only ten per cent to community leadership. All roles except administrative ones were considered more enjoyable and more important in the minister's performance of his vocation than the role of community leader, and ministers considered themselves least effective in this role. The preaching and pastoral roles were regarded as most enjoyable and most important, and the clergymen felt that their effectiveness was greatest in these roles, too.[58]

These findings shed light on much of what has been said above about the introversion of the churches and the individualism of Protestant piety. The high priority assigned to the pastoral role may be interpreted as an attempt to supplement the sense of in-group solidarity fostered by involvement of members in "church activities" with a sense of personal closeness to the minister. "This combination of organizational activity and personal loyalty to the minister weaves the fabric of the organization church, which is a substitute for residential community [that is, for the genuine sense of being rooted in a neighborhood, which has been lost as a result of high residential mobility]."[59] The high priority assigned to the preaching role is an expression of the attempt on the part of Protestant ministers to develop a "pseudopersonal charismatic leadership" as a substitute for the authority of the church, which is also eviscerated in American Protestantism. Kenneth Underwood sums it up in these words:

> In many of the Protestant churches it is difficult for the pastor to find a consensus of belief that is the product of a religious community; there does not seem to be any priesthood of believers. The main categories of analysis and occasions of disciplined study have been supplied by the special political and economic associations of the city. No groups of laymen bring before the congregations their vigorous examination of the significance of their faith for specific areas of culture—business, labor, press, politics. There are only the Sunday sermons, the social gatherings of the church with attendance chosen by ages and sex, the "big program meeting" with guest speakers answering perfunctory questions on a "one-night stand"; and from these no conviction with a common point of reference or loyalty emerges to withstand the cohesive force of the secular disciplines of the community.[60]

Small wonder that the introversion of church life also manifests itself in reliance upon "multitudinist" techniques of communication. The assumption that individuals can be "reached" as well by a mimeographed announcement as they can by a face-to-face confrontation is disproved by the OHC program in Newfield and other cities mentioned. The multitudinist approach overlooks the fact than an appeal directed to everyone-in-general, in the name of religion-in-general, becomes an appeal to no one, or at any rate an appeal which can easily be dodged. Instead of a sober encounter between two members of the community of faith and commitment, in which one communicates to the other a challenge to action in the name of their Lord, isolated clients of the religious organization receive a printed notice which may be perused without being taken to heart, and which they feel no moral pressure to take seriously.

The lamentable characteristics of the introverted church are summed up in a phrase which, rightly understood, comprehends much of what has been criticized in the foregoing pages: it is "the tacit truce on engagement." The meaning of the term *engagement*, which derives from contemporary French existentialism, is best conveyed by reference to something normally described by the verb "to engage": the meshing of gears. Gears are engaged when they meet and bite into each other, when first one gear and then another sets others in motion and causes them to perform the work for which they were made. Christians are engaged, are living in engagement, when they are encountering one another honestly and courageously in a common effort to discover the will of God for them, individually and collectively, and to strengthen one another in doing it.

The concept of "engagement" can be illuminated by contrasting it with another concept often employed in popular discussions of the Church; namely, "togetherness" or "belongingness." Many churchgoers define Christian fellowship in these debased terms: they think that the be-all and end-all of the church is to provide a place where nice folks can dress up in nice clothes and smile nicely and say nice things to each other and never disagree. They mistakenly think that it is un-Christian to talk about controversial subjects or to offend the sensibilities of anyone in the group by discussing unpleasant realities. Peter Berger has given a beautiful example of the bad faith which results in a tacit truce on engagement in his book *The Noise of Solemn Assemblies*. Berger declares that the churchgoers of this country have a silent understanding with their clergyman that he can preach on anything he wants to just as vigorously as he pleases—so long as he doesn't "mean business," that is, so long as he lets the matter drop after the sermon. The symbol of this tacit truce on engagement is the smiling handshake with which our worship services usually end. This handshake is a reassuring sign to the congregation that the Word of Judgment can be forgotten as soon as the "church lets out."[61] Another explanation of lack of engagement is to be found in Vidich and Bensman's description of the gentleman's agreement entered into by the people of the town, an agreement not to disturb the peace of mind of anyone by allowing truth to rear its disconcerting head:

> There is silent recognition among members of the community that facts and ideas which are disturbing to the accepted system of illusions are not to be verbalized. . . .
>
> In terms of unconscious interpersonal technique, this requires that a particular individual have a fairly sensitive knowledge of the illusions held by another person and, in interacting with him, he must act and respond to the illusion as a reality. On the other hand, one does not support a person who has completely lost his illusions. This is a *faux pas* and an insult and contrary to all forms of interpersonal etiquette; in such cases the relationship is carried on on the basis of formal greetings and inconsequential small talk. . . .[62]

A truce on engagement is appealing to both clergymen and laymen, for it enables all parties concerned to hide from themselves, from each other, and (one is tempted to hope) from God those disquieting pangs of conscience which continually threaten to shatter the feeling of self-satisfaction that most persons continually seek to build up and protect. If there is no engagement between pastor and parishioners, or between laymen, or between members of the same family, one is able to read a newspaper account of misery and injustice in one's own community without being motivated to do anything about it except sigh regretfully; one is able to hear a sermon on the subject of Christian responsibility without doing anything more than make resolutions which are never carried out; one is able to postpone or rationalize away the decision about whether or not he is called upon to sign a nondiscriminatory pledge or take action in some other way to combat racial injustice. If one is touched only by "spectator influences"—if one is never confronted by other Christians who are willing to take the risk of revealing their fears, doubts, and convictions about God's will and who expect the same in return—it is easy to remain nothing more than a spectator, or a very occasional and halfhearted actor, in the life of the Church in the world.

How does the tacit truce on engagement manifest itself? There are grounds for suspecting the existence of an unspoken contract to this effect when liaison between Catholics and Protestants is as difficult as it was in Newfield, and when the participation of one group is so long delayed and so minimal. One suspects it when Christian community is defined in terms of smiling "fellowship" and when evangelism becomes co-optation of people of similar socio-economic status.[63] One suspects it when large numbers of laymen refuse to respond to a questionnaire on a "touchy" moral issue, when parishioners "just don't want to talk about" an ethical responsibility that has been called to their attention by the pastor, or when the pastor hears about objections to the OHC "by the grapevine" instead of through forthright personal conversation. One suspects it when people complain about a "lack of balance" in a church's program, for this may mean that a steady round of "activities" has become a device to protect people from effective involvement in any one concern. One suspects it when people are reluctant to acknowledge conflicting interests on the part of different groups in society, or when they assume that conflict can be avoided by education or by allowing time to pass. One suspects it, too, when a group of ministers fail to raise questions about a program of social action in a meeting where this program is planned—yet fail to give more than token support (if that much) to the program when it is launched, and fail to evaluate the completed action. (The minutes of the Clergy Fellowship meetings in the months following the OHC campaign yield no indication that such evaluation ever took place.) And one suspects an unwillingness to face engagement when a minister gives no support to a religiously sponsored community project because he views it as another minister's "baby," or when he says he intends to support it later but never does. But the prize illustration of this failing in Newfield was the refusal of a Christian layman who was a realtor to attend a meeting of the Council of Churches Social Action Committee for the purpose of explaining the position of real estate agents on the matter of residence and race. As one of the members of the Committee remarked, "One almost prefers the misguided zeal of someone like Angus Mc-Crory* to this kind of evasion."

To argue that engagement is a vital component of the Christian life, and that it ought to be cultivated in the life of any community of Christians, is not to ask for perpetual agreement or unfailing cooperation. It is simply to say that genuine *koinonia* calls for more than "good breeding" or the avoidance of hostility or antagonistic cooperation in preserving "major values such as peace, harmony, good will, and order within the fellowship."[64] It calls for the truth spoken in love, even (and especially) when the truth is a threat to the security, pride, or ambitions of a parish or an individual. It calls for the voicing of misgivings and criticisms, and for an openness to reappraisal and a willingness to risk or admit failure on the part of those whose ideas or plans are questioned. It suggests that an honest sharing of one's very being is far more important than pleasantness, propriety, or cultural precedent—"what nice people do"—in personal relations between Christians. The tacit truce on engagement is a violation of moral wisdom because in many instances it is a counter-suggestion cue which conveys to other Christians the assurance that the sleeping dog of protective complacency will be left lying undisturbed.

Part of the problem of nonengagement is faulty techniques of communication, and this can be solved to some extent through increased technical wisdom. Sermons delivered with the purest of intent and the warmest of zeal can be ruined by the presence in them of counter-suggestion cues. The total impact of a minister's leadership can be thoroughly vitiated by too great a reliance upon the efficacy of sermons, and a well-conceived program of religious education can be hampered by insufficient emphasis upon group learning situations rather than upon individual learning. Experiments in communication and the learning process may suggest many new approaches to church leaders, and certainly they must be continually alert

* The outspoken segregationist realtor who resigned from the mayor's Displaced Housing Committee. See pp. 43-45.

and open to (as well as competent to criticize!) new insights of this kind.

The tacit truce on engagement is caused, however, by something far more difficult to eradicate than ignorance about effective techniques of communication. It is caused by an understandable reluctance on the part of most human beings, including those whose ostensible religious commitment theoretically fortifies them against this reluctance, to be genuinely open to criticism, or even mild disapproval, from others. But so long as Christians share a culturally defined notion of "good breeding" which tells them that it is impolite for one man to challenge another's behavior, or even his motivations, in the interests of larger goals to which they are both supposedly committed, they will fall short of the kind of painful transformation of their way of living that the Christian gospel requires. As long as one Christian is afraid to criticize another because he fears criticism in return, the fellowship of the church will not be the *koinonia* of the disciples of Jesus Christ; it will be mere "togetherness" and "belongingness."

GUIDELINES FOR RENEWAL

The hardness of heart exposed in the introversion of church life can only be remedied if Christians have the moral wisdom to realize that the Church is not a building, a group of like-minded people who come to it on Sunday morning, or even the denomination with which it is affiliated. They must realize that the purpose of congregational life is not the achievement of institutional ends such as swelling membership rolls, a fatter budget, or even a "happier fellowship" of people who "really enjoy doing things at the church." In the words of an eloquent spokesman for renewal in the Church through revitalization of the lay apostolate,

> The orientation of Christians when they gather together as the church, the *ekklesia*, for worship and study, must always be toward their return to their life in dispersion in the world as salt or leaven. For the life of the church must be made aware of the concrete problems of obedience and witness in the world.[65]

Without a clear affirmation of this fundamental theological principle, all other attempts to renew the vitality of Christian commitment will fail.

Interestingly enough, recent theories of urban political and economic processes suggest a maxim of technical wisdom that is the almost exact counterpart of the maxim of moral wisdom just stated. Social analysts who view metropolitan affairs as "an ecology of games" emphasize by implication the need for some institution to furnish insights regarding what is needed for the common good, not just what would be good for it, and to provide an impetus in that direction by formulating policy proposals which would serve the common good.[66] The political arena as it now exists is little more than a market place in which various factions bid against each other for policies which will promote their own interests, and the politician is simply the broker who ratifies compromises reached by the strongest factions. As many political philosophers (notably Joseph Tussman and John Courtney Murray in recent years)[67] have warned, policy arrived at through the conjectured "invisible hand" of the market is not likely to be any more satisfactory than a philosophy or an economy derived from the clash of competing groups:

> To be sure, some of what Walter Lippmann has called "the public philosophy" affects both politicians and other game-players. This indicates the existence of roles and norms of a larger, vaguer game with a relevant audience that has some sense of cricket. This potentially mobilizable audience is not utterly without importance, but it provides no sure or adequate basis for support in the particular game that the politician or anyone else is playing. Instead of a set of norms to structure enduring role-playing, this audience provides a cross-pressure for momentary aberrancy from gamesmanship or constitutes just another hazard to be calculated in one's play.[68]

The vacuum existing in this model of the political process ought to be filled in a significant way by the religious institutions of our society. Churches ought to be fellowships in which a commitment to the common good is cultivated and nourished —a commitment much deeper than a vague "sense of cricket," and much more consistent and reliable than "a cross-pressure

for momentary aberrancy from [self-interested] gamesmanship."
Churches ought to be forums where men who are more committed to serving the good of the individuals who make up
human society as a whole than they are to serving the interests
of some parochial segment of society, men who identify themselves more with this role than with any role as player in
some other interest group game, come together to identify
the problems of the society, define its pressing needs, and
formulate policy recommendations to meet these needs.
Churches ought to be places, in sum, where men with a shared
understanding of moral wisdom (and a common fidelity to
its implications) bring together the diverse kinds of technical
wisdom pertinent to the various vocational games in which
they are engaged and bring forth, in honest engagement with
one another, guidelines for public policy which protect the
just interests of all groups in the society yet enforce responsibility on all. To repeat, this uncommon reality can come to
pass only if the conception of the Church as servant in the
world is passionately affirmed.

This interpretation of the theological identity of the church
and of its normative social function has obvious implication for
the clergyman's image of himself and his role responsibilities.
If he is something other than the hired hand of a local congregation, then time spent on administrative duties serving
only institutional ends should have low priority. If the church
is something other than a client-oriented organization dedicated to the satisfaction of the emotional needs of parishioners,
then time spent in "fellowshipping," pastoral visitation, and
even some kinds of pastoral counseling must be downgraded
in importance. If the purpose of the gathering of the congregation is largely for dispersal into the world as salt and leaven,
then the content of sermons and religious education may have
to be altered substantially, and the role of community organizer may assume much greater significance. Thus, to illustrate
by taking issue with one of the Newfield ministers, it would
not be at all self-evident that one should assign higher priority
to one's pastoral responsibility to visit a sick person than one
assigns to one's responsibility to increase his ability as a com-

munity leader by attending an important public gathering. And it would most assuredly not be self-evident that the criterion for one's decision would be the wishes of those who pay one's salary!

Finding a remedy for the hardness of heart exemplified in indifference to social ills is also dependent in considerable measure on increased technical wisdom. This must be primarily of two kinds: greater sophistication in social analysis (that is, in understanding the political, economic and social forces at work in the modern world, and the sociological principles by which the interplay of these forces may be interpreted) and greater awareness of what is actually happening day by day in community, nation and world. Because Christian Realism has made a substantial impact upon theological education, the importance of knowledge in sociology, psychology, economics, and political science has been recognized in many quarters, and courses aimed at cultivating some rudimentary sophistication in these fields have been added to the curriculum in a good number of seminaries. The theory is that a clergyman who received this kind of training will continue to educate himself in these disciplines after he leaves seminary, and that he will educate his parishioners in a similar fashion through his influence on the program of parish activities and through his personal influence on the members of the church. This theory is frequently expressed in the practice of churches staffed by well-trained leaders: Sunday School classes, special study groups, and sermons deal with Christian responsibility in regard to various social concerns.

But all too often this theory fails to work out. The role-expectations placed upon a pastor by his denomination, his congregation, and himself give a higher priority to traditional tasks of the ministry than to the cultivation of technical wisdom. Overwhelmed by the demands of the more traditional roles, and overwhelmed also by the complexity of social issues and the superabundance of conflicting interpretations of these issues, the minister finds it easy to forget the good resolutions he may have had when leaving seminary about systematically renewing his store of technical wisdom.

No easy solution to this dilemma recommends itself. It would probably be vain simply to exhort the overburdened pastor to stay up a little later each night and add just a little more to his reading load. A more practical suggestion, and one which has the merit of providing for a higher degree of engagement among ministers and laymen on vital public issues, would involve setting up what might be called "Church Forums on Social Concerns." Such forums would be composed of individuals willing to commit themselves to keep up with two or three worth-while periodicals in the field of public affairs or social science, and to keep other participants advised of the import of exceptionally significant articles appearing in the journals for which each of them is responsible. Communication would be centered in weekly or bi-weekly meetings of participants, but the new ideas accruing from the forums would also filter down to nonparticipants in the community as well as to those in the churches. Such forums would help to produce an atmosphere favorable to intense awareness of social problems, forthright discussion of ethical responsibilities and corporate action. According to one highly regarded social ethicist, large numbers of American businessmen are eager for engagement of this kind:

> These men want study and discussion in the Church that has the rigor and quality they experience elsewhere. They want it directed to their loneliness, their loss of courage to act, their fuzziness about how their varied roles are to be meaningfully related, their guilt and remorse over the hurt and suffering they inflict, the truth they keep from others, the elite snobbery they develop in the process of producing their "most important product—progress."[69]

Church forums on social concerns would provide a creative channel for expressing and enlarging interest in the moral dimensions of one's vocational involvement. They might also stimulate a desire for engagement among churchgoers that could be used to enhance the value of sermons, as the experience of a student pastor in Europe suggests:

> Each Sunday morning the student pastor passed out small cards, giving the topic and text for the following Sunday service, [listing] readings for each day of the week and two or

three key questions for the congregation to think on. The following Sunday, after the final benediction and hymn, the chaplain stepped out of the pulpit and walked down the center aisle. Those concerned came forward and in a "talk back" session with questions and comments they completed the translation of the Word.

By such means as this, in which the congregation assumes an active role in relation to the sermon, the moral earnestness of the occasion is accented and the binding quality of the sermon is developed. The preacher has then a clear view of whom he is addressing. The proclamation ceases to be entertainment, and the first step at least is taken to imbue preaching with that quality the New Testament calls "edifying."[70]

Enhanced effectiveness in the strategy and tactics of social action also depends upon fuller acceptance of two maxims of moral wisdom advocated in this book. The first is the supremacy of justice as the crucial norm in social ethics; the second is the necessity for, and the legitimacy of, the use of power in working for proximate goods in society. Justice itself is of course not immune to misinterpretation by those who define it in ideologically tainted terms—but it is probably less vulnerable to misinterpretation or manipulation than principles such as order, love or freedom, all of which have been used repeatedly, and are still being used, by dominant groups for the suppression of others. And surely it is clear from the record of history that oppression can never be warded off or terminated without the use of power beyond that of persuasion. Man's capacity for injustice makes the use of power necessary; man's capacity, and his desire, for a just human community makes the responsible use of power possible.

The most important single assertion of technical wisdom pertaining to strategic effectiveness is that a variety of tactics must be employed and coordinated in the battle for desired goals. Just as there is no single model for the "community power structure" that holds for all metropolitan areas, but rather many different types of power structure resulting from unique local circumstances,[71] there is no single line of attack which can be counted on to insure victory. As the model for secondary strategy discussed in Chapter Eight suggests, direct action is necessary in dealing with some targets, whereas behind-the-scenes negotiation works better with others—and coordinated attack by agencies specializing in different tactics is often the best way of inducing target decision-makers to grant the goals being sought. Perhaps the most valuable advice one can give to church leaders is a caveat against the "position of the church" fixation deplored by William J. Cook.* Policy-makers at all levels agree that church delegations which approach them with fixed formulas for social salvation in the form of idealistic resolutions arouse little interest, and oftentimes arouse considerable antagonism and resistance.[72] What policy-makers appreciate is new information or fresh analysis which suggests new factors to be considered or new policy alternatives. What they appreciate, in addition, is a willingness on the part of church spokesmen to engage them in dialogue on the moral ramifications of various policy options, rather than a posture of moral superiority which implies little comprehension of the dilemmas faced by the policy-maker and little faith in his integrity or good faith.

A specific idea of potentially great importance in strategy at the community or congregational level is suggested by theories concerning group leadership now current in American sociological circles. According to George Homans, whose book on *The Human Group* remains a classical statement of theory on this subject, every group needs a "father" and a "mother"; that is, every group needs one person whose role it is to socialize them in the values for which the group stands and to make certain that all members of the group perform the tasks for which they are responsible, and another person whose role it is to offer personal warmth and emotional acceptance to individual members.[73] It is difficult for one person to fulfill both roles. At the office party, the boss or the supervisor may step out of their roles as life-and-death authority or whip-cracker, and sentiments may be expressed or behavior tolerated which would be inappropriate under ordinary circumstances. But everyone knows that the occasion is atypical, and

*See above, p. 204.

that the first working-day after the holidays will find every-body in the office back in his proper role.

If this theory is correct, it may be extremely difficult for one man to be both a prophet and a pastor to his parishioners. If it is true that loving acceptance and uncompromising de-mands cannot be effectively given by the same person in a group, the conscious (but unannounced!) role differentiation by teams of clergymen might provide the optimum combina-tion of prophetic authority and pastoral warmth in the ministry of a parish or in the ministry of service to a community. This arrangement might help solve the difficulties of clergymen who, operating in an ethos perceived by most parishioners as designed to meet their needs instead of to make demands upon them, are unable to convey the conviction that they "mean business" when they preach prophetic sermons.

The possible utility of conscious role-differentiation runs parallel to a final recommendation which relates to both tech-nical and moral wisdom, both effectiveness and sensitivity. It is a recommendation suggested to the author by an unforget-table conversation three years ago with the late H. Richard Niebuhr, for many years a teacher of Christian Ethics at Yale Divinity School. Professor Niebuhr observed that, in reflecting on the tragic sight of the hysterical white mothers of New Orleans at the time of the first school desegregation there, he saw the failure of the Church in the South in a new light. The faces of those mothers, contorted with hatred for the few little Negro children who braved their shrieks of rage and scorn, revealed nothing so much as *fear*. These women, said Niebuhr, were literally scared to death: white supremacy, the fundamental principle on which their whole understanding of their identity was based, had been called into question by desegregation of the schools, and they were terrified. Their understanding of their very being was threatened, and they were moved to horror as they contemplated the abyss of non-being which integration meant to them.

But this could not have happened had the Church been faith-ful in communicating to them a self-understanding focused on their identity as children of God. If they had really learned from the Church that their being did not depend upon their being white, or middle-class, or American, or anything else of this kind, but rather upon their being loved by God, they would not have been so afraid. They would have seen more clearly, too, that the barriers of race, class, and nationality (and the pride which erects these barriers) are not only evil, but quite unnecessary and therefore silly. So the failure of the Church, concluded Niebuhr, was not only in neglecting to preach the Word of God's judgment against the sin of racial injustice but also, and perhaps even more, in neglecting to preach and to incarnate in its own life as an institution and as a force in society the Word of God's grace.

Thus an investigation of Christian social action returns in the end to the question of theology. The examination of a social problem and a particular effort to help resolve it comes back to the intellectual-spiritual problem of the source and measure of all human efforts to do what is right and achieve what is good. It is well that this is so—for awareness of injustice is bound to remain grievously limited or suppressed, and efforts to secure justice are likely to degenerate into a selfish fight for parochial interests, unless men are sparked by, and wholly committed to, the conviction that the ground of all being —in the language of faith, God—is a force that heals the dichotomy within each human being and reconciles the estrangement which separates them from one another.[74] Whether or not men use the language of faith is less important than their being grasped by, and submitting their wills to, this power, for without it no man can work unreservedly and unremittingly for social justice.

APPENDICES

APPENDIX A

NOTES ON THE POINT OF VIEW AND METHODOLOGY

This work is concerned not only with the *ought* which Christian faith pronounces in human society, but also with the *is* of a particular society which is far from being the Kingdom of God on earth; that is why it is an empirical study. On the other hand, every phase of the study is informed by the *ought* of Christian value-orientation as found in the mind of one Protestant observer; therefore, it is an evaluative study. Because the purpose of the study was to develop insights regarding effective Christian social action, significance has been considered a more important criterion for the formulation of questions to be asked, compilation of data and evaluation than rigorous obedience to the accepted rules of strict sociological methodology. The author has endeavored to avoid being unduly impressionistic, but he has counted it more important, from the standpoint of social ethics, to be thought-provoking than to be "safe." Insights concerning the pressures which seem to be operating upon the Christian people of Newfield have been regarded as more important than statistical proof as to the exact location and intensity of these pressures—and it has been thought better to risk exaggeration than to fail to articulate insights which appear to be well founded and which suggest answers as to why social action by churchmen is often so ineffective.

Judged in terms of strict sociological methodology, the conclusions advanced in this study are not absolutely reliable. The sample of clergymen interviewed is small, as is the sample of nonsupporters who replied to the questionnaire, and some of the differences of opinion between different groups of respondents used as the basis for generalizations in Chapter Six are not statistically significant according to the X^2 method of measurement. As a result, no truly scientific validity for the insights drawn from the study can be claimed. It can be claimed, however, that the patterns of attitude and behavior discerned here may serve to alert clergymen and lay Christians involved in similar kinds of social action to possible reactions on the part of the people with whom they are working; con-

sequently, their approaches to these people should be rendered
more effective. Analysis of findings does not necessarily have to be
rigorously scientific in order to provide helpful guidance to
practitioners.

This is not to say, certainly, that moralists should be content
simply to "play hunches." They should be constantly seeking to
avail themselves of the technical wisdom provided by social science,
and they should be very grateful that social scientists have a concern for the discipline of scientific methodology. But in cases where
social science has not shown an interest in seeking answers to urgent questions that are of concern to the moralist—and in cases
where social scientists are apparently unwilling to ask the most
pressing questions because they have not yet perfected their tools
of investigation—the moralist must go ahead and try to find answers
in as careful a manner as possible. The practitioner of social ethics
should not engage in action without the benefit of systematic obser-
vation of the situation in which he is operating, but he cannot afford
to postpone action until findings of absolutely unimpeachable reliability are available. He must formulate programs of action based
on intelligent inferences from the most systematic observations that
he can make with the resources at his command.

No apology is made, furthermore, for the normative judgments
which have been advanced regarding the *is* of the Newfield situation in the light of the *ought* contained in the prophetic tradition
of Jewish-Christian faith.. The author does feel compelled, however, to confess his misgivings about the extent to which he has
been successful in distinguishing between realistic norms and utopian
norms for judging the behavior and attitudes of Christians°. If, for
example, the Newfield clergymen have been excoriated for failing
to think and act with a degree of wisdom and heroism that one can
hardly expect of men with their background and their present parish
responsibilities, then the criticism passed on them may be unfair.
So far as these particular clergymen are concerned, only judgments
based on realistic norms defined in terms of actual conditions are
relevant. But the point of the study is not to pass judgment on these
ministers. It is rather to discern the factors operative in one situation which supported, or militated against, effective Christian social action, and to set forth the implications of the existence of these
factors for the Church. In some cases, perhaps, these implications
call for a downward revision of utopian ideals in the formulation
of a realistic Christian social philosophy. It is also true, however,
that the realistic norms which emerge from and apply to similar ventures of Christian social action demand an upward revision of the

---

° This distinction is suggested by Joseph Fichter, *Dynamics of a City
Church* (Chicago: University of Chicago Press, 1951), pp. 259-60.

actual level of conduct exhibited by churchmen. Some of the implications of this study for the training of ministers, for the self-understanding of ministers and laymen, and for the daily life of the local
church have been drawn in the text of the study.

The foregoing remarks help to explain the methods used to obtain and interpret data in the three phases of empirical investigation
involved in this study. For the inventory of housing conditions
among Negroes in Newfield the sample desired was the entire Negro population of the area. This sample was compiled through the
use of municipal records and through the additional knowledge of
a Negro citizen who had lived in Newfield all his life. The list
which was obtained through these procedures was not absolutely
complete, and all families included on the list could not be contacted; however, a comparison of the number of families contacted
with the number of families listed in the 1960 census (adjusted for
continuing in-migration since that census was made) indicates that
about ninety per cent of the Negro families in the area were reached.
An interview schedule of five pages was administered to the head of
household, or to an adult member of the household who was qualified
to be a respondent, by thirteen students of the University over a
two-week period. A sixth page giving information about the general
condition of the residence and the conditions under which the interview was conducted was also filled out by the student after
concluding the interview. The average time consumed in an interview was between forty-five minutes and one hour. Most items on
the schedule called for a simple quantitative response or a "Yes/
No" answer, but there were several open-ended questions, and interviewers were encouraged to record verbatim comments made by
respondents at every opportunity. The coding of the completed interview schedules presented no serious problems because of the nature
of the questions asked; replies to the open-ended questions could
readily be classified according to categories implicit in the remarks
of the respondents and the written comments of the interviewers.

The second phase of empirical investigation was the most important
part of the study, but it was also the one which presented the
most difficulty. The principle that governed selection of the clergymen to be interviewed was simply that of representative inclusive-
ness; that is, an attempt was made to include in the sample a
representative of each theological position and each parish situation
found in the community. This explains why the sample contained
more Protestant ministers than Roman Catholic priests. The interview schedule was made up almost entirely of open-ended questions,
and a tape recorder was used to insure complete accuracy in the
recording of responses. Interviews lasted from forty-five minutes
to one hour and a half. Tentative categories for analysis were set

up during the construction of the interview schedule, but a number of these proved to be inapplicable, and the final set of categories used was determined primarily by a careful reading of the accumulated data. It must be acknowledged, of course, that the predispositions of the analyst may have introduced some distortion into the study at this point: the categories suggested to him are not necessarily the most significant ones, and countervailing themes in the testimony of the respondents may have been overlooked. It is also quite possible that even though what the respondents said was accurately recorded, what they meant by their responses was inaccurately or inadequately interpreted. Despite these dangers, though, the writer remains convinced that the information sought could only have been obtained through the use of open-ended questions, and he hopes that the reader is convinced by the documentation in Chapter Four that the themes highlighted in the presentation of the findings were not imposed upon the testimony of the clergymen.

The questionnaire for laymen was composed mainly of "Yes/No" and multiple choice questions, with additional comment by the respondent encouraged at many points. An attempt was made to get a response from fifty persons who signed the open housing covenant and fifty persons who did not sign it in four churches: the two churches which carried out the housing covenant appeal most effectively, one other Protestant church and one other Roman Catholic church. Eleven hundred questionnaires (with stamped return envelopes) were mailed—two hundred and fifty in each parish except in one where the pastor refused to allow the questionnaire to be sent to his parishioners unless it were sent to the entire mailing list of active members. Most of the respondents availed themselves of the opportunity to write comments in their own words in the spaces provided on the questionnaire, and with few exceptions these comments could be grouped under obvious analytical categories. Thus coding presented no problems.

APPENDIX B

THE GREATER NEWFIELD OPEN HOUSING COVENANT

The card which was used to collect signatures for the open housing covenant had the pledge printed on one side and interfaith endorsements on the other side. The first side reads:

GREATER NEWFIELD'S OPEN HOUSING COVENANT

We the undersigned:

Believe that all persons have the moral and legal right to rent, buy or build a home anywhere without any restrictions which are based upon race, religion or national origin:

Believe it to be in the best interests of the Greater Newfield Area that all persons of goodwill take an active role in bringing about freedom of housing opportunity. We will welcome the purchase or rental of housing and/or apartments in our neighborhood by any responsible and law abiding citizen of whatever race, religion or national origin, and we will work with him to build, to maintain, and to improve a community which is good for all.

If under 21 please

check here ....

Tel. No ....

Signature

....

Name (please print)

....

Address

....

Your signature grants approval for the use of
your name in the local newspaper

The second side read:

INTERFAITH ENDORSEMENTS OF GREATER NEWFIELD'S OPEN HOUSING COVENANT

JEWISH

I support the principle of equal housing opportunties for all and urge the members of our congregation to follow non-segregated practices in the selling, buying, and leasing of residential housing.

I call upon our people to examine the moral imperatives of Judaism and to translate them into concrete action to remove housing discrimination.

October 12, 1961.

RABBI AARON NEUMANN
Congregation Bethel

CATHOLIC

We believe:

that God, the Father, is the Creator of all men and that His Image is impressed upon the soul of each individual.

that Jesus Christ died for all mankind, that all might be saved.

that the Holy Ghost sanctifies every child of God.

These are our principles, our ideals. These principles must be applied to our lives. The love of God in our hearts must be extended to all men in all phases of life. Hence, we should do all in our power to help all, regardless of race, creed or nationality.

We plead with our people to conform their convictions to their ideals.

October 14, 1961.

REV. CHARLES SLOAN, PASTOR
Church of St. Michael
Diocesan Consultor, Diocese of Newfield

PROTESTANT

Believing that God has supremely expressed His love for man in Jesus Christ, and believing that we have been called to witness to this love in our world and in our community,

We affirm the right of all persons to seek housing in, and to be welcomed by, the community of their choice without discrimination by reason of race, creed, or national origin.

EXECUTIVE COMMITTEE OF THE
GREATER NEWFIELD COUNCIL OF
October, 1961.   *CHURCHES*

NOTES

Notes For Chapter One

1. Joseph B. Robison, "Legislation Against Bias—Possibilities and Limitations," *The Journal of Intergroup Relations*, I, 1 (Winter 1959--60), 39.

2. Davis McEntire, *Residence and Race*° (Berkeley: University of California Press, 1960), p. 5.

3. This memorable phrase was used—with great feeling—by a Negro delegate to the National Conference of the National Committee Against Discrimination in Housing, April 25-26, 1963, in Washington, D.C.

4. Housing and Home Finance Agency, *Our Nonwhite Population and Its Housing: The Changes Between 1950 and 1960* (Washington: Housing and Home Finance Agency, 1963), pp. 1-6.

5. RR, pp. 52-53.

6. Housing and Home Finance Agency, *Potential Housing Demand of Nonwhite Population in Selected Metropolitan Areas* (Washington: Housing and Home Finance Agency, 1963), p. ii.

7. "Residential Desegregation: The Church's New Frontier," *Social Progress*, XLIX, 1 (September 1958), 8.

8. See especially Goodwin B. Watson, *Action for Unity* (New York: Harper and Brothers, 1947), Dwight W. Culver, *Negro Segregation in the Methodist Church* (New Haven: Yale University Press, 1953), Edmund D. Soper, *Racism: A World Issue* (Nashville: Abingdon-Cokesbury Press, 1947), John LaFarge, *The Catholic Viewpoint on Race Relations* (Garden City, New York: Hanover House Books, Doubleday and Company, 1956), William Stuart Nelson (ed.), *The Christian Way in Race Relations* (New York: Harper and Brothers, 1948), W.A. Visser 'tHooft, *The Ecumenical Movement and the Racial Problem* (New York: Columbia University Press, 1951), Frank S. Loescher, *The Protestant Church and the Negro* (New York: Association Press, 1948), Naomi Friedman

°For the sake of convenience, this frequently cited work will be referred to in the notes hereafter as RR.

Goldstein, *The Roots of Prejudice Against the Negro in the United States* (Boston: Boston University Press, 1948), and Buell G. Gallagher, *Color and Conscience: The Irrepressible Conflict* (New York: Harper and Brothers, 1946).

9. L.C. Kesselman, *The Social Politics of FEPC* (Chapel Hill: University of North Carolina Press, 1948).

10. Bureau of Social Science Research, "Availability of Apartments for African Diplomats" (Washington: Bureau of Social Science Research, 1962). Cf. the testimony of G. Mennen Williams, Assistant Secretary of State for African Affairs, United States Commission on Civil Rights, *Housing in Washington* (Washington: Government Printing Office, 1962), pp. 125-129.

11. Clement Vose, *Caucasians Only* (Berkeley: University of California Press, 1959), p. 60.

12. RR, pp. 94-95. Cf. Leo J. Linder, "The Social Results of Segregation in Housing," *Lawyers Guild Review*, XVIII, 1 (Spring 1958), 2-11.

13. For a cool statistical analysis of the extent to which the national economy and Negroes suffer from discrimination, see Eli Ginsberg, *The Negro Potential* (New York: Columbia University Press, 1956). For a perceptive description of the vicious circle of poverty, lack of opportunity and loss of incentive, see Michael Harrington, *The Other America* (New York: The Macmillan Company, 1963). For a passionate shriek of rage from a Negro who has experienced what it means to live in the black ghetto, see James Baldwin, *The Fire Next Time* (New York: Dial Press, 1963).

14. Baldwin, *op. cit.;* Eric C. Lincoln, *The Black Muslims in America* (Boston: Beacon Press, 1960), pp. 3-32; E.U. Essien-Udom, *Black Nationalism* (Chicago: University of Chicago Press, 1962), pp. 302-7; Louis E. Lomax, *When the Word Is Given* (Cleveland and New York: The World Publishing Company, 1963), pp. 22-32, 109-211.

15. Lincoln, *op. cit.*, pp. 35-38. Cf. Hylan Lewis, *Blackways of Kent* (Chapel Hill: University of North Carolina Press, 1955).

16. A fuller explanation of the concepts of relative deprivation and relative status is found below, pp. 152-53, and the relevant reference to a scholarly work in which these concepts are elaborated is given in footnote 8 of Chapter Eight.

17. RR, p. 223.

18. In a recent discussion of professional ethics by a group of bankers, one member of the group admitted that "he would be constrained to discharge any employee who helped a customer find a lower rate of interest than the one which seemed most desirable from the bank's point of view." See Victor Obenhaus, "Bankers," in

Cameron P. Hall (ed.), *On-the-Job Ethics* (New York: The National Council of The Churches of Christ in the U.S.A., 1963), p. 8.

19. In Chicago, for example, one study showed that "Negroes, on the average, paid $15 a month more for [housing]—in spite of the fact that the average Negro family income ($3,223) is only 54 per cent of the average white family ($5,835)." A similar investigation of housing obtained by Connecticut families displaced by urban renewal disclosed that "most of the relocated white home purchasers bought houses under $20,000 in all-white neighborhoods, about half of the considerably fewer Negro family home purchasers paid $20,000 or more for homes in racially mixed neighborhoods," and that "only six per cent of the displaced white families consisting of adults and children under 16 paid $80 or more monthly rental—in contrast to 29 per cent of the Negroes and 42 per cent of the Puerto Ricans." See John David Maguire, "The Human Factor in Urban Renewal," *Christianity and Crisis*, XXIII, 24 (January 20, 1964), 264.

20. Gordon W. Allport, *Prejudice* (Garden City, New York: Doubleday Anchor Books, Doubleday and Company, 1958), pp. 161-72.

21. Jack Greenberg, *Race Relations and American Law* (New York: Columbia University Press, 1959), pp. 279-83..

22. RR, pp. 248-50. For some eloquent personal testimony by a realtist, see United States Commission on Civil Rights, *Housing in Washington* (Washington: Government Printing Office, 1962), pp. 188-97.

23. S. Garry Oniki, "Residential Desegregation: Confrontation for the Churches," *Christianity and Crisis*, XXI, 9 (May 29, 1961), 91-95 and Kenneth Underwood and Elden Jacobson, "Probing the Ethics of Realtors," *Christianity and Crisis*, XXI, 9 (May 29, 1961), 96-99.

24. United States Commission on Civil Rights, *1961 United States Commission on Civil Rights Report on Housing* (Washington: Government Printing Office, 1961), p. 51.

25. RR, p. 289.

26. The author heard this statement more than once while hunting for a place to live in Washington, D.C.

27. Greenberg, *op. cit.*, pp. 276-79.

28. A rich account of what happened in Deerfield is provided in Harry and David Rosen, *But Not Next Door* (New York: Ivan Obolensky, Inc., 1962).

29. Greenberg, *op. cit.*, p. 278.

30. RR, pp. 185-87.

31. For a lively fictional version of the gambits employed by various parties for whom residential integration is a potential threat or opportunity, see Keith Wheeler, *Peaceable Lane* (New York: Simon and Schuster, 1960). Cf. RR, p. 289.

32. This tactic was reported to the author by a Yale student whose father was a realtor in a Chicago suburb.

33. Leadership Conference on Civil Rights, *Federally Supported Discrimination* (New York: Futuro Press, 1961), p. 46.

34. Greenberg, *op. cit.*, p. 292.

35. L.K. Northwood, "The Threat and Potential of Urban Renewal," *The Journal of Intergroup Relations,* II, 2 (Spring 1961), 108.

36. *Ibid.*, p. 109.

37. Maguire, *op. cit.*, p. 263, reports that many Negro spokesmen "have begun to charge that urban renewal is really Negro removal and a process of chasing slums around." He adds, "One Connecticut resident threw up his hands in horror at the thought of relocating again and said: 'I've been renewed out of Norfolk and Philadelphia already.'"

38. Northwood, *op. cit.*, p. 110.

39. *Ibid.*

40. Loren Miller, "The Metro-Urban Complex," *The Journal of Intergroup Relations,* III, 1 (Winter 1961-62), 60.

41. RR, pp. 301-5.

42. Leadership Conference on Civil Rights, *Federally Supported Discrimination* (New York: Futuro Press, 1961), pp. 45-46.

43. *Ibid.*, p. 48.

44. RR, pp. 219-37; United States Commission on Civil Rights, *1961 United States Commission on Civil Rights Report on Housing* (Washington: Government Printing Office, 1961), pp. 27-80.

45. National Committee Against Discrimination in Housing, *Equal Opportunity in Housing* (New York: National Committee Against Discrimination in Housing, 1963), Appendix C.

46. *Trends in Housing,* VII, 1 (January-February 1963), 6.

47. RR, pp. 301-7.

48. RR, pp. 315-46.

49. Edward Rutledge and William R. Valentine, "Cooperation Agreements in Housing Administration," *The Journal of Intergroup Relations,* I, 3 (Summer 1960), 11.

50. This confession of exasperation and despair was made to the author by a famous civil liberties attorney in conversation at the

meeting of the National Committee Against Discrimination in Housing in Washington, D.C. in the spring of 1963.

51. National Committee Against Discrimination in Housing, *op. cit.*, pp. 1-3.

52. Frances Levenson and Margaret Fisher, "The Struggle for Open Housing," *The Progressive*, XXVI, 12 (December 1962), 28.

53. James A. Tillman, Jr., "In Defense of Neighborhood Stabilization," *The Journal of Intergroup Relations*, III, 4 (Autumn 1962), 11-13; United States Commission on Civil Rights, *Housing in Washington* (Washington: Government Printing Office, 1962), pp. 350-418.

54. Levenson and Fisher, *loc. cit.*

55. Harry Elmer Barnes, *The Twilight of Christianity* (New York: The Vanguard Press, 1929).

56. Gerhard Lenski, *The Religious Factor* (Garden City, New York: Doubleday and Company, 1961), pp. 2-3, 8-10.

57. J.M. Yinger, *Religion, Society and the Individual* (New York: The Macmillan Company, 1957), pp. 224-26.

58. *Union Seminary Quarterly Review*, XVI, 2 (January 1961), 195-96.

59. Will Herberg, *Protestant-Catholic-Jew* (Garden City, New York: Doubleday and Company, 1955), p. 15. For a slightly modified view on the subject by the same author, see "Religion in a Secularized Society," *Review of Religious Research*, III, 3 (Spring 1962), 145-58. For a challenge to this viewpoint, see J.M. Yinger, "Religion and Social Change: Problems of Integration and Pluralism Among the Privileged," *Review of Religious Research*, IV, 3 (Spring 1963), 129-48.

60. The phrase, "the quiet revolution," was suggested by a television program describing new efforts on the part of churches to meet social needs, shown by a major network in the spring of 1963. The favorable estimate of the growing social consciousness of churchmen has been voiced by several leaders involved in religiously sponsored activities on behalf of racial justice since January, 1963. It should be noted, however, that the optimism of thoughtful observers is not unlimited, and it is based upon a hope for the future more than it is upon evidence in the past. For example, Mathew Ahmann, Executive Director of the National Catholic Conference for Interracial Justice, and editor of *Race: Challenge to Religion*, an anthology of some of the speeches delivered at the National Conference on Religion and Race in Chicago during January, 1963, has characterized 1963 as "the year of the mouse" In a speech at Union Theological Seminary, New York City, January 8, 1964, Dr. Ahmann

voiced gratitude and guarded optimism in comparing the energy expended by religious groups on behalf of social justice in race relations during 1963 to efforts in previous years; he warned, however, that so far this notable expenditure of energy had produced much in the way of new organizational machinery but little in the way of new breakthroughs in the struggle against segregation and discrimination.

61. National Conference on Religion and Race, *Summary of Conference Recommendations.*

62. According to a report in *The Ecumenist,* II, 2 (January-February 1964), 32, the nineteen cities which are already implementing follow-up efforts in line with recommendations of the Chicago conference are: Boston, Chicago, Columbia (Missouri), Des Moines, Detroit, Gary, Kansas City (Missouri), Lexington (Kentucky), Little Rock, Milwaukee, Omaha, Pittsburg, St. Louis, San Francisco, Seattle, Syracuse, Toledo, Washington, D.C. and the state of Delaware. "The Chicago Conference is credited with helping avert a major riot by placing religious leaders in the streets in a community in which a Negro family had moved." It has also formulated "a program to mobilize the purchasing power of the churches and synagogues to use against discriminatory lending and hiring practices," has made plans for a series of television programs highlighting the urgency of the demand for racial justice, and "is carrying out a campaign to enlist clergy support throughout Illinois for the civil rights bill now pending in Congress."

63. Tape recordings and mimeographed copies of some of the speeches made at a conference in Lincoln, Nebraska in early September, 1963, are available from the Commission on Religion and Race of the National Council of Churches of Christ in the U.S.A., 475 Riverside Drive, New York 27, N.Y.

Notes For Chapter Two

1. William W. Cooney, "[Newfield]: A Sociological and Economic Study" (unpublished Master's thesis, Department of Government, Wesleyan University, 1935), pp. 17-18.

2. *Ibid.,* p. 53.

3. *Ibid.,* p. 59.

4. By 1922 there were 2,500 persons from this locality in Newfield. See Clayton F. Hewitt, "A Political Survey of [Newfield]" (unpublished Master's thesis, Department of Government, Wesleyan University, 1957), pp. 7-8.

5. Cooney, *op. cit.,* p. 25. Assimilation was retarded by the fact that there was no pressing need to learn English (since there were

so many "home folks" in Newfield who spoke the dialect of the Sicilian town from which they had immigrated).

6. *Ibid.*, pp. 24-25.

7. *Ibid.*, p. 81.

8. *Ibid.*, pp. 83-84.

9. *Ibid.*, Appendix 1.

10. *Ibid.*, p. 57.

11. *Ibid.*, Appendix 4 and Hewitt, *op. cit.*, p. 5.

12. Hewitt, *op. cit.*, p. 77.

13. *Ibid.*, pp. 13ff.

14. *Ibid.*, p. 11.

15. Walter H. Sangree, "Mel Hyblaeum" (unpublished Master's thesis, Department of Anthropology, Wesleyan University, 1952), p. 32.

16. Cooney, *op. cit.*, p. 46.

17. Hewitt, *op, cit.*, p. 25.

18. *Ibid.*, p. 27.

19. *Ibid.*, p. 22.

20. *Ibid.*, p. 21.

21. *Ibid.*, p. 24.

22. *Ibid.*, p. 22.

23. Newfield *Review*, October 24, 1961.

24. Hewitt, *op. cit.*, p. 87.

25. *Ibid.*, pp. 87-88.

26. Newfield *Review*, February 17, 1960.

27. *Ibid.*, March 26, 1960.

28. Interview with Dr. John Wallace, Member of the Social Action Committee of the Greater Newfield Council of Churches, January 23, 1961.

29. Newfield *Review*, February 16, 1961.

30. *Ibid.*, March 27, 1961.

31. *Ibid.*, March 28, 1961.

32. *Ibid.*, May 10, 1961.

33. *Ibid.*

34. *Ibid.*

35. Lawson was so quoted by McCrory at a public meeting in the City Hall, May 26, 1961.

36. Newfield *Review*, June 26, 1961.

37. *Ibid.*, June 30, 1961.

38. Minutes of the meeting of the Social Action Committee of the Greater Newfield Council of Churches, July 26, 1961.

39. *Ibid.*, September 13, 1961.

40. Newfield *Review*, September 18, 1961.

41. The author was present at this meeting of the Clergy Fellowship. Jackson's remark was made to him as he departed from the meeting.

42. Interview with the Reverend Harold Baldwin, Chairman of the Social Action Committee of the Greater Newfield Council of Churches, October 19, 1961.

43. Manuscript of Dr. Kerr's address delivered at the semi-annual meeting of the Greater Newfield Council of Churches, October 16, 1961.

44. Interview with the Reverend Harold Baldwin, Chairman of the Social Action Committee of the Greater Newfield Council of Churches, October 19, 1961.

Notes For Chapter Three

1. Some experts are of the opinion that "even were the migration to cease tomorrow, it would make relatively little difference to the future trend of Negro population increase" in Northern cities. High birth rates insure that "virtually all cities will have sizable Negro percentages in no more than a decade or two." See Grier, Eunice and George, *The Impact of Race on Neighborhood in the Metropolitan Setting* (Washington: Washington Center for Metropolitan Studies, 1961), pp. 10-11. It is likely, however, that "the 'push' from the South may grow stronger as the consequence of growing white antagonisms following attempts to enforce the Supreme Court's nonsegregation decisions." See Morton Grodzins, *The Metropolitan Area As a Racial Problem* (Pittsburgh: University of Pittsburgh Press, 1958), pp. 4-5.

2. United States Department of Labor Bulletin S-3, *The Economic Situation of Negroes in the United States* (Washington: Government Printing Office, October 1960), p. 13. "Private household workers" comprise 36.9% of the national nonwhite female work force.

3. *Ibid.*, pp. 13-15.

4. Henry G. Stetler, *Attitudes Toward Racial Integration in Connecticut* (Hartford: The Commission on Civil Rights of the State of Connecticut, 1961), p.11.

5. Henry Clark, "The Housing Conditions of Negroes in [Newfield]" (Public Affairs College, Wesleyan University, 1961), p. 5.

Notes For Chapter Four

1. The concept of "cues" as crucial determinants of response in an ambiguous intergroup situation is an important ingredient in the understanding of prejudice and discrimination. If discriminatory behavior is indeed caused primarily by a social context in which most participants believe such behavior is expected of them in that particular situation, it can be short-circuited by a countervailing act on the part of some other participant (so long as the latter's knowledge of what is expected in the situation is not doubted). In ambiguous situations, particularly, the first action taken by any participant provides a cue which very frequently is accepted and imitated by others. See Verne H. Fletcher, "Collective Dimensions in Interracial Behavior," *The City Church*, XI, 4 (September-October 1960), 2-11; Marguerite Hofer, "Strategies in Race Relations for Ministers, Church and Community Leaders" (Pittsburgh, 1959); and Melvin L. Kohn and Robin M. Williams, "Situational Patterning in Intergroup Relations," *American Sociological Review*, XXI, 2 (April 1956), 164-74.

Notes For Chapter Five

1. Newfield *Review,* October 17, 1961.

2. The Jewish rabbi admitted that he felt mildly annoyed over being asked to give his blessing to a *fait accompli,* and he felt that the Roman Catholics would have had better grounds than he for annoyance because of their status as the largest single religious group in the city.

3. Newfield *Review,* November 25, 1961.

4. *Ibid.,* October 27, 1961.

5. "Proclamation" of the Mayor of Newfield, November 14, 1961.

6. Newfield *Review,* November 15, 1961.

7. Minutes of the NAACP meeting, January 27, 1962.

8. Minutes of the Committee for Middle-Income Housing, February 15, 1962.

9. Interview with Father Sloan, April 16, 1962.

Notes For Chapter Six

1. An excellent summary of expert opinion on the benefits and possible draw-backs of equal-status contact is given in Edward P. Suchman, John P. Dean and Robin M. Williams, *Desegregation: Some Propositions and Research Suggestions* (New York: Anti-Defamation League of B'nai B'rith, 1958), pp. 47-56.

2. The family was mentioned as an important influence on the respondent's decision by a significantly higher percentage of Roman Catholics. Because Catholics were not exposed to other influences in the same way or to the same extent that Protestants were, little can be made of the findings of this study on that point. It should be noted, however, that the correlation between Catholicism and strong family ties suggested here has recently been confirmed in Lenski, *op. cit.*, pp. 193-97.

3. Confirmation of this assumption in regard to the race issue is provided in Earnest Q. Campbell and Thomas F. Pettigrew, *Christians in Racial Crisis* (Washington: Public Affairs Press, 1959), pp. 41-62. These authors discovered that the most poorly educated churchgoers in Little Rock were the most adamantly opposed to both integration and "church meddling" in public affairs.

4. This finding indicates that education, although it tends to reduce prejudice in certain ways, is no panacea for prejudiced behavior or attitudes. A recent analysis of research concerning the relationship between these two variables concludes that "on many issues, the educated show as much prejudice as the less educated, and on some issues they show more. They appear no more concerned than others with problems of discrimination and prejudice." See Stember, Charles Herbert, *Education and Attitude Change* (New York: Institute of Human Relations Press, 1961), p. 168 and *passim.*

Notes For Chapter Seven

1. The primacy of justice as the relevant norm for social ethics is a theme which has been forcefully developed by several modern Christian ethicists, notably by Paul Tillich in *Love, Power, and Justice* (New York: Oxford University Press, 1954) and Reinhold Niebuhr in innumerable books and essays, including especially (in addition to specific citations given in footnotes below) *The Destiny of Man* (New York: Charles Scribner's Sons, 1943), pp. 244-56 and *Moral Man and Immoral Society* (New York: Charles Scribner's Sons, 1932), pp. 1-22, 257-77. The author's conviction that the achievement of proximate goals which make for a more tolerable degree of justice is more important than preoccupation with the beliefs or intentions of the moral agent is expounded in Henry Clark, *The Ethical Mysticism of Albert Schweitzer* (Boston: Beacon Press, 1962), pp. 144-58.

2. Reinhold Niebuhr, *The Destiny of Man*, p. 248.

3. *Ibid.*

4. Reinhold Niebuhr, *Moral Man and Immoral Society*, p. 234.

Niebuhr answered the critics of his realism two years later, admitting their worst charge and defending his position without apology:

> This wholly pragmatic and relativistic analysis of the problem of violence obviously fails to arrive at an absolute disavowal of violence under all circumstances. It is therefore tainted with the implied principle that the end justifies the means. This is supposedly a terrible Jesuitical maxim which all good people must abhor. Yet all good people are involved in it.

See *An Interpretation of Christian Ethics* (New York: Meridian Books, 1956), p. 174.

5. Henry Clark, "Can Property Be Private?" *Christianity and Crisis*, XXI, 23 (January 8, 1962), 236-38. Cf. Paul Ramsey, *Christian Ethics and the Sit-In* (New York: Association Press, 1961), pp. 17-39.

6. This phrase has become a shibboleth for several generations of theological students. Enchanted by the grandeur of Mr. Eliot's poetry, they overlook the consequences of taking this posture seriously. The passage in which the phrase occurs is found in the last speech of *Murder in the Cathedral*, in *The Complete Poems and Plays of T. S. Eliot* (New York: Harcourt, Brace and Company, 1952), p. 196.

7. Earl Raab and Seymour M. Lipset, *Prejudice and Society* (New York: Anti-Defamation League of B'nai B'rith, 1959), p.18.

8. *Ibid.*

9. *Ibid.*, pp. 22-39.

Notes For Chapter Eight

1. The conceptual framework employed in this chapter was suggested in part by several important books which seek to make explicit a model of political influence which might have wide applicability in American communities. The most helpful of these sources are Edward C. Banfield, *Political Influence* (Glencoe: The Free Press, 1961); Martin Meyerson and Edward C. Banfield, *Politics, Planning and the Public Interest* (Glencoe: The Free Press, 1955); and James Q. Wilson, *Negro Politics: The Search for Leadership* (Glencoe: The Free Press, 1960).

2. A study of racial attitudes in the state where Newfield is located reveals that the drive for school desegregation in the South "heightened consciousness of the [racial] problem" among residents of the state, and had the effect of arousing greater sympathy for Negroes' demands for equal rights. See Henry G. Stetler, *Attitudes*

Toward Racial Integration in Connecticut (Hartford: The Commission on Civil Rights of the State of Connecticut, 1961), pp. 16-21.

3. The important phenomenon referred to in the phrase marked off by quotation marks is analyzed in detail in Kenneth E. Boulding, *The Organizational Revolution* (New York: Harper and Brothers, 1953).

4. For a concise summary of policy statements on race relations by religious bodies in this country as of 1958, see Campbell and Pettigrew, *op. cit.*, pp. 137-70. A compilation of later pronouncements on this issue is to be found in *Interracial News Service*, XXXII, 1 (January-February 1961). A special pamphlet giving "Denominational Statements with Reference to Fair Housing Practices" was published in April, 1961, by The Department of Racial and Cultural Relations of the National Council of Churches of Christ in the U.S.A. Most of the major denominations passed strong resolutions on racial justice during 1963, and many of them set up special commissions to carry out "crash programs" (often involving powerful economic sanctions on their own member churches) in this area of concern.

It should be noted that although every clergyman interviewed in Newfield was familiar with the general position of his denomination on race relations, only one was acquainted with its pronouncements on housing in particular.

5. Interview with Professor Floyd Walker of the Department of Government of the University, July 10, 1961.

6. Newfield *Press*, September 13, 1961.

7. Interview with the Reverend Larry Oliver, November 16, 1961.

8. Robert K. Merton, *Social Theory and Social Structure* (Glencoe: The Free Press, 1957), pp. 227-30, 234-35, 241, 248.

9. The pervasiveness of avoidance was most poignantly revealed to the author by a casual statement made by a member of the University Study Committee who was a lifetime resident of Newfield. In relating a conversation with a local Negro, he remarked, "This guy was from the South, so naturally he didn't trust white people." It was obvious from the off-hand nature of this remark that such an attitude was so much to be taken for granted that its significance required no comment.

10. Interview with a member of the University Study Committee who was also an officer in the local branch of the NAACP, February 8, 1962. One of the two poor leaders referred to was popularly thought to have been guilty of at least extraordinary incompetence in the handling of branch funds.

11. For example, the average attendance at branch meetings was approximately fifteen to twenty persons, out of a membership of about one hundred and fifty, and the attendance of the highly publicized special meeting on the new civil rights law in housing included only about forty Negroes—but attendance at the branch's fall social event, a gala dinner-dance held in one of the most fashionable night clubs of the area, was one hundred sixty.

12. Stetler, *op. cit.*, p. 29.

13. According to a noted historian, the experience of the Depression heightened the symbolic value of real estate for virtually all middle-class suburban citizens who lived through it. Property came to symbolize the security which had been lost once and must never be lost again, and the symbolic (as well as the pecuniary) value of a self-owned home in a good neighborhood was especially important to immigrant families. See Oscar Handlin, *The Newcomers* (Cambridge: Harvard University Press, 1959), pp. 64-68.

14. One reliable informant, a long-term resident of Newfield who was familiar with real estate ownership patterns in the community, estimated that almost ninety per cent of rental housing units in dwellings other than large apartment buildings belonged to persons of Italian extraction. This estimate was borne out by a study of rental housing conducted by members of the Butler Memorial Congregational Church Social Action Committee.

15. Wilson, *op. cit.*, pp. 169-213, 300-2.

16. Morton Deutsch and Mary Evans Collins, *Interracial Housing: A Psychological Evaluation of a Social Experiment* (Minneapolis: University of Minnesota Press, 1951). Cf. Daniel M. Wilner, Rosabelle Price Walkley and Stuart W. Cook, *Human Relations In Interracial Housing* (Minneapolis: University of Minnesota Press, 1955).

17. Deutsch and Collins, *op. cit.*, pp. 76-103, 122. The quotations used here are taken from a condensed version of the Deutsch and Collins study found in William Petersen (ed.), *American Social Patterns* (Garden City, New York: Doubleday Anchor Books, 1956), pp. 35, 41, 50.

18. This highly pertinent consideration was suggested to the author by Mrs. Helen Baker of the American Friends Service Committee in Washington, D.C., May 10, 1963.

19. Martin E. Marty, *The New Shape of American Religion* (New York: Harper and Brothers, 1958), pp. 134-137.

20. Oliver Popenoe and Laura Popenoe, "The Greater Washington Good Neighbor Campaign 1961: A Report on How It Was Done" (Washington: National Capital Clearing House for Neighborhood Democracy, 1961), p. 5.

21. Blizzard's study of ministers' ranking of their role responsibilities also shows that preaching is considered to be of prime importance. See Samuel Blizzard, "The Minister's Dilemma," *The Christian Century*, LXXIII, 17 (April 25, 1956), 508-10. An elaboration of this point is to be found below, pp. 213-14. Cf. J.M. Gustafson, "An Analysis of the Problem of the Role of the Minister," *The Journal of Religion*, XXXIV, 3 (July 1954), 187-91.

22. Interview with the Reverend Robert A. Spivey, Acting Chaplain at Williams College and a leader in organizing the Williamstown fair housing campaign, December 30, 1963.

23. Interviews with various Newfield realtors, June 13-15, 1963.

24. James B. Conant, *Slums and Suburbs* (New York: McGraw-Hill Book Company, 1961), pp. 33-35.

25. Interview with an official of the Health and Welfare Council of Washington, D.C., July 18, 1962.

26. Interview with an official of the Civil Rights Division of the AFL-CIO, July 18, 1962.

27. Interview with a social worker on the staff of the Howard University Community Service Project in the Forty-Ninth Precinct, July 19, 1962.

28. Lloyd A. Marcus, *The Treatment of Minorities in Secondary School Textbooks* (New York: Anti-Defamation League of B'nai B'rith, 1962).

29. Some infuriating data on "credit gouging" is contained in Hillel Black, *Buy Now, Pay Later* (New York: Pocket Books, Inc., 1962), pp. 122-48.

30. Saul Alinsky, *Reveille for Radicals* (Chicago: University of Chicago Press, 1946), pp. 177-83.

31. Interview with Mr. Al Mermin, New Haven, Connecticut, June 29, 1961.

32. This information was obtained from a member of the Connecticut Civil Rights Commission who spoke on the subject of American race relations at a conference of The Society for Religion in Higher Education, Drew University, August 24-29, 1962.

33. Interview with the priest in charge of Fides House, a Roman Catholic settlement house in Washington, D. C.

34. See Lee Rainwater, *And the Poor Get Children* (Chicago: Quadrangle Books, 1960).

35. Sophia M. Robison, John A. Morsell and Edna A. Merson, "Summary of Survey on Country-Wide Instances of Open Occupancy Housing" (New York: Committee on Civil Rights in Manhattan, 1957), pp. 16-18.

36. Alfred S. Kramer, "The Churches and Race Relations," *Interracial News Service*, XXXIV, 1 (January-February 1963), 4-5.

37. RR, p. 280.

38. This principle was illustrated by the contrasting experience of two ministers in a metropolitan area where Negro entry into previously all-white areas is a matter of great concern for many white parishioners. One pastor thought it would be best to meet the issue head-on: he advised the governing body of his church in advance that Negroes would soon be moving into a new housing development nearby, and asked them to articulate a policy on the admission of Negroes into the church. Anxieties had time to mushroom; opposition had time to crystallize—and the policy voted on was one of nonadmission for nonwhites. The other pastor said nothing, but when the new housing development was opened for occupancy, he organized evangelical teams to call on *all* new residents and to invite the religiously unaffiliated to join their congregation. As a result of this "normal" approach, several Negro applicants for membership were accepted into the church on the day when all new members from the new housing development were inducted. (This story was related to the author by the Reverend George W. Webber of New York City.)

39. RR, pp. 199-217. A more detailed version of the same material is available in Eunice Grier and George Grier, *Privately Developed Interracial Housing* (Berkeley and Los Angeles: University of California Press, 1960).

40. RR, pp. 208ff.

41. Michael A. Bamberger and Nathan Lewin, "The Right to Equal Treatment: Administrative Enforcement of Antidiscrimination Legislation," *Harvard Law Review*, LXXIV, 3 (January 1961), 589.

42. *Ibid.;* cf. pp. 528-32.

43. *Ibid.*, p. 589.

44. *Ibid.*, p. 550.

45. Speech at Yale University, March, 1960.

46. RR, p. 279.

47. Bamberger and Lewin, *op. cit.*, p. 557.

48. *Ibid.*, p. 541.

49. *Ibid.*, p. 543.

50. James G. Heller, "How Urban Renewal Can Be Used to Cure Ghetto Blight," *The Journal of Intergroup Relations*, III, 4 (Autumn 1962), 333.

51. George B. Nesbitt and Marian P. Yankauer, "The Potential

for Equalizing Housing Opportunity in the Nation's Capital," *The Journal of Intergroup Relations*, IV, 1 (Winter 1962-63), 93.

52. James Q. Wilson, "The Strategy of Protest," *The Journal of Conflict Resolution*, V (September 1961), 294ff.

53. Interview, May 10, 1963.

54. Wilson, *op. cit.*, p. 298.

55. *Ibid.*, p. 299.

56. *Ibid.*

57. Such a situation now prevails in New York City. The seriousness of the problem of urban housing for low-income families appears all the greater in the light of a recent report by the agency in charge of repossession to the effect that rental revenues charged by the city in operating a tenement are not sufficient to cover the cost of needed repairs. The inadequacy of a laissez-faire approach could hardly be more obvious, or the need for at least a short-term subsidy from public funds more urgent. See New York *Times*, February 12, 1964.

58. New York *Times*, January 9, 1964.

59. Interview with Mrs. Helen Baker, May 10, 1963.

60. Interview with an official of HHFA who has a key responsibility for low-income demonstration housing in Philadelphia, May 24, 1963.

61. Jane Jacobs, *The Death and Life of Great American Cities* (New York: Random House, 1961), pp. 321-34.

62. *Ibid.*, pp. 335-6.

63. *Ibid.*, pp. 11, 127, 295ff., 314, 326, 332.

64. Peter Marcuse, "Benign Quotas Reexamined," *The Journal of Intergroup Relations*, III, 2 (Spring 1962), 114.

65. *Ibid.*, p. 115.

66. *Ibid.* Mr. Marcuse's argument on this point can also be used in connection with the controversy over "compensatory discrimination" favoring Negroes, the case for which is stated very persuasively by Whitney Young, head of the National Urban League, in The New York *Times Magazine*, October 6, 1963, pp. 43, 129, 131.

Notes For Chapter Nine

1. Reports on the number of signatures obtained in New Haven and Hartford were obtained in personal conversation with individuals who had worked in the open housing covenant campaign held in these cities. The figure on Des Moines comes from Gerald Rasmussen, "Let's Open the Doors in Des Moines" (Des Moines, 1959).

2. Kenneth W. Underwood, *Protestant and Catholic* (Boston: Beacon Press, 1957), p. 307.

3. *Ibid.*, p. 308.

4. *Ibid.*, p 316.

5. *Ibid.*, Cf. Liston Pope, *Millhands and Preachers* (New Haven: Yale University Press, 1942), pp. 162-86 for a similar account of the indifference and inaction exhibited by ministers living in the midst of a social crisis.

6. Robert Friedrichs, "Christians and Residential Exclusion," *The Journal of Social Issues*, XV, 4 (Winter 1959), 21.

7. James A. Tillman, Jr., *Journey Without End* (Minneapolis: Greater Minneapolis Interfaith Fair Housing Program, 1960), p. 8 and Appendix 1, p. 5.

8. Lenski, *op. cit.*, p. 24.

9. Charles Glock and Benjamin Ringer, "The Political Role of the Church as Defined by its Parishioners," *Public Opinion Quarterly* (Winter 1954-55), pp. 337-47.

10. Herbert E. Stotts and Paul Deats, Jr., *Methodism and Society: Guidelines for Strategy* (New York and Nashville: Abingdon Press, 1962), pp. 43-44, 330.

11. Robert S. Lynd and Helen Merrell Lynd, *Middletown* (New York: Harcourt, Brace, and Company, 1929), p. 345.

12. *Ibid.*

13. These three categories for understanding racial injustice are provided in Kyle Haselden, *The Racial Problem in Christian Perspective* (New York: Harper and Brothers, 1959), pp. 67-152.

14. Sermon at Battell Chapel, Yale University, January 21, 1962.

15. The Interfaith Steering Committee sought to remedy this difficulty by persuading representatives of various civic and fraternal organizations to introduce the covenant to their members. This attempt was merely an after-thought, though, and it was not carefully planned nor systematically carried out.

16. One of the most notable experiments designed to test the relative merits of learning based on lectures and on group discussion is that reported in Kurt Lewin, "Group Decision and Social Change," in Eleanor E. Maccoby, Theodore M. Newcomb and Eugene L. Hartley, *Readings in Social Psychology*, 3rd ed. rev. (New York: Henry Holt and Company, 1958), pp. 330-44. The shortcomings of exhortation and the comparative advantages of group learning techniques are also outlined in Allport, *op. cit.*, pp. 444-62, and Robin M. Williams, *The Reduction of Intergroup Tensions* (New York: Social Science Research Council, 1947), pp. 64-74.

17. Gibson Winter, *The Suburban Captivity of the Churches* (New York: The Macmillan Company, 1962), p. 158.

18. Peter Berger. *The Noise of Solemn Assemblies* (Garden City, New York: Doubleday and Company, 1961), pp. 102-3. The ratification of inauthentic existence in a phoney "O.K. world" is associated by Berger with Sartre's concept of "bad faith." Declares Berger: "A religious establishment such as ours is highly conducive to 'bad faith'. That is, religion provides the individual with the means by which he can hide from himself the true nature of his existence." In *The Precarious Vision* (Garden City, New York: Doubleday and Company, 1961), pp. 85-100, Berger illustrates the meaning of "bad faith" more fully, saying, "We understand a man to be in bad faith who excuses himself by pointing to his social role and to the ideologies in which the role is enveloped" (p. 89). On the same page, he adds, "Bad faith means that society assists us in hiding our own actions from our awareness. The role becomes a moral alibi."

19. Underwood, *op. cit.*, pp. 85, 89.

20. *Ibid.*, p. 121.

21. The term, and the discussion of its meaning which follows in the text, comes from Louis Schneider and Sanford M. Dornbusch, *Popular Religion* (Chicago: University of Chicago Press, 1958), pp. 96-101.

22. Herberg, *op. cit.*, pp. 116-17.

23. Underwood, *op. cit.*, p. 313.

24. *Ibid.*, p. 312.

25. *Ibid.*, p. 313.

26. Talk by the Director of the University Study before the Clergy Fellowship, September 20, 1961; address by Dr. Arnold Kerr, October 16, 1961.

27. Underwood, *op. cit.*, p. 314.

28. *Ibid.*, p. 345.

29. *Ibid.*

30. *Ibid.*, p. 329.

31. *Ibid.*, p. 313.

32. *Ibid.*, p. 327.

33. William J. Cook, "U.S. Publics and Foreign Policy Process," a paper presented to the annual conference of The American Society for Christian Social Ethics, Louisville, Kentucky, January 25, 1963, p 2.

34. *Ibid.*

35. Reinhold Niebuhr, *An Interpretation of Christian Ethics* (New York: Meridian Books, 1956), pp. 158, 159.

36. Reinhold Niebuhr, "Christian Faith and Social Action," in John Hutchison, *Christian Faith and Social Action* (New York: Charles Scribner's Sons, 1953), p. 241.

37. Reinhold Niebuhr, *An Interpretation of Christian Ethics*, p. 174. (For the complete statement about the end justifying the means, see above, footnote 4 in Chapter Seven.)

38. Niebuhr as paraphrased in Donald B. Meyer, *The Protestant Search for Political Realism* (Berkeley and Los Angeles: University of California Press, 1960), p. 229.

39. Campbell and Pettigrew, *op. cit.*, p. 102.

40. *Ibid.*

41. *Ibid.*, p. 103.

42. Schneider and Dornbusch, *op. cit.*, pp. 106-11.

43. Peter Berger, *The Noise of Solemn Assemblies*, p. 37. Berger asserts: "What the church has said to him might conceivably have bearing on his private life. But it is quite irrelevant to his involvement in public life."

44. Peter Berger and Gibson Winter are sometimes accused of ending up with a position of this kind, but their criticisms of American religious life are almost conservative compared to some that one hears voiced by the young Turks of Protestantism at conferences where theological education is being discussed. The ideal of "religionless Christianity" in a "world come of age" is allegedly found in the writings of Dietrich Bonhoeffer; at any rate, the young generation of German Protestants who are enamored with this notion claim Bonhoeffer as their patron saint and, his banner held aloft, make bold to attack the ramparts of traditional understandings of Christianity and the Church.

45. Marty, *op. cit.*, and James M. Gustafson, *Treasure in Earthen Vessels* (New York: Harper and Brothers, 1961) represent this position.

46. Underwood, *op. cit.*, p. 306.

47. *Ibid.*, p. 314.

48. *Ibid.*, p. 273. Cf. William J. Cook's condemnation of the "position-of-the-church" fixation," p. 204 above.

49. The concepts referred to by enclosure in quotation marks have been brought into the consciousness of American intellectuals and social analysis by David Riesman, *et al.*, *The Lonely Crowd* (New Haven: Yale University Press, 1950) and Maurice Stein, *The Eclipse of Community* (Princeton: Princeton University Press, 1960).

50. Underwood, *op. cit.*, pp. 120-21.

51. Arthur J. Vidich and Joseph Bensman, *Small Town in Mass Society* (Princeton University Press, 1958), pp. 241-52.

52. Winter, *op. cit.*, pp. 59-76.

53. *Ibid.*, p. 42.

54. *Ibid.*, pp. 111-12.

55. *Ibid.*, p. 119.

56. *Ibid.*, pp. 161-62.

57. Robert Wesley Brown, "Open Housing Covenants in Northern California" (Menlo Park, California, 1961), p. 7.

58. Blizzard, *loc. cit.*

59. Winter *op. cit.*, pp. 105.

60. Underwood, *op. cit.*, pp. 110-11.

61. See p. 172.

62. Vidich and Bensman, p. 303.

63. Winter, *op. cit.*, pp. 61ff.

64. Campbell, *op. cit.*, p. 195.

65. George W. Webber, "EHPP: Emerging Issues," in Robert Lee, (ed.), *Cities and Churches* (Philadelphia: The Westminster Press, 1962), p. 171.

66. Norton E. Long, "The Local Community as an Ecology of Games," in Edward C. Banfield (ed.), *Urban Government* (Glencoe: Free Press, 1961), p. 405.

67. Joseph Tussman, *Obligation and the Body Politic* (New York: Oxford University Press, 1960) and John Courtney Murray, *We Hold These Truths* (New York: Sheed and Ward, 1960).

68. Long, *loc. cit.*

69. Kenneth W. Underwood, "Social Ethic in the New Era," in Arthur Walmsley (ed.), *The Church in a Society of Abundance* (New York: The Seabury Press, 1963), p. 56.

70. Franklin H. Littell, "Reflections on the Project and its Product", in Hall, *op. cit.*, p. 132.

71. Some of the most important sources to be consulted in this connection are Floyd A. Hunter, *Community Power Structure* (Chapel Hill: University of North Carolina Press, 1952); Robert A. Dahl, *Who Governs* (New Haven: Yale University Press, 1961); and Nelson W. Polsby, *Community Power and Political Theory* (New Haven: Yale University Press, 1963). For additional sources, see Banfield (ed.) *op. cit.*, p. 414.

72. Cook, *loc. cit.* The same viewpoint was voiced by most of the experienced Washington spokesmen—including Clarence Mitchell, head of the Washington Bureau of the NAACP and Edward Synder of the Friends Committee on National Legislation—who addressed the Seminar on Civil Rights and the Governmental Process, Washington, D.C., January 20-22, 1964.

73. George C. Homans, *The Human Group* (New York: Harcourt, Brace and Company, 1950), pp. 245-52. Cf. Gibson Winter, *Love and Conflict* (Garden City, New York: Doubleday and Company, 1958), pp. 43-44. In Winter's words, "Anyone who exercises leadership can expect to be disliked. . . . Most of us want to be liked, so it is hard to pay this price for leadership. . . . In America, at least, no one likes to be led. . . . The man with the best ideas and suggestions is exercising real leadership. It soon develops that the man with the best ideas is not very well liked. . . . Groups need a leader . . . , but they also need a member who is well liked and who can keep everyone together. . . . A strong and effective group develops when this best-liked person allies himself with the leader who is making the suggestions. If the best-liked person will support the leader, the group can move ahead and work out its problems."

74. The author's convictions on this theme are expressed in *The Ethical Mysticism of Albert Schweitzer* (Boston: Beacon Press, 1962), pp. 171-78.